America as a World Power, 1872–1945

America as a World Power, 1872–1945

edited by

ROBERT H. FERRELL

University of South Carolina Press
Columbia, South Carolina

AMERICA AS A WORLD POWER, 1872–1945

First HARPER PAPERBACK edition published 1971.

This edition published by the University of South Carolina
Press, Columbia, S.C., 1971, by arrangement with Harper Paper-
backs, from whom a paperback edition is available (HR/1512).

International Standard Book Number: 0-87249-244-3
Library of Congress Catalog Card Number: 70-171359

Suggested Library of Congress classification furnished by
McKissick Memorial Library of the University of South Carolina:
E183.7.F

Manufactured in the United States of America

For Lila and Carolyn, again

Contents

Acknowledgments

Any editor or author works with the help of friends, and for the present volume I am much indebted to Cynthia Russett for advice on the chapter concerning Darwinism; to Eugene P. Trani for several fine Theodore Roosevelt letters; and to William M. Franklin for sage advice on government publications. William Crane of the Fort Wayne (Indiana) Public Library was wonderfully efficient in helping with the collection of materials. It was also a privilege to work in his beautiful library with its huge store of books. May I thank my hosts and friends in Belgium where this volume was finished during a year of teaching and study at the Catholic University of Louvain: Omer de Raeymaeker, scholar and teacher; Mrs. G. Lercangée of the American Studies Center, Royal Library, Brussels, always eager to bring out more books; the USIS Library in Brussels; and especially Dorothy Moore Deflandre of the Belgian-American Foundation, director of Fulbright activities in Belgium, a marvelously efficient and sensitive representative of the government of the United States. It is pleasant to acknowledge the help of Richard B. Morris, a good friend, for excellent reading of the manuscript and judicious suggestions for its improvement. And a thank you to Vivi Mannuzza and the hardworking staff at Harper & Row.

R. H. F.

Foreword

The following volume represents the second of a three-volume documentary history of American diplomacy from its beginning in 1775 to the present day. *Foundations of American Diplomacy* covers the period from the opening of the American Revolution through the year of the Geneva arbitration, 1872. The present volume, *America as a World Power*, treats the diplomatic record to the end of World War II. The third, *America in a Divided World*, will consider the era from 1945 to the present.

RICHARD B. MORRIS,
General Editor

Introduction

I

OF THE three themes of this volume on American diplomacy from 1872 to 1945—empire, democracy, and security—the first is in many ways the most interesting, if the least important. It is least important because the American empire in its larger outline, protectorates in Central America and the Caribbean and possession of the Philippine Islands, did not last. But it is the most interesting because the diplomacy of empire, even the diplomacy of getting rid of empire, had a rhetoric and an energy entirely lacking in the more prosaic pursuits of advancing democracy throughout the world and ensuring the security of the United States.

Empire was preeminently a task for Americans who lived at the turn of the twentieth century, and there was little evidence of any popularity of the idea prior to the mid-1880s. If an observer of the nation's hopes and prospects in the year 1872, when the United States government had written finis to its Civil War diplomacy with the Geneva arbitration against Great Britain, had asked any group of intelligent Americans whether the country's policy ever might turn imperial, he would have been greeted with derision. There had never been an imperial era in American history, so his auditors would have told him. The nation had taken its continental territory by virtue of manifest destiny. The country had no imperial ambitions. In 1872 his auditors would have said that the country desired nothing so much as peace and quiet, no large schemes, so that Americans could devote their talents to business, which was the nation's prime interest, not any such occupation as sending countrymen out to obscure places of the world for obscure reasons.

It was not until the mid-1880s, with the beginning of a new American navy of steam and steel, and with the entering into the American consciousness of the notions of Darwinian thought, that opinion began to change, and even then it required another decade before the nation was ready to take up the burdens of imperial greatness. The influence of the new navy and the new Darwinian ideas is not altogether easy to analyze, for it may be that even ideas and the weapons necessary to realize them do not mean that there will be a result. If it is true that great armaments and great rivalries produce great wars, then the world today—in the 1970s—not merely is in far worse shape than ever before; indeed war should have begun twenty years ago. But in the context of the 1880s and especially the 1890s, it seems clear that the new cruisers and battleships coming off the ways, and the clear, almost too clear, philosophy of John Fiske, Captain Alfred T. Mahan, Theodore Roosevelt, and their supporters pointed toward the splendid little war, as John Hay described it, that broke out in 1898.

Meanwhile, new opportunities prepared the country for conflict. The first of these was over the Samoan Islands, an archipelago set down obscurely in the South Pacific, so remotely that even at the present writing many Americans could not tell the location of the Samoas within thousands of miles. McKinley's avowed ignorance about the Philippines in 1898 would have applied far more easily to the Samoas. And yet Secretaries of State Thomas F. Bayard and James G. Blaine made the Samoas into an issue with Imperial Germany, and forced first a condominium in 1889 including Great Britain, and a decade later a partition into German and American Samoa.

The second of the opportunities to focus American imperial ambition came with the revolution in the Hawaiian Islands in January, 1893, an affair which in its background and immediate cause was more local than imperial. The revolutionists dearly desired annexation to the United States, and Minister John L. Stevens supported them, and only the chance changing of administrations in Washington, from the imperial ideas of Benjamin Harrison to the "little America" beliefs of Grover Cleveland, prevented annexation at that moment. Later, in the midst of the Spanish-American War, the Hawaiians entered the American empire.

The third and fourth issues of the time that raised the possibility of imperial tasks were both over events in Latin America—the *Baltimore* affair of 1891, and the Venezuelan affair of 1895. In the former, involving an attack by a mob on unarmed American sailors on leave in the city of Valparaiso, the American government eventually—and properly, considering the provocation—demanded redress, and the Chilean government abjectly gave in, although not before an admirable naval commander, Robley D. (Fighting Bob)

Evans, opposed a concentration of the Chilean navy in Valparaiso harbor. In the Venezuelan affair, the most important expression of American overseas power prior to the Spanish War, the administration of Grover Cleveland told the British government (which was supporting an enlargement of the territory of British Guiana, at the expense of Venezuela) that the Monroe Doctrine was in force; Cleveland invoked the doctrine, for the first time since its announcement seventy-two years before. Succeeding generations of historians of the United States would read with almost incredulity the high point of the lecture that Secretary of State Richard Olney read to the British over Venezuela:

> Today the United States is practically sovereign on this continent, and its fiat is law upon the subjects to which it confines its interposition. Why? It is not because of the pure friendship or good will felt for it. It is not simply by reason of its high character as a civilized state, nor because wisdom and justice and equity are the invariable characteristics of the dealings of the United States. It is because, in addition to all other grounds, its infinite resources combined with its isolated position render it master of the situation and practically invulnerable as against any or all other powers.

Olney's adversary, Lord Salisbury, with some annoyance pointed out that the occasion was hardly worth the words bestowed upon it. According to Ambassador Bayard,

> At the conclusion of my reading and statement, his Lordship made courteous expression of his thanks, and expressed regret and surprise that it had been considered necessary to present so far-reaching and important a principle and such wide and profound policies of international action in relation to a subject so comparatively small.

The occasion was more important than Salisbury thought because of what it meant for the future. After 1895 he and his successors would be extremely careful with the proud Americans and the proudest of all American doctrines.

Then, at last, came the war with Spain, with its remote causes probably the new feeling of manifest destiny inspired by the Darwinian ideology, and also the existence of a new navy eager to demonstrate its prowess, and with the more immediate cause the inhumanity of Spanish policy in Cuba, which cried out for intervention. The Cuban revolution had broken out in 1895, and events approached a point where, as Senator Henry Cabot Lodge said in a letter of January, 1898, "There may be an explosion any day in

Cuba which would settle a great many things." The explosion occurred on the evening of February 15, 1898, outside the hull of the battleship *Maine* anchored in Havana harbor, and apparently touched off the ship's magazines. Within a few weeks the nation was at war for the first time since 1865.

It is a perplexing task for an American of the present era, with its menacing international affairs, to look back upon the spirit of the war of 1898, which is as remote from the present day as would be a galleon from a guided-missile cruiser. How the country could so wholeheartedly join in a campaign against a nation such as Spain, possessing a fraction of the population (eighteen million v. seventy-five million), boasting a navy of a few antique warships hardly fit to go to sea, is difficult to imagine. Commodore George B. Dewey's flagship *Olympia*, decommissioned at the Philadelphia Navy Yard in 1922 but never scrapped, was rescued from the ship-breakers a few years ago, refurbished, towed out of the yard and anchored along a pier in downtown Philadelphia, where schoolchildren and incredulous historians now may go aboard for the charge of fifty cents to see the very ship that took American empire to the Philippines. On the bridge are two large golden footprints, immortalized in bronze, which show where Dewey stood when he gave his famous firing order to Captain Gridley. It is difficult indeed to see the *Olympia* tied up in its latter-twentieth century setting and realize that seventy and more years ago the nation went wild when it heard that Dewey had sunk the Spanish squadron at Manila and was about to plant the American flag in lands close to Japan and China. The exhilaration and exultation, the enthusiasm, that marked the three short months of the Spanish-American War are almost imcomprehensible to a present-day generation, born to detest war.

The war of 1898 marked the apogee of American imperial ambition. Ever afterward, the acquisition of imperial tasks never seemed quite so attractive and eventually became downright unattractive. The war possessed the United States of the Philippine Islands and thereby almost immediately embroiled the nation in the international politics of the Far East. American imperialism in the Philippines, one should say, was more missionary and civilizing than imperial. The burden of conquest in the Islands was not easy to take up, and the United States probably would not have taken it up in a simple spirit of imperialism. The Filipino rebellion, ending in 1902, made the embarrassment the more real, except for such unabashedly imperial men as Theodore Roosevelt—and it is possible to argue that the rebellion affected even him, as not long thereafter he began to wish the country could rid itself of the Philippines. Nor, one should add, was the subsequent involvement in the affairs of the Far East an imperial venture in the usual sense, as the United States did not gain any territory and was in truth trying to protect territory not belonging to it, the territory of China, from the increasing rapacity of the Imperial Japanese Government.

The burdens of imperialism became increasingly inconvenient, if difficult to throw off. The documents that follow show how carefully the United States government sought to protect the Chinese and to avoid trouble with the Japanese. It was anxious work, and the end was not in sight even in 1945 when General Douglas MacArthur's troops occupied Tokyo, and when (to remark the situation in 1945 is only to show how temporary it was) the Nationalist government of Generalissimo Chiang Kai-shek returned to Nanking after an absence of eight years.

To be sure, some of the more imperial diplomacy of the United States was in Central America and the Caribbean, where the Spanish-American War had demonstrated the urgent need of an Isthmian canal. The battleship *Oregon*, present on the west coast at the outbreak of the conflict, had to round Cape Horn on a long voyage to take part in the action at Santiago de Cuba. In quick succession came the protectorates and quasi-protectorates: Cuba in 1901–04, Panama in 1903, the Dominican Republic in 1904, Nicaragua in 1911, Haiti in 1915. The intervention in Mexico in 1914, and again in 1916, was not so immediately related to the Canal as were the other interventions, but the feeling that the United States needed to make sure of its neighbors dominated that intervention as it did the others.

Proof that the Americans are not by nature, but only by occasion and for short duration, imperial, came when after the World War of 1914–18 the dangers, real or imaginary, of a German interference with the canal transit disappeared, and after a suitable pause in the 1920s, the American government withdrew from all its responsibilities except for Puerto Rico, the Virgin Islands, and the Canal Zone. Puerto Rico is free to go its own way, but has chosen not to do so. The Virgin Islands are probably too small for independence. In the Canal Zone the United States modified the treaty of 1903 in 1936 and again in 1955 and it is now an open question as to how long the American government will continue to rule there.

It was, then, a heady but short-lived experience with imperialism, and in American possession today are only remnants of what to individuals at the turn of the century seemed the sure signs of a future great American empire akin to those of Britain and France and Germany. The Samoas are still in American custody but almost forgotten. Hawaii has received statehood. The Philippines have been wobbling in independence for a generation. There are a few other islands, such as Guam and Midway. There is the Trust Territory of the Pacific Islands, the principal importance of which seems to be as a testing ground for atomic weapons. A great idea in American foreign policy thus rose and fell, within living memory.

II

The second of the ideas set out in the documents to follow is, as President Woodrow Wilson announced on April 2, 1917, in his war message to Congress, making the world safe for democracy. Here was a phrase by the greatest phrasemaker in American history that has rung down through the years since its utterance that darkening evening in the House Chamber, as the lights gleamed throughout the great room, and members of the Senate and House listened as the President explained the reasons why war was necessary. When Wilsonian views passed into disrepute in the 1920s, it was easy to criticize the phrase spoken on April 2, and many people were impelled to say that such a goal, so world-wide a vision, was too much for the republic of the New World. Perhaps it has proved too much of a goal, and maybe also it was not properly the nation's business. But in the twentieth century a great deal of American diplomacy has been devoted to supporting the peoples of the world against autocracy and privilege. And who, really, could fail to be moved by Wilson's peroration that fateful evening in Washington, those hauntingly eloquent sentences uttered now so long ago:

It is a distressing and oppressive duty, Gentlemen of the Congress, which I have performed in thus addressing you. There are, it may be, many months of fiery trial and sacrifice ahead of us. It is a fearful thing to lead this great peaceful people into war, into the most terrible and disastrous of all wars, civilization itself seeming to be in the balance. But the right is more precious than peace, and we shall fight for the things which we have always carried nearest our hearts, —for democracy, for the right of those who submit to authority to have a voice in their own governments, for the rights and liberties of small nations, for a universal dominion of right by such a concert of free peoples as shall bring peace and safety to all nations and make the world itself at last free. To such a task we can dedicate our lives and our fortunes, everything that we are and everything that we have, with the pride of those who know that the day has come when America is privileged to spend her blood and her might for the principles that gave her birth and happiness and the peace which she has treasured. God helping her, she can do no other.

Even the American imperialists were in favor of democracy. It is indeed possible to contend that mixed with the dreams of the imperialists was a large feeling for democracy, a desire to advance the fortunes of democratic government everywhere. As Wilson told Sir William Tyrrell in regard to Latin America, "I am going to teach the South American republics to elect good men." Wilson's ambassador to the Court of St. James's, Walter Hines Page, in October, 1913, informed Sir Edward Grey that the United States might have to intervene in Mexico. "In that event," the ambassador continued,

the United States would go into Mexico, and they would hold the elections with bayonets round every polling station to ensure that the people voted secretly and with freedom, so that the result of the election might be the choice of the people.

Grey expressed a fear that such action might be a large operation. Page replied that "however many millions it cost, if the American people decided to act they would vote anything that was required." American aims everywhere in Latin America were democratic, even if the means to this end were not. The hopes of the imperialists that they would bring democracy to their charges may have been rationalizations, to use the American academic word; they may have been verbal façade, icing or frosting on a cake of economic and patriotic desire; and yet somehow the talk of democratizing the Western Hemisphere was not simply talk. After all, the issue that brought on the war in 1898, Cuba, was primarily a humane issue. The document in this present volume which sets out Senator Red-

field Proctor's view of Cuba early in 1898 is a document with
strong democratic overtones. The essence of Proctor's argument
was that the Cubans deserved to govern themselves:

> I have endeavored to state in not intemperate mood what I saw and
> heard, and to make no argument thereon, but leave everyone to
> draw his own conclusions. To me the strongest appeal is not the
> barbarity practiced by Weyler nor the loss of the *Maine* . . . but
> the spectacle of a million and a half of people, the entire native
> population of Cuba, struggling for freedom and deliverance from
> the worst misgovernment of which I ever had knowledge. . . . I
> am not in favor of annexation: not because I would apprehend any
> particular trouble from it, but because it is not wise policy to take
> in any people of foreign tongue and training, and without any
> strong guiding American element. The fear that if free the people
> of Cuba would be revolutionary is not so well founded as has been
> supposed, and the conditions for good self-government are far more
> favorable. The large number of educated and patriotic men, the
> great sacrifices they have endured, the peaceable temperament of
> the people, whites and blacks, the wonderful prosperity that would
> surely come with peace and good home rule, the large influx of
> American and English immigration and money, would all be strong
> factors for stable institutions.

The participation of the United States in the World War in
1917–18 and the Paris Peace Conference of 1919 was, to be sure,
the prime illustration of democracy as an idea in American foreign
policy. It is quite true that the issue precipitating the United States
into the European conflict was not democracy but neutral rights,
an ancient principle in American foreign relations that went back
to its first American statement in the Plan of 1776. When Wilson
presented to Congress the various reasons for going to war, he
talked mostly about neutral rights. It was only in the midst of his
speech that he used the phrase which ever after would haunt both
his admirers and critics. Nonetheless, once he had said it, the
phrase caught on, and the rest of the speech was soon forgotten. It
came to constitute his entire European program. The peoples of
Europe, accustomed to hearing about national rights, suspecting
with good reason that the formal treaties of alliance were not the
only agreements among the powers, either the Central Powers or
the Allies, seized upon "The world must be made safe for democracy," and for a short time became as enamoured of it as were the
Americans. It was an old idea in American foreign policy, which at
the outset of the Republic was known as republicanism, and

became known as democracy during the era of Andrew Jackson. Its appearance in 1917–18, after a considerable talk about it during the turn-of-the-century imperial era, was nothing new in American foreign relations. But the wonderful rhetoric with which President Wilson clothed this idea seemed to renew its strength and send it forth to conquer the world.

The failure of this idea at Paris, its sublimation into glowing remarks by the statesmen at the same time that they were fulfilling their secret wartime pledges, seemed to shock the American people, who somehow were not prepared to contend in peacetime for what they had fought in war. In retrospect it is saddening to see how the Americans, after helping win a great war, expected their principles to triumph almost without effort—were willing to take the wartime enthusiasms and immediate postwar evocations of their Associates as a sign that everything was well. Perhaps the Americans had not had enough experience with the problems of Europe, being more accustomed to those of Latin America and even of Asia, and were not prepared to discover how intractable some of the Old World's problems were, even if approached with the new formula of national self-determination, or democracy.

When the Treaty of Versailles failed in the Senate for reasons only partly related to its merits, the American people dropped, perhaps permanently, their hope that the world could be made safe for democracy. As a leading idea of American foreign policy, democracy disappeared in 1919, and has not been heard from since. This was a pity, as it is at least arguable that in the years since the Second World War, when the nation found itself attacked by world communism, it would have helped the national morale and foreign policy had there been more faith in democracy, more willingness to assert the founding principle of American government as good for all peoples in all times, less willingness to be "realistic," as a postwar word had it, and deal with whatever regime was at hand and not try to change it.

III

The last principle illustrated in the forthcoming documents is that of security—national security. From the beginning of the government of the United States there has been concern for the republic's existence. Here too was no novel principle, although after the War of 1812 any concern for the nation's security diminished greatly, and little more was heard of it until the 1930s.

Parenthetically one must remark that during the imperial era there was talk of security of the Panama Canal, a possible threat from Imperial Germany. Nothing ever developed. There was meanwhile a feeling that the nation could defend the Canal, whatever the challenge, even after initial losses and confusions. After all, American wars had been a series of initial confusions followed by an intrepid summoning of courage and then the inevitable triumph.

Also parenthetically, one must say that American participation in the World War in 1917–18 was not for reasons of security. There was little talk of balance of power, except to belittle such a notion as European, outmoded by the new doctrine of self-determination. It should have been obvious to President Wilson that in 1917 the balance in Europe was far out of order, that it was in the interest of American security to enter the European war to redress that balance. Secretary of State Robert Lansing understood the threat to American security in 1917. Wilson did not, and entered the war largely for reasons of neutral rights, which he soon replaced with the idea of making the world safe for democracy.

Not until the rise of the second German threat, when Chancellor Adolf Hitler's nation began to develop a strength hitherto unknown in time of peace in Europe, and especially when the German leader's ambitions in 1938–39 became crystal clear, did the United States government begin to seek allies in a fight to preserve its security. The allies appeared first in Latin America, where the Americans hastily advanced the idea of the good neighbor and elaborated a set of doctrines for the hemisphere—that its territorial waters were not subject to interference, and that there should be no transfer of colonial territory from one Old World country to another.

Even then, President Franklin D. Roosevelt moved with agonizing slowness to involve the country in the European conflict, and did not make a commitment of importance until the fighting had gone on for a year. The President appears at first to have thought that the British and French could fight America's battles, that the United States in Europe might pursue the policy of Britain in the eighteenth century, when the British hired mercenaries to fight their Continental enemies. Not until the French suddenly went down in June, 1940, did Roosevelt begin to see that something more than munitions and cheery words were necessary to preserve American security. There followed the destroyers-bases deal of September 2, 1940, the first serious effort to aid the British beyond the normal bounds of neutrality. As the President informed Congress:

> Preparation for defense is an inalienable prerogative of a sovereign state. Under present circumstances this exercise of sovereign right is essential to the maintenance of our peace and safety. This is the most important action in the reinforcement of our national defense that has been taken since the Louisiana Purchase. Then as now, considerations of safety from overseas attack were fundamental.

This was some exaggeration. The bases were not as important as the Louisiana Purchase. Nor were the destroyers of great moment to the British; despite Prime Minister Winston Churchill's cables about the need for destroyers, fifty old "four-stackers" were not going to make the difference in Europe. The destroyers-bases deal, though, was a symbol of what America might do in the future, and before long the President undertook a major move of substance, the lend-lease proposition which he began to talk about privately in the autumn of 1940, and openly in press conferences about the time of the new year.

With passage of the Lend-Lease Act on March 11, 1941, the United States made an irretrievable move in defense of its national security. Indeed, the formal title of this move, as it passed through Congress, was An Act to Promote the Defense of the United States. The critics of the President sensed that lend-lease was the formal turning point in a new defense of American security that would so widen the commitments and responsibilities of the government that American foreign policy never would be the same again, and there was vociferous if ultimately futile objection to the act. In the course of the objection there was comment that the President soon would be trying to convoy ships to Europe carrying the goods produced under lend-lease, and critics of the act prevailed upon Congress to write a proviso into the law that "nothing in this Act shall be construed to authorize or to permit the authorization of convoying by naval vessels of the United States." Some months later, in September, 1941, the President slyly got around this problem by using a German submarine's attack on the United States destroyer Greer (after the Greer had been following the submarine for more than three hours, broadcasting its position to a nearby British plane) as an excuse for instituting convoys against, as FDR put it, the rattlesnakes of the Atlantic ("but when you see a rattlesnake poised to strike, you do not wait until he has struck before you crush him. These Nazi submarines and raiders are the rattlesnakes of the Atlantic"). Lend-lease required convoying, for it was futile to make goods for Britain—and, after Hitler's attack in June, 1941, Russia—without providing the means for the materials to reach their destination.

It is therefore safe to say that with passage of lend-lease and the ensuing institution of convoying, the United States became an undeclared belligerent in the European war, in protection of its security.

Unknown to most Americans at the time, and unsuspected by leading officials, the security of the country was more immediately in jeopardy from the Japanese. The Roosevelt administration in early November, 1941, had toyed with the idea of a modus vivendi with Japan, some arrangement that would stave off hostilities, preserve the amenities of friendship, until the defenses of the Philippines and other places were in better order. A contingent of 21,000 troops was scheduled to sail from a west coast port for the Philippines on December 8. When word got out in Washington of a possible temporary arrangement with the Japanese, there was an outcry. Churchill remarked that it would mean a "thin diet for Chiang Kai-shek." Chiang's supporters pressed the administration unmercifully. Secretary Hull gave up any idea of compromise and on November 26, 1941, presented the two Japanese ambassadors then in Washington with a set of propositions, in two sections. Section II, points 3 and 4, were the crucial demands:

> 3. The Government of Japan will withdraw all military, naval, air and police forces from China and from Indochina.
> 4. The Government of the United States and the Government of Japan will not support—militarily, politically, economically—any government or regime in China other than the National Government of the Republic of China with capital temporarily at Chung-king.

It was, then, a restatement of the second open-door note of 1900, forty-one years later! Unknown to Secretary Hull and the President, at that very moment the Pearl Harbor attack fleet—six carriers, two battleships, a full complement of cruisers, destroyers, and submarines—sailed from a fog-shrouded northern Japanese port.

Within days the Japanese struck with a success that brought consternation to leaders of the American government. Of course, after the initial worries subsided it became evident that the Pacific coast at least—although this said nothing for Hawaii, not to mention the Philippines—was fairly safe, that the distances probably were too far for the Japanese attack fleet even if that fleet had managed to come undetected to the Hawaiians. The days lengthened, with no further sign of the Pearl Harbor task force. The fleet returned to Japan undetected.

After the nation recovered its nerve, it became apparent once more that the principal long-range threat to American security during the Second World War was from Europe, from the forces of Hitler. The German conqueror had occupied the whole of Western Europe, except for Sweden, Switzerland, Portugal, and such satellites as Spain and Italy. Nothing seemed to stand in his way. The presumption in 1941, and even for many months into 1942, was that he might well win against Russia, in which case he would turn his attention to the New World and end any possible challenge from that quarter.

In retrospect, the threat to American security in the Western Hemisphere may not have been as dire as it seemed in the first months of American participation in the Second World War, and yet one can never be certain as to what Hitler might have done had he possessed the opportunity. It is true that no Nazi plans existed to attack the United States, or even for troops to cross over from Africa to the hump of Brazil and attack South America. The Germans had not planned that far. After the end of the war it appeared that the German high command had not even planned the attack upon Britain with any thoroughness, and did not begin planning for the attack upon Russia until the summer of 1940. There was not the iron-bound certainty to German policy which contemporaries gave to it. Still, Hitler detested Americans, considering them the creatures of Hollywood. What was there to America, he once said, except "millionaires, beauty queens, stupid records, and Hollywood?" If he had become the new Genghis Khan, winning in Russia, establishing himself upon the European heartland, he might have taken his New Order to the New World.

President Roosevelt thought so, and made the Grand Alliance in hope that it could prevail. The President did his best to hold together the alliance, proving more willing than later critics thought he should have been to go to the corners of the earth to visit the dictator of Russia. First the President, at Casablanca in January, 1943, tied American security to the unconditional surrender of Germany, Italy, and Japan. He then did everything possible to show his concern for the continuing struggle of the Russians. Teheran and Yalta, the two wartime summit conferences considered in the documents which follow, were the high points of this quest. The first conference was a get-together, but as William M. Franklin recently has shown—in Some Pathways in Twentieth-Century History, Daniel R. Beaver, ed. (1969)—it was more than that, for most of the decisions set down at Yalta were anticipated in the discussions at Teheran. Yalta, of course, held in the one-time summer palace of the last Tsar, was an evidence of American and British desire for continuation of the comradeship in arms. The decisions for the Far East, later so criticized, were only an indication that the Western Allies believed Russia had lost far too much in the wars of the twentieth century and deserved a return to the territorial status quo of 1904, before the Russo-Japanese War.

Then came the end of the war. If ever there was a refutation of the phrase later announced by General MacArthur, "There is no substitute for victory," it was the victory of 1945, which was as complete a victory as a grand alliance ever had won in all the annals of Europe's or the world's wars. That briefly golden year 1945, which had seemed the close of so long an effort, turned out to be the beginning of another. Pursuing a policy of security, Americans had failed to obtain it, discovering that, as in the case of other policies, just when they believed they had come to the moment of triumph, it disappeared into the mists of uncertainty.

. . . In the lowest vertebrate animal, the amphioxus, the cerebrum and cerebellum do not exist at all. In fishes we begin to find them, but they are much smaller than the optic lobes. In such a highly organized fish as the halibut, which weighs about as much as an average-sized man, the cerebrum is smaller than a melon-seed. Continuing to grow by adding concentric layers at the surface, the cerebrum and cerebellum become much larger in birds and lower mammals, gradually covering up the optic lobes. As we pass to higher mammalian forms, the growth of the cerebrum becomes most conspicuous, until it extends backwards so far as to cover up the cerebellum, whose functions are limited to the conscious adjustment of muscular movements. In the higher apes the cerebrum begins to extend itself forwards, and this goes on in the human race. The cranial capacity of the European exceeds that of the Australian by forty cubic inches, or nearly four times as much as that by which the Australian exceeds the gorilla; and the expansion is almost entirely in the upper and anterior portions. But the increase of the cerebral surface is shown not only in the general size of the organ, but to a still greater extent in the irregular creasing and furrowing of the surface. This creasing and furrowing begins to occur in the higher mammals, and in civilized man it is carried to an astonishing extent. The amount of intelligence is correlated with the number, the depth, and the irregularity of the furrows. A cat's brain has a few symmetrical creases. In an ape the creases are deepened into slight furrows, and they run irregularly, somewhat like the lines in the palm of your hand. With age and experience the furrows grow deeper and more sinuous, and new ones appear; and in man these phenomena come to have great significance. The cerebral surface of a human infant is like that of an ape. In an adult savage, or in a European peasant, the furrowing is somewhat marked and complicated. In the brain of a great scholar, the furrows are very deep and crooked, and hundreds of creases appear which are not found at all in the brains of ordinary men. In other words, the cerebral surface of such a man, the seat of conscious mental life, has become enormously enlarged in area; and we must further observe that it goes on enlarging in some cases into extreme old age. . . .

The . . . highest method of forming great political bodies is that of *federation*. . . . Here there is no conquest, but a voluntary union of small political groups into a great political group. Each little group preserves its local independence intact, while forming part of an indissoluble whole. Obviously this method of political union requires both high intelligence and high ethical development. In early times it was impracticable. It was first attempted, with brilliant though ephemeral success, by the Greeks, but it failed for want of the device of representation. In later times it was put into operation, with permanent success, on a small scale by the Swiss, and on a great scale by our forefathers in England. The coalescence of shires into the kingdom of England, effected as it was by means of a representative assembly, and accompanied by the general retention of local self-government, afforded a distinct precedent for such a gigantic federal union as men of English race have since constructed in America. The principle of federation was there, though not the name. And here we hit upon the fundamental contrast between the history of England and that of France. The method by which the modern French nation has been built up has been the Roman method of conquest with incorporation. As the ruler of Paris gradually overcame his vassals, one after another, by warfare or diplomacy, he annexed their counties to his royal domain, and governed them by lieutenants sent from Paris. Self-government was thus crushed out in France, while it was preserved in England. And just as Rome achieved its unprecedented dominion by adopting a political method more effective than any that had been hitherto employed, so England, employing for the first time a still higher and more effective method, has come to play a part in the world compared with which even the part played by Rome seems insignificant. The test of the relative strength of the English and Roman methods came when England and France contended for the possession of North America. The people which preserved its self-government could send forth self-supporting colonies; the people which had lost the very tradition of self-government could not. Hence the dominion of the sea, with that of all the outlying parts of the earth, fell into the hands of men of English race; and hence the federative method of political union—the method which contains every element of permanence, and which is pacific in its very conception—is already assuming a sway which is unquestionably destined to become universal.

Bearing all this in mind, we cannot fail to recognize the truth of the statement that the great wars of the historic period have been either contests between the industrial and the predatory types of society or contests incident upon the imperfect formation of great political aggregates. Throughout the turmoil of the historic period —which on a superficial view seems such a chaos—we see certain definite tendencies at work; the tendency toward the formation of larger and larger political aggregates, and toward the more perfect maintenance of local self-government and individual freedom among the parts of the aggregate. This two-sided process began with the beginnings of industrial civilization; it has aided the progress of industry and been aided by it; and the result has been to diminish the quantity of warfare, and to lessen the number of points at which it touches the ordinary course of civilized life. With the further continuance of this process, but one ultimate result is possible. It must go on until warfare becomes obsolete. The nineteenth century, which has witnessed an unprecedented development of industrial civilization, with its attendant arts and sciences, has also witnessed an unprecedented diminution in the strength of the primeval spirit of militancy. It is not that we have got rid of great wars, but that the relative proportion of human strength which has been employed in warfare has been remarkably less than in any previous age. In our own history, of the two really great wars which have permeated our whole social existence,—the Revolutionary War and the War of Secession,—the first was fought in behalf of the pacific principle of equal representation; the second was fought in behalf of the pacific principle of federalism. In each case, the victory helped to hasten the day when warfare shall become unnecessary. In the few great wars of Europe since the overthrow of Napoleon, we may see the same principle at work. In almost every case the result has been to strengthen the pacific tendencies of modern society. Whereas warfare was once dominant over the face of the earth, and came home in all its horrid details to everybody's door, and threatened the very existence of industrial civilization; it has now become narrowly confined in time and space, it no longer comes home to everybody's door, and, in so far as it is still tolerated, for want of a better method of settling grave international questions, it has become quite ancillary to the paramount needs of industrial civilization. When we can see so much as this lying before us on the pages of history, we cannot fail to see that the final extinction of warfare is only a question of time. Sooner or later it must come to an end, and the pacific principle of federalism, whereby questions between states are settled, like questions between individuals, by due process of law, m..st reign supreme over all the earth.

As regards the significance of Man's position in the universe, this gradual elimination of strife is a fact of utterly unparalleled grandeur. Words cannot do justice to such a fact. It means that the wholesale destruction of life, which has heretofore characterized evolution ever since life began, and through which the higher forms of organic existence have been produced, must presently come to an end in the case of the chief of God's creatures. It means that the universal struggle for existence, having succeeded in bringing forth that consummate product of creative energy, the Human Soul, has done its work and will presently cease. In the lower regions of organic life it must go on, but as a determining factor in the highest work of evolution it will disappear.

The action of natural selection upon Man has long since been essentially diminished through the operation of social conditions. For in all grades of civilization above the lowest, "there are so many kinds of superiorities which severally enable men to survive, notwithstanding accompanying inferiorities, that natural selection cannot by itself rectify any particular unfitness." In a race of inferior animals any maladjustment is quickly removed by natural selection, because, owing to the universal slaughter, the highest completeness of life possible to a given grade of organization is required for the mere maintenance of life. But under the conditions surrounding human development it is otherwise. There is a wide interval between the highest and lowest degrees of completeness of living that are compatible with maintenance of life. Hence the wicked flourish. Vice is but slowly eliminated, because mankind has so many other qualities, beside the bad ones, which enable it to subsist and achieve progress in spite of them, that natural selection—which always works through death—cannot come into play. The improvement of civilized man goes on mainly through processes of direct adaptation. The principle in accordance with which the gloved hand of the dandy becomes white and soft while the hand of the labouring man grows brown and tough is the main principle at work in the improvement of Humanity. . . .

3. Navalism

A. ALFRED THAYER MAHAN

THE IDEA that life was a race, and that nations as well as individuals raced (racism, one might with humor describe it) was easy to believe in post-Civil War America. One of the believers was a middle-aged navy captain, Alfred Thayer Mahan, who lectured at the new Naval War College in Newport, Rhode Island, in the latter 1880s and published his lectures in 1890. Here, to be sure, was a book with as much long-range influence as the work of Darwin published thirty-one years before. Mahan wrote a scholarly interpretation of the rise of English sea power which today seems too technical for readers, and perhaps was not altogether interesting for readers of his day; but the introductory chapter made some remarks about the importance of sea power that etched themselves into the minds of influential individuals of Mahan's time. These men, in positions of public influence not merely in the United States but in Britain, Germany, and Japan, translated Mahan's conclusions into the naval ambitions of their own countries, and urged the prophet's injunctions, variously interpreted, upon their own countrymen. Mahan's book was not even responsible for the rebirth of the American navy, as two of his footnotes, reprinted in the document that follows, attest: the Naval Act of 1890, which provided the first modern battleships for the United States Navy, ships of the Oregon class which saw action in 1898, had passed Congress before his book was published. Nor was he responsible for the interpretations of his views offered abroad, or the subsequent great naval race after the turn of the twentieth century between Great Britain and Germany, which resulted in the rippling flashes and booming of great guns at Jutland on that sad late afternoon in May, 1916. He simply had the luck to publish his book at a time when men of affairs were looking for excuses to build new modern navies of iron and steel, with rifled guns and heavy armor. The navies then became instruments of the new manifest destinies of the new naval powers.

. . . To turn now from the particular lessons drawn from the history of the past to the general question of the influence of government upon the sea career of its people, it is seen that that influence can work in two distinct but closely related ways.

SOURCE: Alfred Thayer Mahan, The Influence of Sea Power upon History: 1660–1783 (Boston, 1890), pp. 81–88.

First, in peace: The government by its policy can favor the natural growth of a people's industries and its tendencies to seek adventure and gain by way of the sea; or it can try to develop such industries and such sea-going bent, when they do not naturally exist; or, on the other hand, the government may by mistaken action check and fetter the progress which the people left to themselves would make. In any one of these ways the influence of the government will be felt, making or marring the sea power of the country in the matter of peaceful commerce; upon which alone, it cannot be too often insisted, a thoroughly strong navy can be based.

Secondly, for war: The influence of the government will be felt in its most legitimate manner in maintaining an armed navy, of a size commensurate with the growth of its shipping and the importance of the interests connected with it. More important even than the size of the navy is the question of its institutions, favoring a healthful spirit and activity, and providing for rapid development in time of war by an adequate reserve of men and of ships and by measures for drawing out that general reserve power which has before been pointed to, when considering the character and pursuits of the people. Undoubtedly under this second head of warlike preparation must come the maintenance of suitable naval stations, in those distant parts of the world to which the armed shipping must follow the peaceful vessels of commerce. The protection of such stations must depend either upon direct military force, as do Gibraltar and Malta, or upon a surrounding friendly population, such as the American colonists once were to England, and, it may be presumed, the Australian colonists now are. Such friendly surroundings and backing, joined to a reasonable military provision, are the best of defences, and when combined with decided preponderance at sea, make a scattered and extensive empire, like that of England, secure; for while it is true that an unexpected attack may cause disaster in some one quarter, the actual superiority of naval power prevents such disaster from being general or irremediable. History has sufficiently proved this. England's naval bases have been in all parts of the world; and her fleets have at once protected them, kept open the communications between them, and relied upon them for shelter.

Colonies attached to the mother-country afford, therefore, the surest means of supporting abroad the sea power of a country. In peace, the influence of the government should be felt in promoting by all means a warmth of attachment and a unity of interest which will make the welfare of one the welfare of all, and the quarrel of one the quarrel of all; and in war, or rather for war, by inducing such measures of organization and defence as shall be felt by all to be a fair distribution of a burden of which each reaps the benefit.

Such colonies the United States has not and is not likely to have. As regards purely military naval stations, the feeling of her people was probably accurately expressed by an historian of the English navy a hundred years ago, speaking then of Gibraltar and Port Mahon. "Military governments," said he, "agree so little with the industry of a trading people, and are in themselves so repugnant to the genius of the British people, that I do not wonder that men of good sense and of all parties have inclined to give up these, as Tangiers was given up." Having therefore no foreign establishments, either colonial or military, the ships of war of the United States, in war, will be like land birds, unable to fly far from their own shores. To provide resting-places for them, where they can coal and repair, would be one of the first duties of a government proposing to itself the development of the power of the nation at sea.

As the practical object of this inquiry is to draw from the lessons of history inferences applicable to one's own country and service, it is proper now to ask how far the conditions of the United States involve serious danger, and call for action on the part of the government, in order to build again her sea power. It will not be too much to say that the action of the government since the Civil War, and up to this day, has been effectively directed solely to what has been called the first link in the chain which makes sea power. Internal development, great production, with the accompanying aim and boast of self-sufficingness, such has been the object, such to some extent the result. In this the government has faithfully reflected the bent of the controlling elements of the country, though it is not always easy to feel that such controlling elements are truly representative, even in a free country. However that may be, there is no doubt that, besides having no colonies, the intermediate link of a peaceful shipping, and the interests involved in it, are now likewise lacking. In short, the United States has only one link of the three.

The circumstances of naval war have changed so much within

the last hundred years, that it may be doubted whether such disastrous effects on the one hand, or such brilliant prosperity on the other, as were seen in the wars between England and France, could now recur. In her secure and haughty sway of the seas England imposed a yoke on neutrals which will never again be borne; and the principle that the flag covers the goods is forever secured. The commerce of a belligerent can therefore now be safely carried on in neutral ships, except when contraband of war or to blockaded ports; and as regards the latter, it is also certain that there will be no more paper blockades. Putting aside therefore the question of defending her seaports from capture or contribution, as to which there is practical unanimity in theory and entire indifference in practice, what need has the United States of sea power? Her commerce is even now carried on by others; why should her people desire that which, if possessed, must be defended at great cost? So far as this question is economical, it is outside the scope of this work; but conditions which may entail suffering and loss on the country by war are directly pertinent to it. Granting therefore that the foreign trade of the United States, going and coming, is on board ships which an enemy cannot touch except when bound to a blockaded port, what will constitute an efficient blockade? The present definition is, that it is such as to constitute a manifest danger to a vessel seeking to enter or leave the port. This is evidently very elastic. Many can remember that during the Civil War, after a night attack on the United States fleet off Charleston, the Confederates next morning sent out a steamer with some foreign consuls on board, who so far satisfied themselves that no blockading vessel was in sight that they issued a declaration to that effect. On the strength of this declaration some Southern authorities claimed that the blockade was technically broken, and could not be technically re-established without a new notification. Is it necessary, to constitute a real danger to blockade-runners, that the blockading fleet should be in sight? Half a dozen fast steamers, cruising twenty miles off-shore between the New Jersey and Long Island coast, would be a very real danger to ships seeking to go in or out by the principal entrance to New York; and similar positions might effectively blockade Boston, the Delaware, and the Chesapeake. The main body of the blockading fleet, prepared not only to capture merchant-ships but to resist military attempts to break the blockade, need not be within sight, nor in a position known to the shore. The bulk of Nelson's fleet was fifty miles from Cadiz two days before Trafalgar, with a small detachment watching close to the harbor. The allied fleet began to get under way at 7 A.M., and Nelson, even under the conditions of those days, knew it by 9:30. The English fleet at that distance was a very real danger to its enemy. It seems possible, in these days of submarine telegraphs, that the blockading forces in-shore and off-shore, and from one port to another, might be in telegraphic communication with one another along the whole coast of the United States, readily giving mutual support; and if, by some fortunate military combination, one detachment were attacked in force, it could warn the others and retreat upon them. Granting that such a blockade off one port were broken on one day, by fairly driving away the ships maintaining it, the notification of its being re-established could be cabled all over the world the next. To avoid such blockades there must be a military force afloat that will at all times so endanger a blockading fleet that it can by no means keep its place. Then neutral ships, except those laden with contraband of war, can come and go freely, and maintain the commercial relations of the country with the world outside.

It may be urged that, with the extensive sea-coast of the United States, a blockade of the whole line cannot be effectively kept up. No one will more readily concede this than officers who remember how the blockade of the Southern coast alone was maintained. But in the present condition of the navy, and, it may be added, with any additions not exceeding those so far proposed by the government,[1] the attempt to blockade Boston, New York, the Delaware, the Chesapeake, and the Mississippi, in other words, the great centres of export and import, would not entail upon one of the large maritime nations efforts greater than have been made before. England has at the same time blockaded Brest, the Biscay coast, Toulon, and Cadiz, when there were powerful squadrons lying within the harbors. It is true that commerce in neutral ships can then enter other ports of the United States than those named; but what a dislocation of the carrying traffic of the country, what failure of supplies at times, what inadequate means of transport by rail or water, of dockage, of lighterage, of warehousing, will be involved

1. [Mahan's footnote] Since the above was written, the secretary of the navy, in his report for 1889, has recommended a fleet which would make such a blockade as here suggested very hazardous.

in such an enforced change of the ports of entry! Will there be no money loss, no suffering, consequent upon this? And when with much pain and expense these evils have been partially remedied, the enemy may be led to stop the new inlets as he did the old. The people of the United States will certainly not starve, but they may suffer grievously. As for supplies which are contraband of war, is there not reason to fear that the United States is not now able to go alone if an emergency should arise?

The question is eminently one in which the influence of the government should make itself felt, to build up for the nation a navy which, if not capable of reaching distant countries, shall at least be able to keep clear the chief approaches to its own. The eyes of the country have for a quarter of a century been turned from the sea; the results of such a policy and of its opposite will be shown in the instance of France and of England. Without asserting a narrow parallelism between the case of the United States and either of these, it may safely be said that it is essential to the welfare of the whole country that the conditions of trade and commerce should remain, as far as possible, unaffected by an external war. In order to do this, the enemy must be kept not only out of our ports, but far away from our coasts.[2]

2. [Mahan's footnote] The word "defence" in war involves two ideas, which for the sake of precision in thought should be kept separated in the mind. There is defence pure and simple, which strengthens itself and awaits attack. This may be called passive defence. On the other hand, there is a view of defence which asserts that safety for one's self, the real object of defensive preparation, is best secured by attacking the enemy. In the matter of sea-coast defence, the former method is exemplified by stationary fortifications, submarine mines, and generally all immobile works destined simply to stop an enemy if he tries to enter. The second method comprises all those means and weapons which do not wait for attack, but go to meet the enemy's fleet, whether it be but for a few miles, or whether to his own shores. Such a defence may seem to be really offensive war, but it is not; it becomes offensive only when its object of attack is changed from the enemy's fleet to the enemy's country. England defended her own coasts and colonies by stationing her fleets off the French ports, to fight the French fleet if it came out. The United States in the Civil War stationed her fleets off the Southern ports, not because she feared for her own, but to break down the Confederacy by isolation from the rest of the world, and ultimately by attacking the ports. The methods were the same; but the purpose in one case was defensive, in the other offensive.

The confusion of the two ideas leads to much unnecessary wrangling as to the proper sphere of army and navy in coast-defence. Passive defences belong

Can this navy be had without restoring the merchant shipping? It is doubtful. History has proved that such a purely military sea power can be built up by a despot, as was done by Louis XIV.; but though so fair seeming, experience showed that his navy was like a growth which having no root soon withers away. But in a representative government any military expenditure must have a strongly represented interest behind it, convinced of its necessity. Such an interest in sea power does not exist, cannot exist here without action by the government. How such a merchant shipping should be built up, whether by subsidies or by free trade, by constant administration of tonics or by free movement in the open air, is not a military but an economical question. Even had the United States a great national shipping, it may be doubted whether a sufficient navy would follow; the distance which separates her from other great powers, in one way a protection, is also a snare. The motive, if any there be, which will give the United States a navy, is probably now quickening in the Central American Isthmus. Let us hope it will not come to the birth too late. . . .

B. The Need for Sea Power

THEODORE ROOSEVELT, *thirty-two years old in 1890, at that time Civil Service Commissioner in Washington, read Mahan's book with enthusiasm, and his review appeared in* The Atlantic Monthly, LXVI *(October, 1890), pp. 563–567.*

Captain Mahan has written distinctively the best and most important, and also by far the most interesting, book on naval history which has been produced on either side of the water for many a long year. Himself an officer who has seen active service and borne himself with honor under fire, he starts with an advantage that no civilian can possess. On the other hand, he does not show the shortcomings which make the average military man an exasperatingly incompetent military historian. His work is in every respect scholarly, and has not a trace of the pedantry which invariably mars

SOURCE: William H. Harbaugh, ed., *The Writings of Theodore Roosevelt* (Indianapolis, 1967), pp. 36–41.

to the army; everything that moves in the water to the navy, which has the prerogative of the offensive defence. If seamen are used to garrison forts, they become part of the land forces, as surely as troops, when embarked as part of the complement, become part of the sea forces.

mere self-conscious striving after scholarship. He is thoroughly conversant with his subject, and has prepared himself for it by exhaustive study and research, and he approaches it in, to use an old-fashioned phrase, an entirely philosophical spirit. He subordinates detail to mass-effects, trying always to grasp and make evident the essential features of a situation; and he neither loses sight of nor exaggerates the bearing which the history of past struggles has upon our present problems. . . .

Captain Mahan's effort is to show the tremendous effect which sea power has had upon the development of certain of the great nations of the world, especially at momentous crises of their history. . . . His discussion of the campaigns and battles, of the strategy and tactics, is full and clear, and written in a perfectly scientific and dispassionate spirit. But this is not his greatest merit. He never for a moment loses sight of the relations which the struggles by sea bore to the history of the time; and, for the period which he covers, he shows, as no other writer has done, the exact points and the wonderful extent of the influence of the sea power of the various contending nations upon their ultimate triumph of failure, and upon the futures of the mighty races to which they belonged.

In the first chapter after the Introduction, he discusses the various elements which go to make up sea power, writing always, as elsewhere throughout the book, with especial heed to the circumstances of the United States at the present time. He shows how sea power is affected by the geographical position, physical conformation, extent, and density of population of a country no less than by the character of the people and of the government. He points out the need of adequate fortifications and navy-yards on all the coast, and incidentally specifies the need at some point on the Gulf Coast, preferably the mouth of the Mississippi; and he lays stress on the necessity of a large commercial marine, if we wish the sea population which alone furnishes a secure base for naval power. . . .

Again, as Captain Mahan shows, our experience in the Civil War is worthless as a test of what we could do against a foreign sea power. It is impossible to imagine a more foolish state of mind than that which accepts the belief in our capacity to improvise means of resistance against the sea power of Europe, ready equipped and armed at all points, because we were successful in overcoming with our makeshifts an enemy even more unprepared

than we were ourselves. It is true that at the end of four years'
warfare we had developed a formidable fleet; but in the event of a
European contest, it is not likely that we should be allowed as
many weeks before the fatal blow fell. There is a loose popular idea
that we could defend ourselves by some kind of patent method,
invented on the spur of the moment. This is sheer folly. There is
no doubt that American ingenuity could do something, but not
enough to prevent the enemy from ruining our coasting-trade and
threatening with destruction half our coast towns. Proper forts,
with heavy guns, could do much; but our greatest need is the need
of a fighting-fleet. Forts alone could not prevent the occupation of
any town or territory outside the range of their guns, or the general
wasting of the seaboard; while a squadron of heavy battleships, able
to sail out and attack the enemy's vessels as they approached, and
possessing the great advantage of being near their own base of
supplies, would effectually guard a thousand miles of coast. Passive
defense, giving the assailant complete choice of the time and place
for attack, is always a most dangerous expedient. Our ships should
be the best of their kind—this is the first desideratum; but, in
addition, there should be plenty of them. We need a large navy,
composed not merely of cruisers, but containing also a full proportion of powerful battleships, able to meet those of any other
nation. . . .

II

New Opportunities

By the latter years of the nineteenth century a new philosophy with international implications, survival of the fittest (as Herbert Spencer, not Darwin, described it), was germinating in the American consciousness, and there was a new navy in the making in American shipyards. The first sure signs of America's new manifest destiny appeared in a series of diplomatic controversies over two Pacific island groups, the Samoas and the Hawaiians, and over American honor and the Monroe Doctrine in, respectively, Chile and Venezuela. The latter controversy did not merely involve the pristine doctrine of American foreign policy, but the most ancient foe of the American people, Great Britain. Its successful conclusion—the British backed down and accepted American help to settle the issue—greatly increased the national desire for more assertiveness in foreign affairs.

4. Samoa

THE INTEREST of the United States in Samoa had emerged as early as the Grant administration, when in 1872 an American naval officer negotiated a treaty with Samoan native chieftains. Although the treaty failed in the Senate, Grant next year dispatched a special agent, Colonel A. B. Steinberger, who for a short time succeeded in setting himself up as premier of the islands. The American government in 1878 arranged for rights to a naval station in Pago Pago. Unfortunately, in the mid-1880s the Samoan kettle began to boil. At a conference in Berlin in 1884 the British and German governments arranged a sort of trade, in accord with which the German government recognized the new British position in Egypt—the British had occupied Egypt in 1882—and the British gave the Germans a free hand in equatorial Africa and the South Seas. Chancellor Otto von Bismarck moved quickly to take the Samoas. He immediately met opposition from the Department of State. Secretary Thomas F. Bayard apparently did not understand that he was dealing with a European arrangement, but was nothing if not vocal in raising the American position to a point of high principle. Three special problems agitated Bayard: a German claim that Consul Dawson in 1881 had protested an occupation of Apia by the German warship Moewe, and had caused the editor of an Apia newspaper to write some hostile articles; that another American consul, by name of Canisius, had inspired King Malietoa (whom the Germans heartily disliked) to write two irreverent letters to the German emperor; and that Consul Greenebaum on May 14, 1886, had proclaimed an American protectorate over the Samoan Islands and hoisted the American flag as a sign thereof.

. . . I am instructed by the President to say that he fully participates in the regrets of Prince Bismarck that the relations of traditional friendship which have subsisted between the United States and Germany unbroken for so many years should be, in any way or degree, disturbed or affected by occurrences in remote islands in which the material interests of both Governments are comparatively insignificant.

This Government has manifested in the most unmistakable manner its desire to avoid all possibilities of difference with the

SOURCE: Thomas F. Bayard to the American minister in Berlin, George H. Pendleton, Jan. 17, 1888, in Foreign Relations of the United States: 1888 (2 vols., Washington, D.C., 1889), I, pp. 595–96, 600–01, 603–04, 607–08.

other treaty powers in Samoa, alike by its action in respect to its consular representation there, and by the exercise of its moral influence to discountenance and prevent those native dissensions which, assuming the form of disaffection towards existing government, have stood as a constant invitation and incentive (of which interested foreigners in the islands have not been slow to avail themselves) to intrigue with native factions to obtain commercial and political supremacy. This policy it has pursued with consistency and good faith, actuated not so much by the idea of any present or probable future commercial interest in that quarter of the globe in which the islands in question lie, as by a benevolent desire to promote the development and secure the independence of one of the few remaining independent territories and autonomous native governments in the Pacific Ocean.

Had the Government of the United States entertained any designs of territorial aggrandizement or of political control in Samoa, they could have been accomplished, it is believed, with much satisfaction to a majority of the natives, and with little opposition from any of them, long prior to the date of either the British or the German treaty. But another and widely different policy has guided the action of the United States in respect to the native communities in the Southern Pacific, and it is not, I apprehend, claiming too much credit for this Government to express the opinion that the example it exhibited of treating with Samoa as an independent state led to a similar course and a similar acknowledgment of native independence in that island group by Germany and Great Britain.

Since that time a regard for the subsequently acquired conventional rights of Germany and Great Britain has been an additional reason for continuing the policy of this Government of respect for native independence. The disinterested position of the United States is strongly emphasized by the promptitude with which the action of Mr. Greenebaum was disavowed by this Government, when he proclaimed an American protectorate over Samoa, in order to counteract the disintegrating and destructive effect upon the then native government, not only of prior acts of the German consul, Dr. Stuebel, which had been protested against by the British consul as well as by Mr. Greenebaum, and some of which, at least, I understood, were not sustained by the Imperial Government, but also of the active and substantial support given by German subjects there resident to those in arms against the government of Malietoa. Without waiting for representation or remonstrance, I at once caused both Germany and Great Britain to be informed of this Government's entire disapproval of Mr. Greenebaum's action, as being unauthorized and at variance with his instructions, and he was soon after recalled.

This Department has never been furnished with evidence as to the reported authorship of the two letters of Malietoa to the Emperor of Germany of the 18th and 28th of May, 1885, nor as to the alleged origin of certain articles in Samoan newspapers, which I have never seen; but in respect to the alleged action of the American consul, Mr. Dawson, in 1881, on the occasion of the landing of a force from His Imperial Majesty's ship Möwe, the documents in the possession of this Department lead to a very different impression of that incident from that which Prince Bismarck has been led to entertain. Not only was the action of the German consul on that occasion, as I am informed, not in agreement with the Samoan Government and the municipal administration, but it was taken without consultation with the acting head of the municipal government, after the disturbance had actually been quelled by the local police, and was complained against by the Samoan King, a copy of whose complaint, dated July 14, 1881, and addressed to Mr. Dawson, as the acting head of the consular and municipal body, is herewith inclosed. But, whatever may be the precise circumstances of the affair, it appears at most merely to involve a personal difference of opinion as to the measures required by an unforseen but brief commotion, and to have had no connection whatever with subsequent disorders in the islands. . . .

The earnest desire of the Government of the United States to perpetuate the native Government of the Samoan Islands and to place it on a secure basis is further evidenced, and its views upon the present situation may be more clearly understood by a review of its action subsequently to the proclamation by Mr. Greenebaum, United States consul, of a protectorate over the islands. . . .

Immediately upon being informed of the consul's action, identical instructions were sent by telegraph, on the 1st of June, 1886, both to yourself and to our minister at London, to say to the Governments to which you were respectively accredited, that the claim of an American protectorate over Samoa by the United States consul there was wholly unauthorized and disapproved, no protectorate by any foreign nation being desired; and further, to suggest to those Governments to authorize their ministers at this capital to confer with me with a view to the establishment of order. Following this were certain practical suggestions which it is unnecessary here to enumerate, the last of which, however, was that a joint declaration should be made by the three powers against annexation or the assumption of a protectorate by any of them. . . .

On the 25th of June last the first formal session of the conference was held in this city, the British and German ministers and myself being present as the representatives of our respective Governments.

Other sessions were held from time to time during the following month, and some points of agreement reached; but owing to my inability to concur in the German proposition, which was substantially assented to, though not in all respects explicitly supported, by the British minister, the conference was, on the 26th of July, adjourned by unanimous consent until the autumn, in order that the members might consult their respective Governments with a view to an agreement on some other scheme of co-operative action.

In substance, the German Government proposed to commit the actual control of the islands to a person to be appointed for a term of five years by the power having the preponderating commercial interests there, the appointment to be renewed on the same terms, and the other powers merely to have the concurrent privilege of approving or refusing to approve the nominee. . . .

It is not strange, therefore, that I was taken wholly by surprise when the German minister called at this Department on the 29th of August last, and left with me a memorandum stating that his Government proposed to independently protect its own interests and rights in Samoa and obtain the satisfaction and reparation deemed to be due to its national honor, and, in case Malietoa was either not willing or not powerful enough to give the necessary satisfaction for the past and sufficient guaranties for the future, to declare war against him and refuse to recognize his Government.

Coupled with this declaration was an assurance that the Imperial Government was far from intending to bring about any change in the political relations which the three powers represented there entertained to Samoa; that, on the contrary, it maintained unaltered the existing treaties and stipulations between

Germany, Great Britain, and the United States with regard to Samoa, as well as the equality of the three treaty powers, and proposed to continue its endeavors to arrive at an understanding as to the reforms necessary to establish lasting peace in these islands.

On the 23d of September the German minister called again and left a memorandum stating that Germany had declared war "against Malietoa personally," and that as soon as she had obtained by his abdication due satisfaction the state of war would cease.

It is not my purpose to enter into an examination of the question how far hostilities of this type can be reconciled with settled principles of international law, or with the independence and autonomy of the country against which such measures are aimed. But it may be stated, as a matter well known, that on the 23d of August last, in less than a month from the date of the adjournment of the conference till the autumn, and before any notification to this Government of such resolve on the part of Germany, the German consul at Apia demanded of Malietoa satisfaction in the form of an apology and indemnity, together with the punishment of alleged Samoan offenders, for certain injuries said to have been suffered by German subjects at the hands of Samoans on the evening of the 22d of March preceding, during the celebration by the former of the anniversary of the birth of His Majesty the Emperor of Germany, as well as a considerable pecuniary indemnity for robberies alleged to have been committed on German plantations during the past four years.

To these demands the King was notified to make reply on the following day, which he did by asking that he be given until the 27th of the month, three days, in order that he might have time to consult his Government and chiefs and make a formal answer.

To this request no reply was made by the German consul, and on the same day, the 24th of August, war was declared.

On the following day Tamasese was proclaimed by the German consul as King of Samoa, against the formal and public protest of the American and British consuls. And on the 17th of September, after having been, since the declaration of war against him, a fugitive, Malietoa gave himself up to the German consul, and was taken on board of the *Bismarck*, the flag ship of the German squadron.

It is not my purpose to comment upon the grounds of the recent

German action in Samoa, as they have been above stated, although I regret that the powerful Government of Germany did not find it possible to take a more liberal view of the conditions of Samoan life and civilization, and the unfortunate situation of the native King, who, in regarding himself as the rightful ruler of the islands, could point, in confirmation of his title, to a long series of acknowledgments of his authority by all three treaty powers. . . .

The conclusion at which I am forced to arrive from this review of recent events in Samoa is that the present unfortunate situation there is due not to any action on the part of the representatives of the United States, but to the fomentation by interested foreigners of native dissensions, and to the desire exhibited in a marked degree by those in charge of local German interests to obtain personal and commercial advantages and political supremacy.

But this communication ought not to be concluded without the statement that, in the opinion of this Government, the course taken by Germany in respect to Samoa upon the temporary adjournment of the conference in this city, as above detailed, can not be regarded as having been marked by that just consideration which the ancient friendship between the United States and Germany entitles this Government to expect . . .

You are at liberty to communicate a copy of this instruction to the German Government. . . .

Bayard and his successor at the Department of State, James G. Blaine, pressed the Germans so hard that Bismarck assembled a conference over Samoa which met in Berlin in 1889 and instituted a three-power condominium of Germany, the United States, and Great Britain. Ten years later the powers signed a treaty partitioning the islands between Germany and the United States, with the British receiving compensation in the form of the Tonga Islands, just south of the Samoas, together with part of the Solomon Islands and some adjustments in West Africa. During the First World War, New Zealand forces occupied the German Samoas, which passed to Britain under the secret wartime treaty dividing Germany's Pacific islands between Britain and Japan, everything south of the equator going to Britain.

5. Hawaii

A. THE CASE FOR ANNEXATION

THE HAWAIIAN Islands long had concerned the United States government, before their political affairs blew into a crisis in 1892–93. Missionaries had gone out to Hawaii early in the century, and the islands were a port of call for American whaling and other vessels. A treaty of 1875 admitted Hawaiian sugar into the United States duty-free, giving the islanders an advantage of nearly two cents a pound over other foreign producers. This same treaty pledged the Hawaiian government not to alienate any port or territory in the kingdom to any other power and thus made the islands virtually a protectorate. A second treaty, negotiated in 1884 and ratified and proclaimed in 1887, set aside Pearl Harbor for exclusive use of the American navy. When the McKinley Tariff Act of 1890 removed the tariff on sugar and gave domestic producers a bounty, the Hawaiian sugar barons suddenly found themselves in trouble; and it has often seemed as if the revolution, and the offer of annexation extended by the white planter regime that succeeded the native dynasty, reflected only a desire to get in on the bounty, rather than having in mind any other revolutionary purpose. Actually the problem in the islands was not so much economic as social. Queen Liliuokalani (known as Queen Lil) was seeking to take over the government, to supplant the authority of the local Americans who had been governing the islands fairly successfully by allowing the dynasty to maintain itself as a figurehead, and they thereupon moved to stop her. The American minister in the islands, John L. Stevens, was glad to assist them. Before the revolution he had related his position in detail to Secretary of State John W. Foster.

. . . One of two courses seems to me absolutely necessary to be followed, either bold and vigorous measures for annexation or a "customs union," an ocean cable from the Californian coast to Honolulu, Pearl Harbor perpetually ceded to the United States, with an implied but not necessarily stipulated American protectorate over the islands. I believe the former to be the better, that which will prove much the more advantageous to the islands, and

SOURCE: Stevens to Foster, Nov. 20, 1892, *Foreign Relations of the United States: 1894, Appendix II, Affairs in Hawaii* (Washington, D.C., 1895), pp. 383–84.

the cheapest and least embarrassing in the end for the United States. If it was wise for the United States, through Secretary Marcy, thirty-eight years ago, to offer to expend $100,000 to secure a treaty of annexation, it certainly can not be chimerical or unwise to expend $100,000 to secure annexation in the near future. To-day the United States has five times the wealth she possessed in 1854, and the reasons now existing for annexation are much stronger than they were then. I can not refrain from expressing the opinion with emphasis that the golden hour is near at hand. A perpetual customs union and the acquisition of Pearl Harbor, with an implied protectorate, must be regarded as the only allowable alternative. This would require the continual presence in the harbor of Honolulu of a United States vessel of war and the constant watchfulness of the United States minister while the present bungling, unsettled, and expensive political rule would go on, retarding the development of the islands, leaving at the end of twenty-five years more embarrassment to annexation than exists to-day, the property far less valuable, and the population less American than they would be if annexation were soon realized.

It may be said that annexation would involve the obligation of paying to the Hawaiian sugar-producers the same rate of bounties now paid to American producers, thus imposing too heavy a demand on the United States Treasury. It is a sufficient answer to this objection to say that it could be specifically provided in the terms of annexation that the United States Government should pay 6 mills per pound—$12 per ton—to the Hawaiian sugar-raisers, and this only so long as the present sugar-bounty system of the United States shall be maintained. Careful inquiry and investigation bring me to the conclusion that this small bounty would tide the Hawaiian sugar-planters over their present alarming condition and save the islands from general business depression and financial disaster. Could justice to American interests in the islands and care for their future welfare do less than this?

To give Hawaii a highly favorable treaty while she remains outside the American Union would necessarily give the same advantages to hostile foreigners, those who would continue to antagonize our commercial and political interests here, as well as those of American blood and sympathies. It is a well authenticated fact that the American sentiment here in 1890, the last year of the great prosperity under the sugar provisions of the reciprocity treaty, was much less manifest than before that treaty had gone into effect, and less pronounced than when Secretary Marcy authorized the negotiation of the annexation treaty in 1854. It is equally true that the desire here at this time for annexation is much stronger than in 1889. Besides, so long as the islands retain their own independent government there remains the possibility that England or the Canadian Dominion might secure one of the Hawaiian harbors for a coaling station. Annexation excludes all dangers of this kind.

Which of the two lines of policy and action shall be adopted our statesmen and our Government must decide. Certain it is that the interests of the United States and the welfare of these islands will not permit the continuance of the existing state and tendency of things. Having for so many years extended a helping hand to the islands and encouraged the American residents and their friends at home to the extent we have, we can not refrain now from aiding them with vigorous measures, without injury to ourselves and those of our "kith and kin" and without neglecting American opportunities that never seemed so obvious and pressing as they do now. I have no doubt that the more thoroughly the bed rock and controlling facts touching the Hawaiian problem are understood by our Government and by the American public, the more readily they will be inclined to approve the views I have expressed so inadequately in this communication. . . .

B. Provisional Rule

AFTER THE revolution Stevens described the events, and made a suggestion to Secretary Foster.

In my 73, of November 8 [omitted here], I gave full information of the surrender of the Queen to the wishes of the Legislature by the formation of a ministry composed of men of intelligence and wealth, possessing the entire confidence of the business men and the more responsible citizens of the country. But this surrender of the Queen and of those surrounding her was only seeming. As soon as the principal appropriations had been voted and the legislative work was nearly concluded, several of the best members having already left for their homes, a remarkable conspiracy was revealed.

SOURCE: Stevens to Foster, Jan. 18, 1893, *Foreign Relations . . . :* *1894*, pp. 386–88.

The undersigned, for the first time since he has been at the head of this legation, January 4 took passage for Hilo and the volcano on the U.S.S. *Boston* for the benefit of the health of himself and of his daughter, it being also desirable that the town of the second importance in the islands should have this attention at the time the *Boston* was making a visit to Hawaii, the chief island in the group. Beyond all doubt, immediately after the *Boston* and myself had left Honolulu the unscrupulous adventurers around the Queen improved the opportunity to push through the Legislature an astounding lottery franchise with the obvious intent to sell it out to the Louisiana lottery men. This was worked by some of the same parties supposed to be of the powerful opium ring whose four points of operation are Vancouver, San Francisco, Honolulu, and Hongkong. They distributed the lottery stock among the native members of the Legislature in large figures.

Notwithstanding the strong opposition of all the best people of the islands, including whites and natives, and the emphatic opposition of the chamber of commerce, the Queen and her palace favorite gave their warmest support to the lottery bill and signed it at once. She was to be immediately compensated by being allowed to proclaim a new constitution, restoring to the Crown the old despotic prerogatives in direct violation of the existing constitution, which provides for the only mode of change, which is by the action of successive legislatures.

Returning on the *Boston* from our Hilo trip on the 14th instant, we found the Legislature was to be prorogued at 12 a. m., one-half hour after my arrival at the legation. The prorogation completed, members of the Legislature, diplomatic corps, judges of the supreme court, and other officials went to the palace by invitation. In the meantime it began to be known in public circles the Queen's intention to proclaim the revolutionary constitution. This resulted in raising an excitement which alarmed her confidants and caused some of them to draw back. This consumed time, so that she could not secure the signatures of her new cabinet as she had expected. In the meantime the diplomatic corps grew weary and left the palace, realizing that the invitation to be present was a trick.

As I had just returned, weary from my voyage, I had not received the invitation, the chamberlain knowing I was absent when he invited the English, Portuguese, French, and Japanese diplomatic representatives the day before. In the short meanwhile I had suspicioned the trick. Finally, the Queen appeared in the throne room, before the supreme judges and other officials, in an extreme passion of anger, and avowed her purpose to postpone her revolutionary constitution for a brief period, and then went upon the balcony and spoke with great passion in the same strain to those around the palace, principally her retainers and the royal guard, her determination to proclaim her constitution at another time. What I have described as to the lottery legislation, the forcing out of the responsible cabinet of November 8 and appointing the lottery cabinet, two of whom had been voted out of the ministry during the legislation session by a two-thirds vote for the best of reasons. It was the lottery bribe and the autocratic design of the Queen that quickly precipitated events.

A mass meeting of the citizens was called to meet on Monday, the 16th, at 2 p. m., which assembled in the largest hall in the city. Short as was the notice, over 1,300 of the principal citizens of Honolulu and from other islands, who happened to be in the city, were in attendance. This meeting included merchants, bankers, professional men, the principal business men, and the mechanics, the chief German and some of the leading English merchants and other nationalities, as well as American residents. It is said such an assemblage was never before equaled in Honolulu. Intelligent American visitors here say that such a public meeting would do credit to a meeting of a similar class of citizens in our best American cities.

The assemblage was a unit in feeling and purpose. The speeches and resolutions are on the printed slips I herewith inclose. This remarkable uprising of the best citizens, including nearly all of the chief property holders, the Tahitian marshal and palace favorite did not dare attempt to suppress. A committee of public safety was at once created to meet the emergency and to prevent anarchy and riot. It was fortunate that the *Boston* was in the harbor. The committee on public safety called on me for aid. I promptly addressed to the commander of the *Boston*, Capt. G. S. Wiltse, the following note:

UNITED STATES LEGATION,
Honolulu, January 16, 1893.
SIR: In view of the existing critical circumstances in Honolulu, including an inadequate legal force, I request you to land marines and sailors from the ship under your command for the protection

of the United States legation and United States consulate, and to secure the safety of American life and property.

Very truly, yours,

JOHN L. STEVENS,
Envoy Extraordinary and Minister Plenipotentiary of the United States.

Capt. G. C. WILTSE,
Commander U.S.S. Boston.

A copy of the call of the committee of public safety for aid is inclosed.

Promptly the men from the *Boston* were landed. Detachments were placed around the legation and the consulate, the principal members having marched to a central hall for shelter and headquarters; the night being at hand, the public anxiety being especially strong as to what might be done by irresponsible persons in the night, the landing of the men of the *Boston* so promptly gave immediate relief to the public anxiety.

As soon as practicable a Provisional Government was constituted, composed of four highly respectable men, with Judge Dole at the head, he having resigned his place on the supreme bench to assume this responsibility. He was born in Honolulu, of American parentage, educated here and in the United States, and is of the highest reputation among all citizens, both natives and whites. P. C. Jones is a native of Boston, Mass., wealthy, possessing property interests in the islands, and a resident here for many years. The other two members are of the highest respectability. The committee of public safety forthwith took possession of the Government buildings, archives, and treasury, and installed the Provisional Government at the heads of the respective departments. This being an accomplished fact, I promptly recognized the Provisional Government as the *de facto* Government of the Hawaiian Islands. The English minister, the Portuguese chargé d'affaires, the French and the Japanese commissioners promptly did the same; these, with myself, being the only members of the diplomatic corps residing here.

All is quiet here now. Without the sacrifice of a single life this change of government has been accomplished. Language can hardly express the enthusiasm and the profound feeling of relief at this peaceful and salutary change of government. The underlying cause of this profound feeling among the citizens is the hope that the United States Government will allow these islands to pass to American control and become American soil. A commission of citizens, duly accredited, will go by the steamer that takes this dispatch to Washington, to state the wishes of the Provisional Government and of the responsible people of the islands, and to give a complete account of the existing state of things here.

It is proper that I should add, that the presence of the *Boston* here has been of the highest importance, and the behavior of officers and men has been admirable. Capt. Wiltse has exercised prudence and great firmness, while he and the undersigned have recognized only accomplished facts and have not allowed the use of the United States force for any but the most conservative reasons.

The change of administration in Washington, from Benjamin Harrison to Grover Cleveland, led to reexamination of the treaty for annexation that Harrison and Secretary Foster had hastily presented to the Senate. Cleveland withdrew the treaty, and sent out a commissioner, James H. Blount, with "paramount" authority to investigate. Paramount Blount, as the commissioner became known to his Hawaiian critics, seized upon Minister Stevens's remark about the ripe pear, and recommended rejection of the treaty, which advice Cleveland accepted. By joint resolution of Congress, the United States government annexed Hawaii in 1898 as a war measure.

6. Chile

A. INCIDENT AT VALPARAISO

INVOLVEMENT *in the politics of islands in the Pacific was one way for Americans to show their new manifest destiny, demonstrating to the nations of Europe that the government of the United States also had ambition to display its power abroad; but it was toward Latin America that the new national mood came most clearly into focus. The American government in 1891 showed friendship toward a regime in Chile which was beset by revolution, and as luck would have it the revolutionists won*

SOURCE: Captain Winfield Scott Schley to the American minister in Santiago, Patrick Egan, Oct. 22, 1891, *Foreign Relations of the United States: 1891* (Washington, D.C., 1892), p. 205.

and almost at once began to express their hostility toward the yanquis.
Trouble broke out when a party of over a hundred officers and men
from the U.S.S. Baltimore went on shore leave at Valparaiso on Octo-
ber 16, 1891, and two crew members visited the True Blue Saloon.

. . . As nearly as the origin of the outbreak can be established, it
may be traced to a quarrel between [Boatswain's Mate Charles
W.] Riggin and a Chilean sailor about 6 p. m. in a saloon. It
appears that Talbot came into the saloon at that moment, and,
approaching them, he states that the Chilean sailor spit in his face
and that he knocked the sailor down. At all events, there appears to
have been a crowd on the outside ready and waiting, as numbers of
men immediately rushed into the saloon and began the assault on
these two men. They escaped and took refuge in a street car then
passing, but were assailed there and dragged from the car, and
Riggin was stabbed in the back many times by the crowd and left
to die in the street. When he was picked up by a shipmate,
Armorer Johnson, and in his arms to be taken to a drug store near
by, a squad of police appeared on the scene and one of the number
deliberately fired upon these two men. One of the shots entered
Riggin's neck, killing him almost instantly.

Talbot escaped with a number of severe stab wounds in the
back, two of which penetrated the lungs, and was arrested by the
police subsequently in a house where he had fled for safety.

Coal-heaver Jerry Anderson was robbed by a mob of least twenty-
five persons in broad daylight, and then knocked down and dan-
gerously stabbed several times in the back, one wound penetrating
the lungs. This occurred before the disturbance later in the afternoon.

Coal-heaver William Turnbull was stabbed eighteen times in
the back and beaten with clubs. As two of the wounds penetrated
the lungs, his condition is most critical [Turnbull died on October
25].

Carpenter's Mate John Hamilton was knocked down with stones
and then stabbed seriously in the buttock, groin, and back, and has
many other bodily injuries. He was afterwards brutally dragged in
an unconscious condition by two policemen to the *carcel*.

Coal-heaver George Panter and Landsman John Davidson were
severely wounded with stones, clubs, and cut with knives. Many
others of the crew were assaulted and stoned and clubbed and cut
with knives, though to a less serious extent. Complaint is made by
several men that after arrest they were "nippered" with catgut

cords and dragged to the station. In one case a lasso or lariat was used.

The fact that a number of the wounds are recognized as bayonet wounds would appear to point to police participation in some few cases, though I am glad to be able to say that there were some instances in which the officers intervened most courageously to protect our men against the mob.

Thirty-six of my men were arrested and detained in prison and in hospital, then examined, and ultimately discharged, as no proof of their guilt could be adduced. I can personally bear witness to the sobriety, orderliness, good behavior, and politeness of my men to Chilean officers up to 5:30 p. m., when I left the shore, returning to my ship. This fact is corroborated later by many eyewitnesses on shore at or after 6 p. m., when the disturbance occurred.

It is believed that the assault was instigated by Chilean sailors recently discharged from the transports, together with the long-shoremen, and that it was premeditated. Several of the men were told to keep within doors after night, as an assault upon them was intended by the crowds. That this was so is shown from the attacks made in widely separated localities in the town while the men were at supper in the hotels and restaurants. It is not believed that the sailors of the Chilean fleet assisted in this work of butchery, as there are instances in which some of them generously assisted our men against the mob and into places of safety, and it is a pleasant duty to dispel this infamous idea as published in the press of Valparaiso.

I can assure you most positively that my men were unarmed and defenseless, and the fact that the police authorities failed to discover an instrument beyond several small pocketknives and a small iron pestle about 4 inches long, such as druggists use, that could deserve the name of a weapon, is a most complete refutation of this charge.

B. Continuing the Confrontation

The navy Department recalled Schley's ship, and replaced it with the U.S.S. Yorktown, Commander Robley D. Evans. Some years later Evans set down his reminiscences, with excerpts from a diary.

SOURCE: A Sailor's Log: Recollections of Forty Years of Naval Life (New York, 1901), pp. 253, 258–60, 296–98.

. . . During my stay at Montevideo I had many cables from the Department regarding the new Chilean cruiser Errazuriz, which for some reason was causing them much anxiety. I found that she was undergoing repairs at Buenos Ayres, and promptly sent an officer in plain clothes to have a look at her. He succeeded in getting on board, and remained more than an hour before he was suspected and invited to leave. During that time he had found out all I wanted to know, and after he had made his report I wired the Secretary her condition, and that he need not worry about her, as I could do her up with the Yorktown in thirty minutes if it became necessary. The news from Valparaiso at this time was alarming. The tension between the two Governments was great, and war might come at any moment.

The instant our new sails were on board I again put to sea. . . .

We found the Baltimore looking warlike and ready for business. The harbour was full of war vessels, and we anchored nearly two miles from the landing; but at that season it made no difference. All the inshore port was filled with the Chilean navy, and a sorry-looking lot they were. . . .

When I had called on Captain Schley, commanding the Baltimore, and reported for duty, I paid my visits of ceremony to the authorities on shore and the senior Chilean naval officers afloat. They were all scrupulously polite to me, but everywhere there was intense hatred for the Baltimore and her crew. At this time I think the feeling was confined to them, and did not extend to us as a nation; but later on it changed and involved everything North American. Captain Schley informed me that he was going north in a few days, probably as soon as the Boston arrived, which I regretted, as I thought he should remain until the trouble about his men had been settled. He was in the midst of a correspondence with the intendente, conducted in the most perfect Castilian, to show, or prove, that his men were all perfectly sober when they were assaulted on shore. I did not agree with him in this, for in the first place I doubted the fact, and in the second it was not an issue worth discussing. His men were probably drunk on shore, properly drunk; they went ashore, many of them, for the purpose of getting drunk, which they did on Chilean rum paid for with good United States money. When in this condition they were more entitled to protection than if they had been sober. This was my view of it, at least, and the one I always held about men whom I commanded.

Instead of protecting them, the Chileans foully murdered these men, and we believed with the connivance and assistance of armed policemen. That was the issue—not the question of whether they were drunk or sober. . . .

One of the performances that had most tried my patience and temper at Valparaiso was the way they ran their torpedo boats about my ship, using her apparently as a target. At first I considered it only as an exhibition of bad manners, but, in view of the various warnings I had had, I concluded that there might be something more serious in it. It was plain to all hands that an effort was being made to impress the officers of the foreign ships in port, who watched closely with their glasses. I was unwilling to play the part which had apparently been assigned me. When they ran at me the second time one of the boats missed my stern by less than six feet. I went to quarters at once and gave orders, if one of them even scratched the paint on the Yorktown, to blow the boat out of the water and kill every man in her, so that there could be no question of an accidental collision. I then saw the officer in charge of the drills, and told him that he certainly had great confidence in the steering gear of his torpedo boats; that if anything should jam so that one of them struck me I would blow her bottom out. He replied that the water in the harbour belonged to his Government, and that he proposed to use it for the purpose of drilling his boats. I answered that I was fully aware of the ownership he had stated, but that the Yorktown and the paint on her belonged to the United States, and that neither must be defaced by his torpedo boats. After this incident they did not run at us so much, though the newspapers encouraged them to do so. . . .

A mail is in, and I have nice letters from friends commending my course at Valparaiso; very satisfactory, but I wish the newspapers would let me alone. Why should they call me "Fighting Bob?" Some of them say they must take my statements with "very large grains of salt." But generally they seem to commend me, which, if one must figure in them, is the best way; but as I see my duty I shall do it, hoping for the approval of the Government. When they send me orders I shall try to follow them. Some of the letters say, "We are waiting for you to stir up the war," and the writers will never know how near I came to doing it. Looking back at it now, I am glad I did just what I did, and in the way I did it. I would not change it if I could. Of course, I could have "stirred up the war," and it may be that people would have justified me, but I could not justify myself. In the discharge of my duty I gave the Chileans a fine chance to fight if they wanted to, and the odds were enough in their favour—nine ships to one. But they backed water every time, and I maintained a dignified and resolute position.

Of course, if they had provoked it I should have engaged their nine ships without hesitation, and the chances would not have favoured my getting the Yorktown out of their harbour. I am glad also that I got away from Valparaiso just when I did, for I am sure that if we had been there when the President's ultimatum came I should have had to open on them, the feeling was so intense. They would have insulted me again, and I should have attacked them. If the Government is going to demand a salute to our flag, and will send a lot of ships, I should like to be in command of one of them. But it is useless to send a single ship, it would only be insulted, as the Chileans respect nothing but force. . . .

C. THE PRESIDENT RESPONDS

COMMANDER Evans remarked in his diary entry, set out above, that it was lucky he got away from Valparaiso before the President's ultimatum reached Chile. President Harrison did not send the Chileans an ultimatum—which according to diplomatic definition must be a demand with a time limit—but simply asked for apology and indemnity in a special message to Congress on January 25, 1892.

. . . The communications of the Chilean Government in relation to this cruel and disastrous attack upon our men, as will appear from the correspondence, have not in any degree taken the form of a manly and satisfactory expression of regret, much less of apology. The event was of so serious a character that if the injuries suffered by our men had been wholly the result of an accident in a Chilean port the incident was grave enough to have called for some public expression of sympathy and regret from the local authorities. It is not enough to say that the affair was lamentable, for humanity would require that expression even if the beating and killing of our men had been justifiable. It is not enough to say that the incident

SOURCE: James D. Richardson, ed., Messages and Papers of the Presidents: 1789–1897 (10 vols., Washington, D.C., 1896–99), IX, pp. 223–26.

is regretted, coupled with the statement that the affair was not of an unusual character in ports where foreign sailors are accustomed to meet. It is not for a generous and sincere government to seek for words of small or equivocal meaning in which to convey to a friendly power an apology for an offense so atrocious as this. In the case of the assault by a mob in New Orleans upon the Spanish consulate in 1851, Mr. Webster wrote to the Spanish minister, Mr. Calderon, that the acts complained of were "a disgraceful and flagrant breach of duty and propriety," and that his Government "regrets them as deeply as Minister Calderon or his Government could possibly do;" that "these acts have caused the President great pain, and he thinks a proper acknowledgment is due to Her Majesty's Government." He invited the Spanish consul to return to his post, guaranteeing protection, and offered to salute the Spanish flag if the consul should come in a Spanish vessel. Such a treatment by the Government of Chile of this assault would have been more creditable to the Chilean authorities, and much less can hardly be satisfactory to a government that values its dignity and honor. . . .

In the same note the attention of the Chilean Government was called to the offensive character of a note addressed by Mr. Matta, its minister of foreign affairs, to Mr. Montt, its minister at this capital, on the 11th ultimo. This dispatch was not officially communicated to this Government, but as Mr. Montt was directed to translate it and to give it to the press of the country it seemed to me that it could not pass without official notice. It was not only undiplomatic, but grossly insulting to our naval officers and to the executive department, as it directly imputed untruth and insincerity to the reports of the naval officers and to the official communications made by the executive department to Congress. It will be observed that I have notified the Chilean Government that unless this note is at once withdrawn and an apology as public as the offense made I will terminate diplomatic relations. . . .

In submitting these papers to Congress for that grave and patriotic consideration which the questions involved demand I desire to say that I am of the opinion that the demands made of Chile by this Government should be adhered to and enforced. If the dignity as well as the prestige and influence of the United States are not to be wholly sacrificed, we must protect those who in foreign ports display the flag or wear the colors of this Government against insult, brutality, and death inflicted in resentment of the acts of their Government and not for any fault of their own. It has been my desire in every way to cultivate friendly and intimate relations with all the Governments of this hemisphere. We do not covet their territory. We desire their peace and prosperity. We look for no advantage in our relations with them except the increased exchanges of commerce upon a basis of mutual benefit. We regret every civil contest that disturbs their peace and paralyzes their development, and are always ready to give our good offices for the restoration of peace. It must, however, be understood that this Government, while exercising the utmost forbearance toward weaker powers, will extend its strong and adequate protection to its citizens, to its officers, and to its humblest sailor when made the victims of wantonness and cruelty in resentment not of their personal misconduct, but of the official acts of their Government. . . .

D. War Averted

FACED WITH *Harrison's stern view of the* Baltimore *affair the Chileans backed down, rather hastily.*

I transmit herewith additional correspondence between this Government and the Government of Chile, consisting of a note of Mr. Montt, the Chilean minister at this capital, to Mr. Blaine, dated January 23; a reply of Mr. Blaine thereto of date January 27, and a dispatch from Mr. Egan, our minister at Santiago, transmitting the response of Mr. Pereira, the Chilean minister of foreign affairs, to the note of Mr. Blaine of January 21, which was received by me on the 26th instant. The note of Mr. Montt to Mr. Blaine, though dated January 23, was not delivered at the State Department until after 12 o'clock m. of the 25th, and was not translated and its receipt notified to me until late in the afternoon of that day.

The response of Mr. Pereira to our note of the 21st withdraws, with acceptable expressions of regret, the offensive note of Mr. Matta of the 11th ultimo, and also the request for the recall of Mr. Egan. The treatment of the incident of the assault upon the sailors

SOURCE: Harrison to Congress, Jan. 28, 1892, Richardson, ed., *Messages . . . 1789–1897*, p. 277.

of the *Baltimore* is so conciliatory and friendly that I am of the opinion that there is a good prospect that the differences growing out of that serious affair can now be adjusted upon terms satisfactory to this Government by the usual methods and without special powers from Congress. This turn in the affair is very gratifying to me, as I am sure it will be to the Congress and to our people. The general support of the efforts of the Executive to enforce the just rights of the nation in this matter has given an instructive and useful illustration of the unity and patriotism of our people. . . .

The government of Chile paid an indemnity of $75,000. Meanwhile the body of Boatswain's Mate Riggin was taken back to the deceased sailor's home city of Philadelphia, where it lay in state in Independence Hall, the first such occasion since the death of Benjamin Franklin in 1790. School children from all over the nation contributed dimes to be melted down into a casting of an urn, surmounted by Riggin's likeness, for presentation to President Harrison. Americans today, visiting the Harrison house in Indianapolis, may examine this huge silver urn, which stands in a place of honor at the top of the stairway to the second floor.

7. Venezuela

A. Applying the Monroe Doctrine

A few years after the Baltimore affair there arose a much more serious controversy with Great Britain over the boundary between British Guiana and Venezuela. The United States government accused the British of seeking to extend the Guiana boundary into Venezuela, violating the Monroe Doctrine. Here was the first formal invocation of the Monroe Doctrine by the United States. The dispute between the British and Venezuela had been running for some years prior to the crisis of 1895–96, in the course of which the British apparently tried to obtain some territory in Venezuela where gold had been discovered. The British government refused American good offices, and flatly refused arbitration out of fear that small nations all over the world then would make false claims and seek arbitration—as everyone knew, the

Source: Cleveland to Olney, July 7, 1895, Henry James, *Richard Olney and His Public Service* (Boston, 1923), pp. 110–111.

besetting sin of arbitrators when facing a confusion of claims and counterclaims was to split the difference. President Cleveland's Secretary of State, Walter Q. Gresham, died suddenly in May, 1895, and Gresham's successor, Richard Olney, who as Cleveland's Attorney General had obtained a reputation for firmness in persuading the President to break strikes, quickly showed the same resolution in foreign affairs. Olney's first action as Secretary was to move against Britain, in support of Venezuela and the Monroe Doctrine. He drew up a long note that was as stiff as anything an American diplomat has ever presented to the government of a great power, and sent it to Cleveland for approval. The President was at a summer house, Gray Gables, on Buzzards Bay, preoccupied for a few days. Olney's daughter later testified that the Secretary underwent the greatest nervous suspense he had ever experienced, until Cleveland shortly replied.

. . . About five hours ago our family was augmented by the addition of a strong plump loud-voiced little girl. Mother and daughter doing well—also the "old man."

I want to thank you for the rubber gloves which came last night. If the bluefish will hang around here a little while longer, I will test their effectiveness.

I read your deliverance on Venezuelan affairs the day you left it with me. It's the best thing of the kind I have ever read and it leads to a conclusion that one cannot escape if he tries—that is, if there is anything of the Monroe Doctrine at all. You show there is a great deal of that and place it, I think, on better and more defensible ground than any of your predecessors—or mine.

Of course I have some suggestions to make. I always have. Some of them are not of much account and some of them propose a little more softened verbiage here and there.

What day after Wednesday of this week can you come and spend a few hours with me that we can go over it together? Mrs. Cleveland sends love to Mrs. Olney. . . .

B. BRITAIN RECOGNIZES AMERICAN INFLUENCE

THE NOTE that Olney on July 20, 1895, dispatched to the American ambassador in London, Thomas F. Bayard (beginning with Bayard in 1893, the United States employed the rank of ambassador on a reciprocal basis for the major diplomatic stations), was—as Cleveland afterward described it—a twenty-inch gun.

SOURCE: Foreign Relations of the United States: 1895 (2 vols., Washington, D.C., 1896), I, pp. 545, 552, 554–55, 557–58.

. . . I am directed by the President to communicate to you his views upon a subject to which he has given much anxious thought and respecting which he has not reached a conclusion without a lively sense of its great importance as well as of the serious responsibility involved in any action now to be taken.

It is not proposed, and for present purposes is not necessary, to enter into any detailed account of the controversy between Great Britain and Venezuela respecting the western frontier of the colony of British Guiana. The dispute is of ancient date. . . .

By the frequent interposition of its good offices at the instance of Venezuela, by constantly urging and promoting the restoration of diplomatic relations between the two countries, by pressing for arbitration of the disputed boundary, by offering to act as arbitrator, by expressing its grave concern whenever new alleged instances of British aggression upon Venezuelan territory have been brought to its notice, the Government of the United States has made it clear to Great Britain and to the world that the controversy is one in which both its honor and its interests are involved and the continuance of which it can not regard with indifference. . . .

That America is in no part open to colonization, though the proposition was not universally admitted at the time of its first enunciation, has long been universally conceded. We are now concerned, therefore, only with that other practical application of the Monroe doctrine the disregard of which by an European power is to be deemed an act of unfriendliness towards the United States. The precise scope and limitations of this rule cannot be too clearly apprehended. It does not establish any general protectorate by the United States over other American states. It does not relieve any American state from its obligations as fixed by international law nor prevent any European power directly interested from enforcing such obligations or from inflicting merited punishment for the breach of them. It does not contemplate any interference in the internal affairs of any American state or in the relations between it and other American states. It does not justify any attempt on our part to change the established form of government of any American state or to prevent the people of such state from altering that form according to their own will and pleasure. The rule in question has but a single purpose and object. It is that no European power or combination of European powers shall forcibly deprive an

American state of the right and power of self-government and of shaping for itself its own political fortunes and destinies. . . .

Is it true, then, that the safety and welfare of the United States are so concerned with the maintenance of the independence of every American state as against any European power as to justify and require the interposition of the United States whenever that independence is endangered? The question can be candidly answered in but one way. The states of America, South as well as North, by geographical proximity, by natural sympathy, by similarity of governmental constitutions, are friends and allies, commercially and politically, of the United States. To allow the subjugation of any of them by an European power is, of course, to completely reverse that situation and signifies the loss of all the advantages incident to their natural relations to us. But that is not all. The people of the United States have a vital interest in the cause of popular self-government. They have secured the right for themselves and their posterity at the cost of infinite blood and treasure. They have realized and exemplified its beneficent operation by a career unexampled in point of national greatness or individual felicity. They believe it to be for the healing of all nations, and that civilization must either advance or retrograde accordingly as its supremacy is extended or curtailed. Imbued with these sentiments, the people of the United States might not impossibly be wrought up to an active propaganda in favor of a cause so highly valued both for themselves and for mankind. But the age of the Crusades has passed, and they are content with such assertion and defense of the right of popular self-government as their own security and welfare demand. It is in that view more than in any other that they believe it not to be tolerated that the political control of an American state shall be forcibly assumed by an European power.

The mischiefs apprehended from such a source are none the less real because not immediately imminent in any specific case, and are none the less to be guarded against because the combination of circumstances that will bring them upon us cannot be predicted. The civilized states of Christendom deal with each other on substantially the same principles that regulate the conduct of individuals. The greater its enlightenment, the more surely every state perceives that its permanent interests require it to be governed by the immutable principles of right and justice. Each, nevertheless, is only too liable to succumb to the temptations offered by seeming special opportunities for its own aggrandizement, and each would rashly imperil its own safety were it not to remember that for the regard and respect of other states it must be largely dependent upon its own strength and power. To-day the United States is practically sovereign on this continent, and its fiat is law upon the subjects to which it confines its interposition. Why? It is not because of the pure friendship or good will felt for it. It is not simply by reason of its high character as a civilized state, nor because wisdom and justice and equity are the invariable characteristics of the dealings of the United States. It is because, in addition to all other grounds, its infinite resources combined with its isolated position render it master of the situation and practically invulnerable as against any or all other powers. . . .

Through carelessness, or perhaps preoccupation, the British government did not respond to Olney's note until after Cleveland had sent in his state of the union message early in December, 1895. When the response came a few days later it was cheeky as well as irascible, and caused Cleveland to be "mad clean through." The President proposed to Congress that the United States draw the boundary, and hold it against all comers. Both Houses of Congress unanimously—almost a record agreement on an issue of foreign affairs—voted funds for the boundary commission. Because of the imminence of the Boer War, and because of the obvious irritation of the government of the United States, the British accepted arbitration. The award of the tribunal in 1899 recognized most of the British territorial claims.

III

The War with Spain

The international implications of survival of the fittest, the launching of the new American navy, the series of diplomatic tests recounted in the preceding chapter—all these forces and factors came to focus upon Cuba beginning in 1895. That focus was further determined by the seeming inability of the government of Spain to handle the political problems of the empire in Cuba. The Cubans had fought an unsuccessful revolution against the mother country in 1868–78. The second revolt, which broke out in 1895, caused such devastation and misery as to invite the people of the United States to lend a hand.

8. The Proctor Speech

THE SINKING of the battleship Maine in Havana harbor on February 15, 1898, raised the temper of many Americans to fever pitch ("Remember the Maine! To Hell with Spain!"). There were other inspirations for war in the first weeks of 1898, such as exaggerations of the New York newspaper press, and the indiscreet letter complaining about the personal weaknesses of President McKinley that the Spanish minister in Washington, Dupuy de Lôme, sent a correspondent in Cuba (the New York Journal obtained a copy of the letter). But one of the principal impulses for war was the unemotional Senate speech by Redfield Proctor of Vermont on March 17, offering an account of a trip to Cuba. Proctor's testimony concerning Spanish military measures in Cuba persuaded many men of good will and intelligence that only intervention by the United States would resolve the Cuban impasse.

Mr. FRYE. Mr. President, the Senator from Vermont [Mr. PROCTOR], a Senator in whom the country has much confidence, and a conservative man, has just returned from a pretty careful investigation of affairs in Cuba, and has expressed a willingness to give to the Senate and the country his views; and some have desired that he may do so at the present moment. I therefore ask the Senator from Florida whether or not he will consent to yield the floor for the present, resuming it again when the Senator from Vermont has finished his statement?

Mr. MALLORY. I yield for that purpose.

Mr. FRYE. I ask unanimous consent of the Senate that the Senator from Vermont may proceed with his statement.

Mr. CHANDLER. I suggest the absence of a quorum, Mr. President.

The PRESIDING OFFICER. The absence of a quorum being suggested, the Secretary will call the roll.

The Secretary called the roll, and the following Senators answered to their names:

Allen,	Berry,	Cannon,	Davis,
Bacon,	Burrows,	Chandler,	Deboe,
Baker,	Butler,	Chilton,	Fairbanks,
Bate,	Caffery,	Clark,	Frye,

SOURCE: 55th Cong., 2d Sess., Congressional Record, pp. 2916–19.

Heitfeld,	Mantle,	Platt, N.Y.	Turley,
Jones, Nev.	Mills,	Proctor,	Turner,
Kenney,	Mitchell,	Quay,	Turpie,
McBride,	Morrill,	Rawlins,	Vest,
McEnery,	Pasco,	Shoup,	Walthall,
McLaurin,	Perkins,	Stewart,	Wetmore.
McMillan,	Pettigrew,	Teller,	
Mallory,	Pettus,	Tillman,	

The PRESIDING OFFICER. Forty-six Senators have answered to their names. A quorum is present, and the Senator from Vermont is recognized.

Mr. PROCTOR. Mr. President, more importance seems to be attached by others to my recent visit to Cuba than I have given it, and it has been suggested that I make a public statement of what I saw and how the situation impressed me. This I do on account of the public interest in all that concerns Cuba, and to correct some inaccuracies that have, not unnaturally, appeared in reported interviews with me.

My trip was entirely unofficial and of my own motion, not suggested by anyone. The only mention I made of it to the President was to say to him that I contemplated such a trip and to ask him if there was any objection to it; to which he replied that he could see none. No one but myself, therefore, is responsible for anything in this statement. . . .

. . . There are six provinces in Cuba, each, with the exception of Matanzas, extending the whole width of the island, and having about an equal sea front on the north and south borders. Matanzas touches the Caribbean Sea only at its southwest corner, being separated from it elsewhere by a narrow peninsula of Santa Clara Province. The provinces are named, beginning at the west, Pinar del Rio, Habana, Matanzas, Santa Clara, Puerto Principe, and Santiago de Cuba. My observations were confined to the four western provinces, which constitute about one-half of the island. The two eastern ones are practically in the hands of the insurgents, except the few fortified towns. These two large provinces are spoken of to-day as "Cuba Libre."

Habana, the great city and capital of the island, is, in the eyes of the Spaniards and many Cubans, all Cuba, as much as Paris is France. But having visited it in more peaceful times and seen its sights, the tomb of Columbus, the forts—Cabana and Morro Castle, etc.—I did not care to repeat this, preferring trips in the country. Everything seems to go on much as usual in Habana. Quiet prevails, and except for the frequent squads of soldiers marching to guard and police duty and their abounding presence in all public places, one sees few signs of war.

Outside Habana all is changed. It is not peace nor is it war. It is desolation and distress, misery and starvation. Every town and village is surrounded by a "trocha" (trench), a sort of rifle pit, but constructed on a plan new to me, the dirt being thrown up on the inside and a barbed-wire fence on the outer side of the trench. These trochas have at every corner and at frequent intervals along the sides what are there called forts, but which are really small blockhouses, many of them more like large sentry boxes, loopholed for musketry, and with a guard of from two to ten soldiers in each.

The purpose of these trochas is to keep the reconcentrados in as well as to keep the insurgents out. From all the surrounding country the people have been driven in to these fortified towns and held there to subsist as they can. They are virtually prison yards, and not unlike one in general appearance, except that the walls are not so high and strong; but they suffice, where every point is in range of a soldier's rifle, to keep in the poor reconcentrado women and children.

Every railroad station is within one of these trochas and has an armed guard. Every train has an armored freight car, loopholed for musketry and filled with soldiers, and with, as I observed usually, and was informed is always the case, a pilot engine a mile or so in advance. There are frequent blockhouses inclosed by a trocha and with a guard along the railroad track. With this exception there is no human life or habitation between these fortified towns and villages, and throughout the whole of the four western provinces, except to a very limited extent among the hills where the Spaniards have not been able to go and drive the people to the towns and burn their dwellings. I saw no house or hut in the 400 miles of railroad rides from Pinar del Rio Province in the west across the full width of Habana and Matanzas provinces, and to Sagua La Grande on the north shore, and to Cienfuegos on the south shore of Santa Clara, except within the Spanish trochas.

There are no domestic animals or crops on the rich fields and pastures except such as are under guard in the immediate vicinity of the towns. In other words, the Spaniards hold in these four western provinces just what their army sits on. Every man, woman, and child, and every domestic animal, wherever their columns have reached, is under guard and within their so-called fortifications. To describe one place is to describe all. To repeat, it is neither peace nor war. It is concentration and desolation. This is the "pacified" condition of the four western provinces.

West of Habana is mainly the rich tobacco country; east, so far as I went, a sugar region. Nearly all the sugar mills are destroyed between Habana and Sagua. Two or three were standing in the vicinity of Sagua, and in part running, surrounded, as are the villages, by trochas and "forts" or palisades of the royal palm, and fully guarded. Toward and near Cienfuegos there were more mills running, but all with the same protection. It is said that the owners of these mills near Cienfuegos have been able to obtain special favors of the Spanish Government in the way of a large force of soldiers, but that they also, as well as all the railroads, pay taxes to the Cubans for immunity. I had no means of verifying this. It is the common talk among those who have better means of knowledge.

All the country people in the four western provinces, about 400,000 in number, remaining outside the fortified towns when Weyler's order was made were driven into these towns, and these are the reconcentrados. They were the peasantry, many of them farmers, some landowners, others renting lands and owning more or less stock, others working on estates and cultivating small patches; and even a small patch in that fruitful clime will support a family.

It is but fair to say that the normal condition of these people was very different from what prevails in this country. Their standard of comfort and prosperity was not high measured by ours. But according to their standards and requirements their conditions of life were satisfactory.

They lived mostly in cabins made of palms or in wooden houses. Some of them had houses of stone, the blackened walls of which are all that remain to show the country was ever inhabited.

The first clause of Weyler's order reads as follows:

I ORDER AND COMMAND.
First. All the inhabitants of the country or outside of the line of fortifications of the towns shall, within the period of eight days, concentrate themselves in the towns occupied by the troops. Any

individual who, after the expiration of this period, is found in the uninhabited parts will be considered a rebel and tried as such.

The other three sections forbid the transportation of provisions from one town to another without permission of the military authority, direct the owners of cattle to bring them into the towns, prescribe that the eight days shall be counted from the publication of the proclamation in the head town of the municipal district, and state that if news is furnished of the enemy which can be made use of, it will serve as a "recommendation."

Many, doubtless, did not learn of this order. Others failed to grasp its terrible meaning. Its execution was left largely to the guerrillas to drive in all that had not obeyed, and I was informed that in many cases the torch was applied to their homes with no notice, and the inmates fled with such clothing as they might have on, their stock and other belongings being appropriated by the guerrillas. When they reached the towns, they were allowed to build huts of palm leaves in the suburbs and vacant places within the trochas, and left to live, if they could.

Their huts are about 10 by 15 feet in size, and for want of space are usually crowded together very closely. They have no floor but the ground, no furniture, and, after a year's wear, but little clothing except such stray substitutes as they can extemporize; and with large families, or more than one, in this little space, the commonest sanitary provisions are impossible. Conditions are unmentionable in this respect. Torn from their homes, with foul earth, foul air, foul water, and foul food or none, what wonder that one-half have died and that one-quarter of the living are so diseased that they can not be saved? A form of dropsy is a common disorder resulting from these conditions. Little children are still walking about with arms and chest terribly emaciated, eyes swollen, and abdomen bloated to three times the natural size. The physicians say these cases are hopeless.

Deaths in the streets have not been uncommon. I was told by one of our consuls that they have been found dead about the markets in the morning, where they had crawled, hoping to get some stray bits of food from the early hucksters, and that there had been cases where they had dropped dead inside the market surrounded by food. Before Weyler's order, these people were independent and self-supporting. They are not beggars even now. There are plenty of professional beggars in every town among the regular residents, but these country people, the reconcentrados, have not learned the art. Rarely is a hand held out to you for alms when going among their huts, but the sight of them makes an appeal stronger than words.

[At this point Proctor turned to the subject of hospitals.] Of these I need not speak. Others have described their condition far better than I can. It is not within the narrow limits of my vocabulary to portray it. I went to Cuba with a strong conviction that the picture had been overdrawn; that a few cases of starvation and suffering had inspired and stimulated the press correspondents, and that they had given free play to a strong, natural, and highly cultivated imagination.

Before starting I received through the mail a leaflet published by the Christian Herald, with cuts of some of the sick and starving reconcentrados, and took it with me, thinking these must be rare specimens, got up to make the worst possible showing. I saw plenty as bad and worse; many that should not be photographed and shown.

I could not believe that out of a population of 1,600,000, two hundred thousand had died within these Spanish forts, practically prison walls, within a few months past from actual starvation and diseases caused by insufficient and improper food. My inquiries were entirely outside of sensational sources. They were made of our medical officers, of our consuls, of city alcaldes (mayors), of relief committees, of leading merchants and bankers, physicians, and lawyers. Several of my informants were Spanish born, but every time the answer was that the case had not been overstated. What I saw I can not tell so that others can see it. It must be seen with one's own eyes to be realized.

The Los Pasos Hospital, in Habana, has been recently described by one of my colleagues, Senator GALLINGER, and I can not say that his picture was overdrawn, for even his fertile pen could not do that. But he visited it after Dr. Lesser, one of Miss Barton's very able and efficient assistants, had renovated it and put in cots. I saw it when 400 women and children were lying on the floors in an indescribable state of emaciation and disease, many with the scantiest covering of rags—and such rags!—sick children, naked as they came into the world; and the conditions in the other cities are even worse. . . .

I had little time to study the race question, and have read

nothing on it, so can only give hasty impressions. It is said that there are nearly 200,000 Spaniards in Cuba out of a total population of 1,600,000. They live principally in the towns and cities. The small shopkeepers in the towns and their clerks are mostly Spaniards. Much of the larger business, too, and of the property in the cities, and in a less degree in the country, is in their hands. They have an eye to thrift, and as everything possible in the way of trade and legalized monopolies, in which the country abounds, is given to them by the Government, many of them acquire property. . . .

. . . It is said that there are about 60,000 Spanish soldiers now in Cuba fit for duty out of the more than 200,000 that have been sent there. The rest have died, have been sent home sick, or are in hospitals, and some have been killed, notwithstanding the official reports. . . .

The dividing lines between parties are the straightest and clearest cut that have ever come to my knowledge. The division in our war was by no means so clearly defined. It is Cuban against Spaniard. It is practically the entire Cuban population on one side and the Spanish army and Spanish citizens on the other.

I do not count the autonomists in this division, as they are so far too inconsiderable in numbers to be worth counting. General Blanco filled the civil offices with men who had been autonomists and were still classed as such. But the march of events had satisfied most of them that the chance for autonomy came too late.

It falls as talk of compromise would have fallen the last year or two of our war. If it succeeds, it can only be by armed force, by the triumph of the Spanish army, and the success of Spanish arms would be easier by Weyler's policy and method, for in that the Spanish army and people believe.

There is no doubt that General Blanco is acting in entire good faith; that he desires to give the Cubans a fair measure of autonomy, as Campos did at the close of the ten-year war. He has, of course, a few personal followers, but the army and the Spanish citizens do not want genuine autonomy, for that means government by the Cuban people. And it is not strange that the Cubans say it comes too late. . . .

I have endeavored to state in not intemperate mood what I saw and heard, and to make no argument thereon, but leave everyone to draw his own conclusions. To me the strongest appeal is not the barbarity practiced by Weyler nor the loss of the *Maine*, if our worst fears [*i.e.*, that the Spanish sank the vessel] should prove true, terrible as are both of these incidents, but the spectacle of a million and a half of people, the entire native population of Cuba, struggling for freedom and deliverance from the worst misgovernment of which I ever had knowledge. But whether our action ought to be influenced by any one or all these things, and, if so, how far, is another question.

I am not in favor of annexation: not because I would apprehend any particular trouble from it, but because it is not wise policy to take in any people of foreign tongue and training, and without any strong guiding American element. The fear that if free the people of Cuba would be revolutionary is not so well founded as has been supposed, and the conditions for good self-government are far more favorable. The large number of educated and patriotic men, the great sacrifices they have endured, the peaceable temperament of the people, whites and blacks, the wonderful prosperity that would surely come with peace and good home rule, the large influx of American and English immigration and money, would all be strong factors for stable institutions.

But it is not my purpose at this time, nor do I consider it my province, to suggest any plan. I merely speak of the symptoms as I saw them, but do not undertake to prescribe. Such remedial steps as may be required may safely be left to an American President and the American people.

9. McKinley's Request for Congressional Action

MINISTER DE LÔME's *letter remarked that President McKinley was "weak and a bidder for the admiration of the crowd," and for many years historians have so described this turn-of-the-century President, pointing to the way in which he gave the Cuban problem to Congress on April 11, 1898. McKinley knew that Congress would vote for intervention and that intervention meant war. Information had just come from the American minister in Madrid that the Spanish were virtually willing to accept American ideas about Cuba, and McKinley referred briefly to this novel development in the last paragraph of his message*

SOURCE: James D. Richardson, ed., *Messages* . . . *1789–1897*, X, pp. 139–40, 143–44, 146–48, 150.

to Congress. Historians have criticized him for rushing the issue at this juncture, for failing to give the Spanish a chance. The precise resting place of McKinley's historical reputation is probably not going to be high—certainly the President of 1898 will never rank as one of the "great" holders of that office—but it may prove higher than McKinley's critics have believed, for it is difficult to see how McKinley could have done anything about Cuba other than urge American intervention. The Spanish government in Madrid was not clear in its supposed capitulation to American demands, and although this issue is too complex to admit discussion in the present pages, it is fair to conclude that the Spanish were not willing to get out of Cuba, unless pried out by force.

Obedient to that precept of the Constitution which commands the President to give from time to time to the Congress information of the state of the Union and to recommend to their consideration such measures as he shall judge necessary and expedient, it becomes my duty to now address your body with regard to the grave crisis that has arisen in the relations of the United States to Spain by reason of the warfare that for more than three years has raged in the neighboring island of Cuba.

I do so because of the intimate connection of the Cuban question with the state of our own Union and the grave relation the course which it is now incumbent upon the nation to adopt must needs bear to the traditional policy of our Government if it is to accord with the precepts laid down by the founders of the Republic and religiously observed by succeeding Administrations to the present day.

The present revolution is but the successor of other similar insurrections which have occurred in Cuba against the dominion of Spain, extending over a period of nearly half a century, each of which during its progress has subjected the United States to great effort and expense in enforcing its neutrality laws, caused enormous losses to American trade and commerce, caused irritation, annoyance, and disturbance among our citizens, and, by the exercise of cruel, barbarous, and uncivilized practices of warfare, shocked the sensibilities and offended the humane sympathies of our people. . . .

The war in Cuba is of such a nature that, short of subjugation or extermination, a final military victory for either side seems impracticable. The alternative lies in the physical exhaustion of the one or the other party, or perhaps of both—a condition which in effect ended the ten years' war by the truce of Zanjon. The prospect of such a protraction and conclusion of the present strife is a contingency hardly to be contemplated with equanimity by the civilized world, and least of all by the United States, affected and injured as we are, deeply and intimately, by its very existence.

Realizing this, it appeared to be my duty, in a spirit of true friendliness, no less to Spain than to the Cubans, who have so much to lose by the prolongation of the struggle, to seek to bring about an immediate termination of the war. To this end I submitted on the 27th ultimo, as a result of much representation and correspondence, through the United States minister at Madrid, propositions to the Spanish Government looking to an armistice until October 1 for the negotiation of peace with the good offices of the President.

In addition I asked the immediate revocation of the order of reconcentration, so as to permit the people to return to their farms and the needy to be relieved with provisions and supplies from the United States, cooperating with the Spanish authorities, so as to afford full relief.

The reply of the Spanish cabinet was received on the night of the 31st ultimo. It offered, as the means to bring about peace in Cuba, to confide the preparation thereof to the insular parliament, inasmuch as the concurrence of that body would be necessary to reach a final result, it being, however, understood that the powers reserved by the constitution to the central Government are not lessened or diminished. As the Cuban parliament does not meet until the 4th of May next, the Spanish Government would not object for its part to accept at once a suspension of hostilities if asked for by the insurgents from the general in chief, to whom it would pertain in such case to determine the duration and conditions of the armistice.

The propositions submitted by General Woodford and the reply of the Spanish Government were both in the form of brief memoranda, the texts of which are before me and are substantially in the language above given. The function of the Cuban parliament in the matter of "preparing" peace and the manner of its doing so are not expressed in the Spanish memorandum, but from General Woodford's explanatory reports of preliminary discussions preceding the final conference it is understood that the Spanish Government stands ready to give the insular congress full powers to settle the terms of peace with the insurgents, whether by direct negotiation or indirectly by means of legislation does not appear.

With this last overture in the direction of immediate peace, and

its disappointing reception by Spain, the Executive is brought to
the end of his effort.

In my annual message of December last I said:

> Of the untried measures there remain only: Recognition of the
> insurgents as belligerents; recognition of the independence of Cuba;
> neutral intervention to end the war by imposing a rational compro-
> mise between the contestants, and intervention in favor of one or
> the other party. I speak not of forcible annexation, for that can not
> be thought of. That, by our code of morality, would be criminal ag-
> gression.

Thereupon I reviewed these alternatives in the light of President
Grant's measured words, uttered in 1875, when, after seven years
of sanguinary, destructive, and cruel hostilities in Cuba, he reached
the conclusion that the recognition of the independence of Cuba
was impracticable and indefensible and that the recognition of
belligerence was not warranted by the facts according to the tests
of public law. I commented especially upon the latter aspect of the
question, pointing out the inconveniences and positive dangers of a
recognition of belligerence, which, while adding to the already
onerous burdens of neutrality within our own jurisdiction, could
not in any way extend our influence or effective offices in the territory of hostilities.

Nothing has since occurred to change my view in this regard, and
I recognize as fully now as then that the issuance of a proclamation
of neutrality, by which process the so-called recognition of belligerents is published, could of itself and unattended by other action
accomplish nothing toward the one end for which we labor—the
instant pacification of Cuba and the cessation of the misery that
afflicts the island. . . .

Nor from the standpoint of expediency do I think it would be
wise or prudent for this Government to recognize at the present
time the independence of the so-called Cuban Republic. Such
recognition is not necessary in order to enable the United States to
intervene and pacify the island. To commit this country now to the
recognition of any particular government in Cuba might subject us
to embarrassing conditions of international obligation toward the
organization so recognized. In case of intervention our conduct
would be subject to the approval or disapproval of such government. We would be required to submit to its direction and to
assume to it the mere relation of a friendly ally.

When it shall appear hereafter that there is within the island a government capable of performing the duties and discharging the functions of a separate nation, and having as a matter of fact the proper forms and attributes of nationality, such government can be promptly and readily recognized and the relations and interests of the United States with such nation adjusted.

There remain the alternative forms of intervention to end the war, either as an impartial neutral, by imposing a rational compromise between the contestants, or as the active ally of the one party or the other.

As to the first, it is not to be forgotten that during the last few months the relation of the United States has virtually been one of friendly intervention in many ways, each not of itself conclusive, but all tending to the exertion of a potential influence toward an ultimate pacific result, just and honorable to all interests concerned. The spirit of all our acts hitherto has been an earnest, unselfish desire for peace and prosperity in Cuba, untarnished by differences between us and Spain and unstained by the blood of American citizens.

The forcible intervention of the United States as a neutral to stop the war, according to the large dictates of humanity and following many historical precedents where neighboring states have interfered to check the hopeless sacrifices of life by internecine conflicts beyond their borders, is justifiable on rational grounds. It involves, however, hostile constraint upon both the parties to the contest, as well to enforce a truce as to guide the eventual settlement.

The grounds for such intervention may be briefly summarized as follows:

First. In the cause of humanity and to put an end to the barbarities, bloodshed, starvation, and horrible miseries now existing there, and which the parties to the conflict are either unable or unwilling to stop or mitigate. It is no answer to say this is all in another country, belonging to another nation, and is therefore none of our business. It is specially our duty, for it is right at our door.

Second. We owe it to our citizens in Cuba to afford them that protection and indemnity for life and property which no government there can or will afford, and to that end to terminate the conditions that deprive them of legal protection.

Third. The right to intervene may be justified by the very serious injury to the commerce, trade, and business of our people and by the wanton destruction of property and devastation of the island.

Fourth, and which is of the utmost importance. The present condition of affairs in Cuba is a constant menace to our peace and entails upon this Government an enormous expense. With such a conflict waged for years in an island so near us and with which our people have such trade and business relations; when the lives and liberty of our citizens are in constant danger and their property destroyed and themselves ruined; where our trading vessels are liable to seizure and are seized at our very door by war ships of a foreign nation; the expeditions of filibustering that we are power- less to prevent altogether, and the irritating questions and en- tanglements thus arising—all these and others that I need not mention, with the resulting strained relations, are a constant men- ace to our peace and compel us to keep on a semi war footing with a nation with which we are at peace.

These elements of danger and disorder already pointed out have been strikingly illustrated by a tragic event which has deeply and justly moved the American people. I have already transmitted to Congress the report of the naval court of inquiry on the destruction of the battle ship *Maine* in the harbor of Havana during the night of the 15th of February. The destruction of that noble vessel has filled the national heart with inexpressible horror. Two hundred and fifty-eight brave sailors and marines and two officers of our Navy, reposing in the fancied security of a friendly harbor, have been hurled to death, grief and want brought to their homes and sorrow to the nation.

The naval court of inquiry, which, it is needless to say, com- mands the unqualified confidence of the Government, was unani- mous in its conclusion that the destruction of the *Maine* was caused by an exterior explosion—that of a submarine mine. It did not assume to place the responsibility. That remains to be fixed.

In any event, the destruction of the *Maine*, by whatever exterior cause, is a patent and impressive proof of a state of things in Cuba that is intolerable. . . .

The long trial has proved that the object for which Spain has waged the war can not be attained. The fire of insurrection may flame or may smolder with varying seasons, but it has not been and it is plain that it can not be extinguished by present methods. The only hope of relief and repose from a condition which can no longer be endured is the enforced pacification of Cuba. In the name of humanity, in the name of civilization, in behalf of endangered American interests which give us the right and the duty to speak and to act, the war in Cuba must stop.

In view of these facts and of these considerations I ask the Congress to authorize and empower the President to take measures to secure a full and final termination of hostilities between the Government of Spain and the people of Cuba, and to secure in the island the establishment of a stable government, capable of maintaining order and observing its international obligations, insuring peace and tranquillity and the security of its citizens as well as our own, and to use the military and naval forces of the United States as may be necessary for these purposes.

And in the interest of humanity and to aid in preserving the lives of the starving people of the island I recommend that the distribution of food and supplies be continued and that an appropriation be made out of the public Treasury to supplement the charity of our citizens.

The issue is now with the Congress. It is a solemn responsibility. I have exhausted every effort to relieve the intolerable condition of affairs which is at our doors. Prepared to execute every obligation imposed upon me by the Constitution and the law, I await your action.

Yesterday, and since the preparation of the foregoing message, official information was received by me that the latest decree of the Queen Regent of Spain directs General Blanco, in order to prepare and facilitate peace, to proclaim a suspension of hostilities, the duration and details of which have not yet been communicated to me.

This fact, with every other pertinent consideration, will, I am sure, have your just and careful attention in the solemn deliberations upon which you are about to enter. If this measure attains a successful result, then our aspirations as a Christian, peace-loving people will be realized. If it fails, it will be only another justification for our contemplated action.

10. The Treaty of Paris

THE WAR *required only about three months, and during the ensuing peace conference at Paris the McKinley administration leisurely made up its mind on two points: whether to accept the Cuban debt (it chose not to), and whether to take the Philippines. Everything then was set down in the peace treaty of December 10, 1898.*

ARTICLE I.

Spain relinquishes all claim of sovereignty over and title to Cuba.

And as the island is, upon its evacuation by Spain, to be occupied by the United States, the United States will, so long as such occupation shall last, assume and discharge the obligations that may under international law result from the fact of its occupation, for the protection of life and property.

ARTICLE II.

Spain cedes to the United States the island of Porto Rico and other islands now under Spanish sovereignty in the West Indies, and the island of Guam in the Marianas or Ladrones.

ARTICLE III.

Spain cedes to the United States the archipelago known as the Philippine Islands. . . .

The United States will pay to Spain the sum of twenty million dollars ($20,000,000) within three months after the exchange of the ratifications of the present treaty.

ARTICLE IV.

The United States will, for the term of ten years from the date of the exchange of the ratifications of the present treaty, admit Spanish ships and merchandise to the ports of the Philippine Islands on the same terms as ships and merchandise of the United States.

SOURCE: *United States Statutes at Large* (Washington, D.C., 1897–99), vol. 30, pp. 1755–59, 1761.

ARTICLE V.

The United States will, upon the signature of the present treaty, send back to Spain, at its own cost, the Spanish soldiers taken as prisoners of war on the capture of Manila by the American forces. The arms of the soldiers in question shall be restored to them.

The time within which the evacuation of the Philippine Islands and Guam shall be completed shall be fixed by the two Governments. Stands of colors, uncaptured war vessels, small arms, guns of all calibres, with their carriages and accessories, powder, ammunition, live stock, and materials and supplies of all kinds, belonging to the land and naval forces of Spain in the Philippines and Guam, remain the property of Spain. Pieces of heavy ordnance, exclusive of field artillery, in the fortifications and coast defences, shall remain in their emplacements for the term of six months, to be reckoned from the exchange of ratifications of the treaty; and the United States may, in the mean time, purchase such material from Spain, if a satisfactory agreement between the two Governments on the subject shall be reached.

ARTICLE VI.

Spain will, upon the signature of the present treaty, release all prisoners of war, and all persons detained or imprisoned for political offences, in connection with the insurrections in Cuba and the Philippines and the war with the United States.

Reciprocally, the United States will release all persons made prisoners of war by the American forces, and will undertake to obtain the release of all Spanish prisoners in the hands of the insurgents in Cuba and the Philippines.

The Government of the United States will at its own cost return to Spain and the Government of Spain will at its own cost return to the United States, Cuba, Porto Rico, and the Philippines, according to the situation of their respective homes, prisoners released or caused to be released by them, respectively, under this article.

ARTICLE VII.

The United States and Spain mutually relinquish all claims for indemnity, national and individual, of every kind, of either Government, or of its citizens or subjects, against the other Government, that may have arisen since the beginning of the late insurrection in Cuba and prior to the exchange of ratifications of the present treaty, including all claims for indemnity for the cost of the war.

The United States will adjudicate and settle the claims of its citizens against Spain relinquished in this article.

Article VIII.

In conformity with the provisions of Articles I, II, and III of this treaty, Spain relinquishes in Cuba, and cedes in Porto Rico and other islands in the West Indies, in the island of Guam, and in the Philippine Archipelago, all the buildings, wharves, barracks, forts, structures, public highways and other immovable property which, in conformity with law, belong to the public domain, and as such belong to the Crown of Spain. . . .

Article IX.

. . . The civil rights and political status of the native inhabitants of the territories hereby ceded to the United States shall be determined by the Congress.

Article XV.

The Government of each country will, for the term of ten years, accord to the merchant vessels of the other country the same treatment in respect of all port charges, including entrance and clearance dues, light dues, and tonnage duties, as it accords to its own merchant vessels, not engaged in the coastwise trade.

This article may at any time be terminated on six months' notice given by either Government to the other.

Article XVI.

It is understood that any obligations assumed in this treaty by the United States with respect to Cuba are limited to the time of its occupancy thereof; but it will upon the termination of such occupancy, advise any Government established in the island to assume the same obligations.

11. Mr. Dooley on the Philippines

THE CONTEMPORARY *humorist Finley Peter Dunne invented a comic Irishman, Martin Dooley, whose place of business was a saloon on Archey Road in the city of Chicago. Here, amid the clangor of the mills and the street traffic, Dooley accustomed himself to talking with his friend, Mr. Hennessy. Dooley's inventor, Dunne, did not think much of taking the Philippines and was convinced of their uselessness when, immediately after the Spanish-American War, America's new charges revolted and occupied the attention of a large part of the United States army until the revolt simmered down in 1902. It especially annoyed Dunne that the American commissioner in the islands, William Howard Taft, was so bland in his pronouncements about the rebellion, claiming that peace reigned almost everywhere.*

" 'Tis sthrange we don't hear much talk about th' Ph'lippeens," said Mr. Hennessy.

"Ye ought to go to Boston," said Mr. Dooley. "They talk about it there in their sleep. Th' raison it's not discussed annywhere else is that ivrything is perfectly quiet there. We don't talk about Ohio or Ioway or anny iv our other possissions because they'se nawthin' doin' in thim parts. Th' people ar-re goin' ahead, garnerin' th' products iv th' sile, sindin' their childher to school, worshipin' on Sundah in th' churches an 'thankin' Hiven f'r th' blessin's iv free govermint an' th' pro-tiction iv th' flag above thim.

"So it is in th' Ph'lippeens. I know, f'r me frind Gov'nor Taft says so, an' they'se a man that undherstands con-tintmint whin he sees it. Ye can't thrust th' fellows that comes back fr'm th' jools iv th' Passyfic an' tells ye that things ar-re no bether thin they shud be undher th' shade iv th' cocoanut palm be th' blue wathers iv th' still lagoon. They mus' be satisfied with our rule. A man that isn't

SOURCE: Louis Filler, ed., *Mr. Dooley: Now and Forever* (Stanford, Calif., 1954), pp. 184, 186–90.*

* For further details about American policy toward the Philippines see the fascinating book by Henry F. Graff, *American Imperialism and the Philippine Insurrection* (Boston, 1969), a volume in the series Testimony of the Times: Selections from Congressional Hearings, under the general editorship of John A. Garraty.

satisfied whin he's had enough is a glutton. They're satisfied an' happy an' slowly but surely they're acquirin' that love f'r th' govermint that floats over thim that will make thim good citizens without a vote or a right to thrile be jury. I know it. Guv'ner Taft says so.

"Says he: 'Th' Ph'lippeens as ye have been tol' be me young but speechful frind, Sinitor Bivridge, who was down there f'r tin minyits wanst an' spoke very highly an' at some lenth on th' beauties iv th' scenery, th' Ph'lippeens is wan or more iv th' beautiful jools in th' diadem iv our fair nation. Formerly our fair nation didn't care f'r jools, but done up her hair with side combs, but she's been abroad some since an' she come back with beautiful reddish goolden hair that a tiara looks well in an' that is betther f'r havin' a tiara. She is not as young as she was. Th' simple home-lovin' maiden that our fathers knew has disappeared an' in her place we find a Columbya, gintlemen, with machurer charms, a knowledge iv Euro-peen customs an' not averse to a cigareet. So we have pinned in her fair hair a diadem that sets off her beauty to advantage an' holds on th' front iv th' hair, an' th' mos' lovely pearl in this ornymint is thim sunny little isles iv th' Passyfic. They are almost too sunny f'r me. I had to come away.

" 'To shift me language suddintly fr'm th' joolry counther an' th' boodore, I will say that nawthin' that has been said even be th' gifted an' scholarly sinitor, who so worthily fills part iv th' place wanst crowded be Hendricks an' McDonald, does justice to th' richness iv thim islands. They raise unknown quantities iv produce, none iv which forchnitly can come into this counthry. All th' riches iv Cathay, all th' wealth iv Ind, as Hogan says, wud look like a second morgedge on an Apache wickeyup compared with th' untold an' almost unmintionable products iv that gloryous domain. Me business kept me in Manila or I wud tell ye what they are. Besides some iv our lile subjects is gettin' to be good shots an' I didn't go down there f'r that purpose.

" 'I turn to th' climate. It is simply hivenly. No other wurrud describes it. A white man who goes there seldom rayturns unless th' bereaved fam'ly insists. It is jus' right. In winter enough rain, in summer plinty iv heat. Gin'rally speakin' whin that throkical sky starts rainin' it doesn't stop till it's impty, so th' counthry is not subjected to th' sudden changes that afflict more northerly climes. Whin it rains it rains; whin it shines it shines. Th' wather fre-

quently remains in th' air afther th' sun has been shinin' a month
or more, th' earth bein' a little overcrowded with juice an' this
gives th' atmosphere a certain cosiness that is indescribable. A light
green mould grows on th' clothes an' is very becomin'. I met a man
on th' boat comin' back who said 'twas th' finest winter climate in
th' wurruld. He was be profission a rubber in a Turkish bath. As f'r
th' summers they are delicious. Th' sun doesn't sit aloft above th'
jools iv th' Passyfic. It comes down an' mingles with th' people. Ye
have heard it said th' isles was kissed be th' sun. Perhaps bitten
wud be a betther wurrud. But th' timprachoor is frequently modified be an eruption iv th' neighborin' volcanoes an' th' inthraduc-
tion iv American stoves. At night a coolin' breeze fr'm th' crather iv
a volcano makes sleep possible in a hammock swung in th' ice-box.
It is also very pleasant to be able to cuk wan's dinner within wan.

" 'Passin' to th' pollytical situation, I will say it is good. Not
perhaps as good as ye'ers or mine, but good. Ivry wanst in a while
whin I think iv it, an iliction is held. Unforchnitly it usually hap-
pens that those ilicted have not yet surrindhered. In th' Ph'lippeens th' office seeks th' man, but as he is also pursooed be th'
sojery, it is not always aisy to catch him an' fit it on him. Th'
counthry may be divided into two parts, pollytically,—where th'
insurrection continues an' where it will soon be. Th' brave but I
fear not altogether cherry army conthrols th' insurrected parts be
martiyal law, but th' civil authorities are supreme in their own
house. Th' diff'rence between civil law an' martiyal law in th'
Ph'lippeens is what kind iv coat th' judge wears. Th' raysult is
much th' same. Th' two branches wurruks in perfect harmony. We
bag thim in th' city an' they round thim up in th' counthry.

" 'It is not always nicessry to kill a Filipino American right away.
Me desire is to idjacate thim slowly in th' ways an' customs iv th'
counthry. We ar-re givin' hundherds iv these pore benighted
haythen th' well-known, ol-fashioned American wather cure. Iv
coorse, ye know how 'tis done. A Filipino, we'll say, niver heerd iv
th' histhry iv this counthry. He is met be wan iv our sturdy boys in
black an' blue iv th' Macabebee scouts who asts him to cheer f'r
Abraham Lincoln. He rayfuses. He is thin placed upon th' grass an'
given a dhrink, a baynit bein' fixed in his mouth so he cannot reject
th' hospitality. Undher th' inflooence iv th' hose that cheers but
does not inebriate, he soon warrums or perhaps I might say swells
up to a ralization iv th' granjoor iv his adoptive counthry. One

gallon makes him give three groans f'r th' constitchoochion. At four gallons, he will ask to be wrapped in th' flag. At th' dew pint he sings Yankee Doodle. Occasionally we run acrost a stubborn an' rebellyous man who wud sthrain at me idee iv human rights an' swallow th' Passyfic Ocean, but I mus' say mos' iv these little fellows is less hollow in their pretintions. Nachrally we have had to take a good manny customs fr'm th' Spanyard, but we have improved on thim. I was talkin' with a Spanish gintleman th' other day who had been away f'r a long time an' he said he wudden't know th' counthry. Even th' faces iv th' people on th' sthreets had changed. They seemed glad to see him. Among th' mos' useful Spanish customs is reconcenthration. Our reconcenthration camps is among th' mos' thickly popylated in th' wurruld. But still we have to rely mainly on American methods. They are always used fin'lly in th' makin' iv a good citizen, th' garotte sildom.

" 'I have not considhered it advisable to inthrajooce anny fads like thrile be jury iv ye'er peers into me administhration. Plain sthraight-forward dealin's is me motto. A Filipino at his best has on'y larned half th' jooty iv mankind. He can be thried but he can't thry his fellow man. It takes him too long. But in time I hope to have thim thrained to a pint where they can be good men an' thrue at th' inquest.

" 'I hope I have tol' ye enough to show ye that th' stories iv disordher is greatly exaggerated. Th' counthry is pro-gressin' splindidly, th' ocean still laps th' shore, th' mountains are there as they were in Bivridge's day, quite happy apparently; th' flag floats free an' well guarded over th' govermint offices, an' th' cherry people go an' come on their errands—go out alone an' come back with th' throops. Ivrywhere happiness, contint, love iv th' shtep-mother counthry, excipt in places where there ar-re people. Gintlemen, I thank ye.'

"An' there ye ar-re, Hinnissy. I hope this here lucid story will quite th' waggin' tongues iv scandal an' that people will let th' Ph'lippeens stew in their own happiness."

"But sure they might do something f'r thim," said Mr. Hennessy.

"They will," said Mr. Dooley. "They'll give thim a measure iv freedom."

"But whin?"

"Whin they'll sthand still long enough to be measured," said Mr. Dooley.

IV

The Far East, 1899–1921

The taking of the Philippine Islands vastly increased American interest in the politics of the far Pacific, in particular the politics of China, and for three generations and more after 1898—indeed, to the present day—the affairs of Asia often have focused the attention of American political leaders. The era was especially full of discussions of principle and policy, down to the opening of the Washington Conference in 1921. It is not unfair to say that whatever successes and failures occurred in American Far Eastern concerns thereafter were largely the results of arguments aired, and positions taken, in the important period 1899–1921.

12. Opening the Door

A. HAY'S ATTEMPT AT A TRADE AGREEMENT

THE PRINCIPLE of the open door, that all nations should enjoy equality of opportunity in the trade of China, was the policy of the United States from the first relations of Americans with the Far East, when the sailing vessel Empress of China went out from Salem to Canton in 1784. In this sense, then, there was nothing extraordinary in the set of propositions that Secretary of State John Hay presented to the powers for approval in 1899. The only novelty of his démarche was that he was asking the powers specifically to agree to what had been American policy.

First. The recognition that no power will in any way interfere with any treaty port or any vested interest within any leased territory or within any so-called "sphere of interest" it may have in China.

Second. That the Chinese treaty tariff of the time being shall apply to all merchandise landed or shipped to all such ports as are within said "sphere of interest" (unless they be "free ports"), no matter to what nationality it may belong, and that duties so leviable shall be collected by the Chinese Government.

Third. That it will levy no higher harbor dues on vessels of another nationality frequenting any port in such "sphere" than shall be levied on vessels of its own nationality, and no higher railroad charges over lines built, controlled, or operated within its "sphere" on merchandise belonging to citizens or subjects of other nationalities transported through such "sphere" than shall be levied on similar merchandise belonging to its own nationals transported over equal distances.

The declaration of such principles by His Imperial Majesty would not only be of great benefit to foreign commerce in China, but would powerfully tend to remove dangerous sources of irritation and possible conflict between the various powers; it would reestablish confidence and security, and would give great additional weight to the concerted representations which the treaty powers

SOURCE: Hay to the American ambassador in St. Petersburg, Charlemagne Tower, Sept. 6, 1899, *Foreign Relations of the United States: 1899* (Washington, D.C., 1901), pp. 140–41.

may hereafter make to His Imperial Chinese Majesty in the interest of reform in Chinese administration so essential to the consolidation and integrity of that Empire, and which, it is believed, is a fundamental principle of the policy of His Majesty in Asia.

Germany has declared the port of Kiao-chao, which she holds in Shangtung under a lease from China, a free port, and has aided in the establishment there of a branch of the imperial Chinese maritime customs. The imperial German minister for foreign affairs has also given assurances that American trade would not in any way be discriminated against or interfered with, as there is no intention to close the leased territory to foreign commerce within the area which Germany claims. These facts lead this Government to believe that the Imperial German Government will lend its cooperation and give its acceptance to the proposition above outlined, and which our ambassador at Berlin is now instructed to submit to it.

That such a declaration will be favorably considered by Great Britain and Japan, the two other powers most interested in the subject, there can be no doubt. The formal and oft-repeated declarations of the British and Japanese Governments in favor of the maintenance throughout China of freedom of trade for the whole world insure us, it is believed, the ready assent of these powers to the declaration desired. . . .

B. The Open Door as Policy

THE REPLIES to Hay's inquiries to the governments of Russia, France, Britain, Germany, Italy, and Japan were hardly encouraging, as some of these nations were more interested in fencing off their new concessions than opening them up; but Hay was reluctant to recognize the polite language of the European powers and Japan for what it was, namely, a refusal of his proposition, and in a circular of March 20, 1900, announced that the open door was in force.

The —— Government having accepted the declaration suggested by the United States concerning foreign trade in China, the terms of which I transmitted to you in my instruction No. —— of ——, and like action having been taken by all the various powers having leased territory or so-called "spheres of interest" in the Chinese Empire, as shown by the notes which I herewith transmit

SOURCE: *Foreign Relations . . . : 1899*, p. 142.

to you, you will please inform the Government to which you are accredited that the condition originally attached to its acceptance —that all other powers concerned should likewise accept the proposals of the United States—having been complied with, this Government will therefore consider the assent given to it by—— as final and definitive.

You will also transmit to the minister for foreign affairs copies of the present inclosures, and by the same occasion convey to him the expression of the sincere gratification which the President feels at the successful termination of these negotiations, in which he sees proof of the friendly spirit which animates the various powers interested in the untrammeled development of commerce and industry in the Chinese Empire, and a source of vast benefit to the whole commercial world. . . .

C. The Boxer Rebellion

Hardly had Hay's announcement of March, 1900, registered with the powers than the Chinese political situation turned into chaos with the Boxer Rebellion. There seemingly was no locus of political authority in China, although the European nations suspected with good reason that the imperial court in Peking was supporting the Boxers' antiforeign excesses. In the midst of the uncertainty as to the fate of the legations and refugees surrounded by Boxer forces in Peking, Hay dispatched an eloquent statement of American policy toward China which has become known as the second open door note. It was, in effect, a plea that the powers not use the occasion of the rebellion to partition the Chinese empire. Because the second note applied to territory, not trade, it was basically different from the first, although the purpose of the United States government remained the same, namely, to support the Chinese people in their slow and, at that moment, agonizing efforts toward political maturity. The Chinese, so Americans believed, needed help, not imperialism.

In this critical posture of affairs in China it is deemed appropriate to define the attitude of the United States as far as present circumstances permit this to be done. We adhere to the policy initiated by us in 1857 of peace with the Chinese nation, of furtherance of lawful commerce, and of protection of lives and prop-

Source: John Hay to American representatives in the major capitals, July 3, 1900, *Foreign Relations of the United States: 1901* (Washington, D.C., 1902), appendix, p. 12.

erty of our citizens by all means guaranteed under extra-territorial treaty rights and by the law of nations. If wrong be done to our citizens we propose to hold the responsible authors to the uttermost accountability. We regard the condition at Pekin as one of virtual anarchy, whereby power and responsibility are practically devolved upon the local provincial authorities. So long as they are not in overt collusion with rebellion and use their power to protect foreign life and property, we regard them as representing the Chinese people, with whom we seek to remain in peace and friendship. The purpose of the President is, as it has been heretofore, to act concurrently with the other powers; first, in opening up communication with Pekin and rescuing the American officials, missionaries, and other Americans who are in danger; secondly, in affording all possible protection everywhere in China to American life and property; thirdly, in guarding and protecting all legitimate American interests; and fourthly, in aiding to prevent a spread of the disorders to the other provinces of the Empire and a recurrence of such disasters. It is of course too early to forecast the means of attaining this last result; but the policy of the Government of the United States is to seek a solution which may bring about permanent safety and peace to China, preserve Chinese territorial and administrative entity, protect all rights guaranteed to friendly powers by treaty and international law, and safeguard for the world the principle of equal and impartial trade with all parts of the Chinese empire. . . .

The interesting part of this declaration was the phrase, "preserve Chinese territorial and administrative entity." In itself no binding pronouncement, indeed subject to some doubt as to its vigor, the phrase underwent a quiet transformation as the years passed, until in the minds of many Americans it became a guarantee of China's territorial integrity.

13. Closing the Door

A. The Taft-Katsura Agreement

IT WAS ONE thing to declare a principle concerning trade and territory, and another to make it prevail. In subsequent years the Far Eastern policy of the United States wavered to such an extent that the late historian A. Whitney Griswold, in a beautifully written but now rather out-of-date volume, The Far Eastern Policy of the United States (1938), argued that American policy was merely a series of assertions and withdrawals, a cyclical experience of hope and failure. The trouble was that the United States government did not want to employ force to back up its policy. Without force it was difficult to obtain the serious attention of the powers interested in Chinese trade and territory, especially the Japanese who, after the turn of the century, began to find China an ever more attractive place for economic and military enterprise.

There were several American moves to stabilize affairs in the Far East, for the betterment of China, and one of them occurred when Secretary of War Taft visited Tokyo in the summer of 1905 and held a conversation with the Japanese premier, Taro Katsura. The resultant "agreed memorandum," to which Roosevelt gave formal consent, was an interesting document.

The following is agreed memorandum of conversation between Prime Minister of Japan and myself:

"Count Katsura and Secretary Taft had a long and confidential conversation on the morning of July 27th. Among other topics of conversations [sic] the following views were exchanged regarding the questions of the Philippine Islands, of Korea, and of the maintenance of general peace in the Far East.

"First, inspeaking [sic] of some pro-Russians in America who would have the public believe that the victory of Japan would be a certain prelude to her aggressions in the direction of the Philippine Islands, Secretary Taft observed that Japan's only interest in the Philippines would be, in his opinion, to have these Islands governed by a strong and friendly nation like the United States, and

SOURCE: John Gilbert Reid, "Taft's Telegram to Root, July 29, 1905," Pacific Historical Review (1940), IX, pp. 69–70.

not to have them placed either under the misrule of the natives, yet unfit for self-government, or in the hands of some unfriendly European power. Count Katsura confirmed in the strongest terms the correctness of his [Taft's] views on the point and positively stated that Japan does not harbor any aggressive designs whatever on the Philippines; adding that all the insinuations of the yellow peril type are nothing more or less than malicious and clumsy slanders calculated to do mischief to Japan.

"Second, Count Katsura observed that the maintenance on [sic] general peace in the extreme East forms the fundamental principle of Japan's international policy. Such being the case, he was very anxious to exchange views with Secretary Taft as to the most effective means of insuring this principle. In his own opinion, the best and in fact the only means for accomplishing the above object would be to form good understanding between the three governments of Japan, the United States and Great Britain which have common interest in upholding the principle of eminence [sic]. The Count well understands the traditional policy of the United States in this respect and perceives fully the impossibilities [sic] of their entering into a formal alliance of such nature with any foreign nation, but in view of our common interests he could [not] see why some good understanding or an alliance in practice if not in name should not be made between those three nations insofar as respects the affairs in the far East. With such understanding firmly formed general peace in these regions should be easily maintained to the great benefit of all powers concerned. Secretary Taft said that it was difficult, indeed impossible, for the President of the United States of America to enter even to any understanding amounting in effect to a confidential informal agreement, without the consent of the Senate, but that he felt sure that without any agreement at all the people of the United States were so fully in accord with the policy of Japan and Great Britain in the maintenance of peace in the far East that whatever occasion arose appropriate action of the Government of the United States, in conjunction with Japan and Great Britain, for such a purpose could be counted on by them quite as confidently as if the United States were under treaty obligations to take [it].

"Third, In [sic] regard to the Korean question, Count Katsura observed that Korea being the direct cause of our [Japan's] war with Russia it is a matter of absolute importance to Japan that a complete solution of the peninsula question should be made as the logical consequence of the war. If left to herself after the war Korea will certainly draw back to her habit of improvidently resuscitating the same international complications as existed before the war. In view of the foregoing circumstances Japan feels absolutely constrained to take some definite step with a view to precluding the possibility of Korea falling back into her former condition and of placing us [Japan] again under the necessity of entering upon another foreign war. Secretary Taft fully admitted the justness of the Count's observations and remarked to the effect that, in his personal opinion, the establishment by Japanese troops of a suzerainty over Korea to the extent of requiring that Korea enter into no foreign treaties without the consent of Japan was the logical result of the present war and would directly contribute to permanent peace in the East. His judgment was that President Roosevelt would concur in his [Taft's] views in this regard, although he [Taft] had no authority to give assurance of this. Indeed Secretary Taft added, that he felt much delicacy in advancing the views he did for he had no mandate for the purpose from the President, and since he left Washington Mr. Root had been appointed Secretary of State and he might seem thus to be trespassing on another's department. He could not, however, in view of Count Katsura's courteous desire to discuss the questions, decline to express his opinions which he had formed while he was temporarily discharging the duties of Secretary of State under the direction of the President and he would forward to Mr. Root and the President a memorandum of the conversation. Count Katsura said that he would transmit the same, confidentially, to Baron Komura [Minister for Foreign Affairs, a delegate to the Portsmouth peace conference]."

Prime Minister quite anxious for interview. If I have spoken too freely or inaccurately or unwittingly, I know you can and will correct it. Do not want to "butt in," but under the circumstances, difficult to avoid statement and so told truth as I believe it. Count Katsura especially requested that our conversation be confined to you [Root] and the President, so have not advised [Minister] Griscom. Is there any objection? If necessary, under your direction, [the Japanese] Foreign Office can give him a copy. . . .

B. TR's ROLE IN THE RUSSO-JAPANESE WAR

THE EXACT meaning of the Taft-Katsura agreement is difficult to ascertain, although it surely must have been something of an accommodation of the views of the United States to those of Japan. There must have been some relation between Taft's recognition of Japanese interest in Korea and Katsura's disavowal of interest in the Philippines. A recent book by Raymond A. Esthus, Theodore Roosevelt and Japan (1966), has contended that there was not a trade-off. Privately both Roosevelt and Taft considered the agreement no bargain. Esthus remarks that nowhere in the private papers of American statesmen of this era is there any evidence of a bargain. Roosevelt in October, 1905, asked Katsura for an explicit disavowal of any bargain, which Katsura gave. But the inquiring student then faces the question of why, if there was no agreement, no bargain, it was necessary to make a memorandum and cable it to Roosevelt for approval. Moreover, as subsequent pages of the present volume will show, the Japanese later made two similar agreements with the United States that were not futile exercises but serious diplomatic statements involving bargains or, at the very least, attempted bargains.

In any event, Roosevelt in the summer of 1905 was carrying out another piece of diplomacy with the Japanese, the mediation of the Russo-Japanese War, in the course of which the President assembled a peace conference at the navy yard in Kittery, Maine, next to Portsmouth, New Hampshire. To bring peace between the two belligerents was a trying task, for the President suspected with reason that both Russia and Japan were likely to despoil China if they could get away with it. Somehow he needed to convince the warring powers that peace and a rough sort of status quo was best for both of them. It was an extremely complicated politique, as he wrote to his close friend and erstwhile tennis companion (at that time posted to the British embassy in St. Petersburg), Cecil Spring (Springy) Rice, July 24, 1905.

Now, oh best beloved Springy, don't you think you go a little needlessly into heroics when you say that "claims of honor must be recognized as the first interest of nations and that honor commands England to abstain from putting any pressure whatever upon Japan to abstain from action which may eventually entail severe sacrifices on England's part"? When I speak of bringing pressure to bear on Japan I mean just such pressure as Emperor William and the

SOURCE: Elting E. Morison, ed., Letters of Theodore Roosevelt (8 vols., Cambridge, Mass., 1951–54), IV, pp. 1283–86.

French Government have sought to bring to bear upon the Czar. It either is or ought to be unnecessary for me to state that I should put the honorable carrying out of plighted faith as above all other considerations, national or personal. I most cordially approve of your position in stating that England must prevent anything like a hostile combination against Japan. As soon as this war broke out I notified Germany and France in the most polite and discreet fashion that in the event of a combination against Japan to try to do what Russia, Germany and France did to her in 1894, I should promptly side with Japan and proceed to whatever length was necessary on her behalf. I of course knew that your Government would act in the same way, and thought it best that I should have no consultation with your people before announcing my own purpose. But I wholly fail to understand the difference in position which makes it proper for France, the ally of Russia, to urge Russia in her own interest (that is, in Russia's interest) to make peace, and which yet makes it improper for England, the ally of Japan, to urge Japan in her own interest (that is, in Japan's interest) to make peace. My feeling is that it is not to Japan's real interest to spend another year of bloody and costly war in securing eastern Siberia, which her people assure me she does not want, and then to find that she either has to keep it and get no money indemnity, or else exchange it for a money indemnity which, however large, would probably not more than pay for the extra year's expenditure and loss of life. If Japan felt that she wanted east Siberia and wanted to drive the Russians west of Lake Baikal the position would be different, and I would say that it was foolish to try for peace; but the Japanese Government have assured me most positively that this is not what they want, and that practically the only territorial cession they wish from Russia is Sakhalin, to which in my judgment they are absolutely entitled. I think that Lansdowne and Balfour (not Chamberlain—his ideals and mine are different) ought to know, what however they must keep absolutely secret, namely, that I undertook this move to bring about peace negotiations only at the request in writing of Japan, made immediately after Togo's victory. Up to that time I had continually advised the Russians to make peace, on the ground that it was their interest to accept defeat rather than to persist in turning defeat into overwhelming disaster. But I took no move toward bringing about peace negotiations until I was requested to do so by Japan, and while I purposely refused to try to find out the exact terms Japan wanted, I received their explicit assurances that they did not want east Siberia as a whole or the acquisition of Russian territory aside from Sakhalin. I do not know what they wish about the dismantling of Vladivostok, or the surrender of the various interned Russian vessels. Of course they expect to succeed to Russia's rights and possessions in Manchuria and to have Korea come within their sphere of influence.

However, most of this talk as to what England ought to do is academic, because I think the Japanese have probably made up their minds just about what they will accept and what they won't.

I was interested in the clipping you sent me from the *Telegraph* containing the special correspondent's account of affairs in St. Petersburg. I should be more impressed by it if I did not have experience at first hand with European special correspondents in Washington. You will note that much of the article is based upon the fact that no advocate of peace was made a Russian plenipotentiary, and especially upon the fact that Witte was not thus made a plenipotentiary. Well, since then Witte has been made a plenipotentiary, which upsets just about one half of the argument of the correspondent in question. However, I am quite prepared to accept much of what the correspondent says as representing the real tone of the amorphous body which in Russia stands as the Government (and incidentally when I feel gloomy about democracy I am positively refreshed by considering the monstrous ineptitude of the ideal absolutism when tried out during the last eighteen months). Witte himself has talked like a fool since he was appointed. The only possible justification of his interviews is to be found in his hope that he may bluff the Japanese; in which he will certainly fail. The correspondent you quote says that Russia will really wish to delay and prolong the peace negotiations. This is possible, but it is just as possible that she will in panic-struck fashion endeavor to hasten them. She has to my personal knowledge occupied both attitudes with great intensity during the last five weeks. At one period during these five weeks the Russian Government took the view that I must not try to hurry them too much and that there was not any need of hurry, and immediately afterwards they turned a somersault and wanted an armistice and immediate action about peace and protested against the delays for which they were themselves responsible. Apparently they have cooled off again somewhat. I made an honest effort to get them an armistice, but I am forced to say that from Japan's standpoint I think that Japan was absolutely right in refusing it, and think so now more than ever after Witte's interview. It may be that there will have to be one more crushing defeat of the Russian army in Manchuria before the Russians wake up to the fact that peace is a necessity. While I most emphatically feel that it is Japan's interest to be moderate in her demands and not to insist up to the point of continuing the war upon anything which is not really vital to her interests, yet I feel even more strongly that Russia must make peace even on hard terms now, under penalty of undergoing disaster which may almost split her empire in sunder and which will certainly take her out of the race for leadership for half a century to come.

There is one thing I am a little puzzled at, and that is why excepting on disinterested grounds the German Emperor should want Russia and Japan to make peace; he has done all he could to bring it about. Of course it may be that he fears lest a continuation of the war result in the internal break-up of Russia, and therefore an impetus to the German revolutionary movement. France has a very obvious motive in seeing peace made. . . .

C. The Root-Takahira Agreement

THE LAST YEARS of the Roosevelt administration saw a considerable diplomacy toward Japan, and concern for the Philippines, and it was in this climate of worry that Secretary of State Elihu Root concluded an agreement with the Japanese ambassador in Washington, Kogoro Taka-hira, which was in the direct line of tradition of the Taft-Katsura agreement. Roosevelt in 1906 had had to face a bad situation in California, where Japanese immigration had created trouble in the public schools; the local school authorities in San Francisco segregated Japanese. The subsequent storm of protest from Japan produced a Gentlemen's Agreement in 1907–08 according to which the Japanese government would not allow laborers to obtain visas to visit the mainland of the United States. Roosevelt in 1907 sent the American fleet on a world-wide tour that included Japan, an excursion which he later claimed in his Auto-biography to have been "the most important service that I rendered to peace." As for the Root-Takahira agreement, presumably another service rendered to peace, it had much more opaqueness than the agreement of three years before, but there must remain at least a suspicion that its deft phrases amounted to an American consent for Japan to go ahead with development of a sphere of interest in southern Manchuria, per-

SOURCE: Takahira to Root, Nov. 30, 1908, *Foreign Relations of the United States: 1908* (Washington, D.C., 1912), pp. 510–11.

haps with the tacit consent of Japan not to attack the Philippines. The reader must make his own judgment, bearing in mind that without any presumption of a bargain this agreement was superfluous, a waste of time for busy men like Root and Takahira.

The exchange of views between us, which has taken place at the several interviews which I have recently had the honor of holding with you, has shown that Japan and the United States holding important outlying insular possessions in the region of the Pacific Ocean, the Governments of the two countries are animated by a common aim, policy, and intention in that region.

Believing that a frank avowal of that aim, policy, and intention would not only tend to strengthen the relations of friendship and good neighborhood, which have immemorially existed between Japan and the United States, but would materially contribute to the preservation of the general peace, the Imperial Government have authorized me to present to you an outline of their understanding of that common aim, policy, and intention:

1. It is the wish of the two Governments to encourage the free and peaceful developments of their commerce on the Pacific Ocean.

2. The policy of both Governments, uninfluenced by any aggressive tendencies, is directed to the maintenance of the existing status quo in the region above mentioned and to the defense of the principle of equal opportunity for commerce and industry in China.

3. They are accordingly firmly resolved reciprocally to respect the territorial possessions belonging to each other in said region.

4. They are also determined to preserve the common interests of all powers in China by supporting by all pacific means at their disposal the independence and integrity of China and the principle of equal opportunity for commerce and industry of all nations in that Empire.

5. Should any event occur threatening the status quo as above described or the principle of equal opportunity as above defined, it remains for the two Governments to communicate with each other in order to arrive at an understanding as to what measures they may consider it useful to take.

If the foregoing outline accords with the view of the Government of the United States, I shall be gratified to receive your confirmation.

I take this opportunity to renew to your excellency the assurance of my highest consideration.

Root *acknowledged the agreement the same day.*

I have the honor to acknowledge the receipt of your note of to-day setting forth the result of the exchange of views between us in our recent interviews defining the understanding of the two Governments in regard to their policy in the region of the Pacific Ocean.

It is a pleasure to inform you that this expression of mutual understanding is welcome to the Government of the United States as appropriate to the happy relations of the two countries and as the occasion for a concise mutual affirmation of that accordant policy respecting the Far East which the two Governments have so frequently declared in the past.

I am happy to be able to confirm to your excellency, on behalf of the United States, the declaration of the two Governments embodied in the following words . . .

D. Proposal for a Chinese Railway

PLAINLY, *American diplomacy in the Far East was finding more accommodation necessary than had appeared at the fin de siècle, when the United States without much thought took the Philippines in the War of 1898 and in the next two years announced the open door policy. A simple act of acquisition had led to an apparently simple statement of American principle, but it seemed as if the Japanese had determined to expand into China and perhaps elsewhere, whether the United States liked it or not. The Philippines stood nearby as a hostage for American good behavior—much as Canada had served American purposes with Great Britain during the nineteenth century. In the administration of President Taft, Secretary of State Philander C. Knox sought a way to give the Chinese government some support, and proposed neutralization of the Chinese railway system.*

In reply to Sir Edward Grey's inquiries reported in his telegram of October 20, Mr. Reid is instructed to present to the foreign office textually the following memorandum:

> Now that there has been signed and ratified by an unpublished imperial decree an agreement by which the American and British interests are to cooperate in the financing and construction of the Chinchow-Tsitsihar-Aigun Railroad, the Government of the United

SOURCE: *Root to Takahira, Foreign Relations . . . . : 1908, p. 511.*
SOURCE: Knox to the American ambassador in London, Whitelaw Reid, Nov. 6, 1909, *Foreign Relations of the United States: 1910* (Washington, D.C., 1915), pp. 234–35.

States is prepared cordially to cooperate with His Britannic Majesty's Government in diplomatically supporting and facilitating this enterprise, so important alike to the progress and to the commercial development of China. The Government of the United States would be disposed to favor ultimate participation to a proper extent on the part of other interested powers whose inclusion might be agreeable to China and which are known to support the principle of equality of commercial opportunity and the maintenance of the integrity of the Chinese Empire. However, before the further elaboration of the actual arrangement, the Government of the United States asks His Britannic Majesty's Government to give their consideration to the following alternative and more comprehensive projects: First, perhaps the most effective way to preserve the undisturbed enjoyment by China of all political rights in Manchuria and to promote the development of those Provinces under a practical application of the policy of the open door and equal commercial opportunity would be to bring the Manchurian highways, the railroads, under an economic, scientific, and impartial administration by some plan vesting in China the ownership of the railroads through funds furnished for that purpose by the interested powers willing to participate. Such loan should be for a period ample to make it reasonably certain that it could be met within the time fixed and should be upon such terms as would make it attractive to bankers and investors. The plan should provide that nationals of the participating powers should supervise the railroad system during the term of the loan and the governments concerned should enjoy for such period the usual preferences for their nationals and materials upon an equitable basis inter se. The execution of such a plan would naturally require the cooperation of China and of Japan and Russia, the reversionary and the concessionaries, respectively, of the existing Manchurian railroads, as well as that of Great Britain and the United States, whose special interests rest upon the existing contract relative to the Chinchow-Aigun Railroad. The advantages of such a plan to Japan and to Russia are obvious. Both those powers, desiring in good faith to protect the policy of the open door and equal opportunity in Manchuria and wishing to assure to China unimpaired sovereignty, might well be expected to welcome an opportunity to shift the separate duties, responsibilities, and expenses they have undertaken in the protection of their respective commercial and other interests, for impartial assumption by the combined powers, including themselves, in proportion to their interests. The Government of the United States has some reason to hope that such a plan might meet favorable consideration on the part of Russia and has reason to believe that American financial participation would be forthcoming. Second, should this suggestion not be found feasible in its entirety, then the desired end would be approximated, if not attained, by Great Britain and the United States diplomatically supporting the Chinchow-Aigun arrangement and inviting the interested powers friendly to complete commercial neutralization of Manchuria to participate in the financing and construction of that line and of such additional lines as future commercial development may demand, and at the same time to supply funds for the purchase by China of such of the existing lines as might be offered for inclusion in this system. The Government of the United States hopes that the principle involved in the foregoing suggestions may commend itself to His Britannic Majesty's Government. That principle finds support in the additional reasons that the consummation of some such plan would avoid the irritations likely to be engendered by the uncontrolled direct negotiations of bankers with the Chinese Government, and also that it would create such a community of substantial interest in China as would facilitate a cooperation calculated to simplify the problems of fiscal and monetary reforms now receiving such earnest attention by the Imperial Chinese Government.

When this proposition came to nothing, Knox set out to force American capital into a new international consortium, which was organizing to finance currency reform and industrial development in Manchuria. The result again was failure, for American financiers did not wish to put money into China without a guarantee from their own government. President Wilson in March, 1913, withdrew government support of this enterprise (although later, during the World War, he revived the consortium idea). The trouble during the Taft administration was that, after the war of 1904–05, Japan and Russia had come into agreement in 1907–10 largely because of the developing alliance system in Europe (Britain had allied with Japan in 1902, and the Russians in 1907). When the two major Far Eastern rivals agreed, it was at the expense of China and involved the partition of Manchuria into two spheres of influence dominated by the two major Manchurian railroads, the Chinese Eastern (Russian) and the South Manchuria (Japanese). Apparently Secretary Knox did not know this.

14. The Future

A. BRYAN INVOKES THE OPEN DOOR POLICY

FOR THE future the major rivalry in the Far East was going to be between Japan and the United States, and this fact became almost clear during the World War of 1914–18. At the outset the Japanese declared

SOURCE: Bryan to the American ambassador in Japan, George W. Guthrie, May 11, 1915, Foreign Relations of the United States:

war on Germany, nominally in support of their ally Britain, actually to seize the German holdings in the Pacific. The British and Japanese governments soon concluded the secret treaty stipulating that all German interests south of the equator would go to Britain, north to Japan. When the Japanese placed twenty-one demands before the Chinese early in 1915, one group of which would have converted China into a satrapy, Secretary of State Bryan protested in a note which has historical interest if only because it was a precursor of the Stimson nonrecognition doctrine of 1932.

Please call upon the Minister for Foreign Affairs and present to him a note textually as follows:

"In view of the circumstances of the negotiations which have taken place and which are now pending between the Government of Japan and the Government of China, and of the agreements which have been reached as a result thereof, the Government of the United States has the honor to notify the Imperial Japanese Government that it cannot recognize any agreement or undertaking which has been entered into or which may be entered into between the Governments of Japan and China, impairing the treaty rights of the United States and its citizens in China, the political or territorial integrity of the Republic of China, or the international policy relative to China commonly known as the open door policy.

"An identical note has been transmitted to the Government of the Chinese Republic."

B. The Lansing-Ishii Conferences

THE JAPANESE waited until the United States government entered the war in 1917, and then pressed for more advantages in China. The Allies —British, French, Italians—sent over missions early in 1917 to adjust their new relations with the American government, but not to take advantage; these missions sought military and supply agreements, and generally were coordinating efforts, not diplomatic missions. The government of Japan sent over perhaps its shrewdest negotiator, Viscount Kikujiro Ishii, and his encounters with Secretary of State Robert Lansing (who had succeeded Bryan in 1915) were a classic example of diplomatic fencing. Lansing conferred with Ishii on September 6, 1917.

The Special Ambassador and I conferred this afternoon for an hour and a half at the Department.

During the first part of the conference the subject discussed was

SOURCE: *Foreign Relations of the United States: The Lansing Papers, 1914–1920* (2 vols., Washington, D.C., 1939–40), II, pp. 432–35.

to what extent Japan had rendered aid in the war, and how it might cooperate more fully with the Allies and this country. . . .

I asked the Ambassador whether he desired to discuss other questions than those immediately pertaining to the war, because if he so desired I was willing to do so—but I thought the supreme object of both Governments at the present moment should be the winning of the war and an understanding as to how we could cooperate to that end.

He said that in view of the fact that he had come here and been so handsomely received by the American people he thought it would be unfortunate not to consider some of the other questions as we had to look forward to a time when the war would be over. He said in the first place he ought to inform me that when he returned to Japan from France, where he was Ambassador in 1915, he stopped in London and saw Sir Edward Grey. Japan at that time had taken Kaio Chau and the German Islands in the South Pacific. He said he told Sir Edward Grey it was the intention of his Government to return Kaio Chau to China, but that no Government in Japan could stand if they did not retain some of the South Sea Islands as "souvenirs" of the war; that it had been a sacrifice for his Government to enter the war, which they were not compelled to do under their treaty of alliance—that is according to the letter of the treaty—but he thought they were according to the spirit. He then went on to say that Sir Edward Grey had practically consented in the readjustment of territory after the war; that the German Islands north of the equator should be retained by Japan, while those south of the equator should go to Great Britain.

I replied that I was glad to know this and appreciated his frankness in telling me, but that I could make no comment on such an agreement at the present time.

I asked him what further questions he wished to discuss and he said to me: "Have you anything to propose in regard to China?"

I replied that I had and while I realized that he would want to consider my proposition before making a reply I would like to present it. I said the proposition was this:

That the co-belligerents against Germany should, jointly or simultaneously, re-declare the "Open Door" policy in a statement which would have a very beneficial effect upon China and I believed upon the world at large, as it was in accord with the principles of commerce to which we all agreed.

The Ambassador seemed a little taken aback by this suggestion and said that of course he should like to consider it and that he appreciated the arguments in its favor although he said he did not know as it was absolutely necessary in view of the fact that Japan had always lived up to the principle.

I replied that Japan had always lived up to any declaration which she had made; that the good faith of Japan could not be questioned; and that upon that this Government always relied and felt no anxiety once the Japanese Government had passed its word.

The Ambassador replied that he felt that Japan had a special interest on account of its position in regard to China, and while its desire was to have China open and free to all countries he felt there might be criticism if there was a bare declaration of the "Open Door" policy without some mention of Japan's special interest.

I replied to him that we recognized the fact that Japan, from her geographical position, had a peculiar interest in China but that to make a declaration to that effect seemed to me needless as it was the result of natural causes and not political; that any such declaration might be interpreted as a peculiar political interest and I was very doubtful whether it would be wise to include it in a reaffirmation of the "Open Door" policy.

The Ambassador said that his Government was of course in favor of the "Open Door" policy; that they would maintain it as they had in the past, but he was not willing yet to say whether he thought it would be a real advantage to reaffirm it.

I said that the "Open Door" policy was peculiarly advantageous to Japan; that if we should return to spheres of influence in which the various powers had a paramount interest in certain sections of China the advantage which Japan had in geographical position would be destroyed; that Japan, with the industrial advantage which she had by reason of cheap and efficient labor and the short distance which she had to carry her goods to the Chinese markets, benefited more than any other of the countries by the "Open Door" policy; that so far as this country was concerned it might be considered advisable to reestablish spheres of influence, but that it was entirely contrary to our policy and principle and we were most anxious to preserve the doctrine in dealing with China. . . .

During the course of the early part of the conversation the Ambassador said that through various channels the German Government had three times sought to persuade Japan to withdraw from the Allies and to remain neutral, but that in every case his Government had firmly rejected the suggestion.

I said to him that I could imagine their seeking some such step as they had planned to attempt it through Mexico as was indicated in the Zimmermann note. I further said to him that it was a matter of no concern to this Government, in view of the fact that Japan's loyalty to an ally, and her reputation for good faith was too well established to be even suspected. . . .

THE TWO *men met again on September 22, 1917.*

Viscount Ishii called at 3:00 p. m. by appointment, and after some preliminary remarks he introduced the subject of the "Open Door" and the suggestion that a redeclaration at this time would be advantageous.

He said that he had heard from his Government and that they did not wish to do anything to affect the *status quo* in China and that it would be hard to explain to the Japanese people why a declaration was made at this time if the suggestion was adopted.

I told him that he must realize that in the present state of the world Japan and the United States were the only countries which could furnish money for the development of China's vast resources; that, if we permitted the gradual restoration of the policy of "spheres of influence", which seemed to be going on, the Allied Governments would look upon us as seeking to monopolize the opportunities; and that it seemed to me that we should unite in every possible way to dispel the impression that we would selfishly seek to take advantage of their wasted condition and build up our own fortunes without thought of those who were fighting the battles of this country and of Japan, as well as their own battles. I said that I thought this was a time when Japan and the United States ought to show a magnanimous spirit and say to them, "We will not take advantage of your calamities as we might do. We will seek no special privileges in China. When this war is over and you begin to rebuild your fortunes by commerce and trade, you will find the markets of China and the opportunities in that land as open and free to you as they are to us." If we redeclared the "Open Door" policy, I told him that is what it would mean, and I asked him if it was not worth while to gain the gratitude and confidence

SOURCE: *Foreign Relations* . . . . : *1914–1920*, pp. 435–36.

of the Allies by an announcement of our purpose to be generous and unselfish in this time when the future must look so dark to them.

The Viscount said that he appreciated all this and that he also realized what I had said before about Japan being the chief beneficiary from the "Open Door" which was manifestly true, but that the Japanese people would be likely to blame the Government if there was nothing said about Japan's "special interest" in China, that the opposition in the Diet would seize upon such an opportunity to attack the Ministry for making a needless declaration, while getting nothing for Japan.

I said to him that if he meant by "special interest" "paramount interest", I could not see my way clear to discuss the matter further; but, if he meant a special interest based upon geographical position, I was not unwilling to take the matter into consideration. I said further that I appreciated his difficulty which pertained to the political situation in Japan and would try and find some formula to satisfy the wishes of his people in case a redeclaration of the "Open Door" policy could be agreed upon in principle.

The Viscount said that he wished I would prepare such a formula first for his consideration and I told him that I would. . . .

PRESIDENT Wilson invited Ishii to the White House, without much result.

DEAR MR. SECRETARY: Thank you for letting me have these [memoranda]. I spent half an hour with Viscount Ishii. I did most of the talking (to let him see my *full* thought) and he seemed to agree throughout in *principle*.

C. AGREEMENT

AT LAST Lansing and Ishii came to an agreement. The Secretary received his Japanese visitor on November 2, 1917.

This morning the Viscount called at the Department and we read over the notes to be exchanged and the confidential protocol accompanying them. We then delivered our respective notes to each other and signed the protocol in duplicate.

SOURCE: Wilson to Lansing, undated, *Foreign Relations . . . . : 1914–1920*, p. 438.
SOURCE: *Foreign Relations . . . . : 1914–1920*, pp. 449–50.

I then asked him about the publication of the notes and he said he had advices from his Government saying that they would publish on the morning of the 7th and that we should publish on the afternoon of the 6th, which would make the time the same. I told the Ambassador that I should make a statement to accompany the publication and I hoped he would be gratified with it.

He then read me a telegram which he had just received from Baron Motono [Japanese Minister of Foreign Affairs] expressing gratification at the completion of the negotiations and congratulating and thanking the Government of the United States and myself.

The Viscount then handed me a statement which he said would be made public in Japan at the same time as the notes, in relation to naval cooperation in the Pacific. The statement had been agreed upon by the Naval authorities of the two Governments. I said we would follow that course also.

The Viscount then spoke of the still pending negotiation between Ambassador Sato and the War Trade Board relative to the exportation of steel in exchange for tonnage. I told him I would see Mr. Jones on the subject and do what I could to bring the negotiation to a satisfactory conclusion.

THE LANSING-ISHII agreement appeared in a formal note presented that same day, November 2, 1917, by Lansing to Ishii.

I have the honor to communicate herein my understanding of the agreement reached by us in our recent conversations touching the questions of mutual interest to our Governments relating to the Republic of China.

In order to silence mischievous reports that have from time to time been circulated, it is believed by us that a public announcement once more of the desires and intentions shared by our two Governments with regard to China is advisable.

The Governments of the United States and Japan recognize that territorial propinquity creates special relations between countries, and, consequently, the Government of the United States recognizes that Japan has special interests in China, particularly in the part to which her possessions are contiguous.

SOURCE: *Foreign Relations of the United States: 1917* (Washington, D.C., 1926), p. 264.

The territorial sovereignty of China, nevertheless, remains unimpaired and the Government of the United States has every confidence in the repeated assurances of the Imperial Japanese Government that while geographical position gives Japan such special interests they have no desire to discriminate against the trade of other nations or to disregard the commercial rights heretofore granted by China in treaties with other powers.

The Governments of the United States and Japan deny that they have any purpose to infringe in any way the independence or territorial integrity of China and they declare, furthermore, that they always adhere to the principle of the so-called "open door" or equal opportunity for commerce and industry in China.

Moreover, they mutually declare that they are opposed to the acquisition by any Government of any special rights or privileges that would affect the independence or territorial integrity of China or that would deny to the subjects or citizens of any country the full enjoyment of equal opportunity in the commerce and industry of China.

I shall be glad to have your excellency confirm this understanding of the agreement reached by us.

D. A Later Development

THE AGREEMENT contained an interesting secret protocol, which Secretary of State Charles Evans Hughes in 1922 quietly embodied in the Nine-Power Treaty of Washington (see below, pp. 204–206). The existence of the protocol did not become public knowledge until long after publication in 1926 of the regular volume of Foreign Relations for the year 1917—until the Lansing papers came back to the Department and were published in a special two-volume set in 1939–40.

In the course of the conversations between the Japanese Special Ambassador and the Secretary of State of the United States which have led to the exchange of notes between them dated this day, declaring the policy of the two Governments with regard to China, the question of embodying the following clause in such declaration came up for discussion: "they (the Governments of Japan and the United States) will not take advantage of the present conditions to

SOURCE: Foreign Relations of the United States: The Lansing Papers (2 vols., Washington, D.C., 1939–40), II, pp. 450–51.

seek special rights or privileges in China which would abridge the rights of the subjects or citizens of other friendly states."

Upon careful examination of the question, it was agreed that the clause above quoted being superfluous in the relations of the two Governments and liable to create erroneous impression in the minds of the public, should be eliminated from the declaration.

It was, however, well understood that the principle enunciated in the clause which was thus suppressed was in perfect accord with the declared policy of the two Governments in regard to China.

V

Colossus of the North

The relations of the United States with Latin America took on a peculiarly intimate quality during the years from the Spanish-American War until at least the end of the First World War, and the reason was that the United States was worrying about the safety of the Panama Canal. When the war of 1914–18 was over, there could be no question of a Caribbean challenge from any European power, least of all the bugaboo of the prewar years, Imperial Germany, and not long thereafter the Colossus of the North changed its policy to the civilities of the good neighbor. This is not to say that American policy did not comprise other concerns and purposes than simply the military protection of the canal route. There can be no question that in the heyday of the new manifest destiny, at least down to 1914 when two of the three Anglo-Saxon-Teutonic powers went to war with each other, the people of the United States felt that they had a special destiny to use the big stick on recalcitrant Latin American nations. Moreover, the American people in these years were filled with a kind of missionary zeal, a desire to clean up and generally improve the quality of life of the peoples south of the Rio Grande. The prevailing reason for policy, however, apart from these two popular desires that happened to coincide with the purposes of the nation's leaders in Washington, was the safety of the canal.

15. Carrying the Big Stick

A. The Platt Amendment

"THERE IS a homely adage which runs, 'Speak softly and carry a big stick; you will go far.' " So spoke Vice President Theodore Roosevelt in an address of September 2, 1901, not many days before an assassin removed William McKinley from the presidency and inaugurated the Roosevelt era. In the next few years the youthful Roosevelt did not hesitate to carry through a Latin American policy of force and vigor, and one of his first acts was to ensure that Cuba, which became independent in 1902, would not lack for American tutelage. The amendment to the army appropriation bill of 1901, which took the name of Senator Orville Platt of Connecticut, but which owed a great deal to the initiative of Secretary of War Root, was written into the Cuban constitution, and then—just to be sure—the Roosevelt administration on July 1, 1904, exchanged ratifications of a treaty between Cuba and the United States.

Whereas the Congress of the United States of America, by an Act approved March 2, 1901, provided as follows:

Provided further, That in fulfillment of the declaration contained in the joint resolution approved April twentieth, eighteen hundred and ninety-eight, entitled, "For the recognition of the independence of the people of Cuba, demanding that the Government of Spain relinquish its authority and government in the island of Cuba, and to withdraw its land and naval forces from Cuba and Cuban waters, and directing the President of the United States to use the land and naval forces of the United States to carry these resolutions into effect," the President is hereby authorized to "leave the government and control of the island of Cuba to its people" so soon as a government shall have been established in said island under a constitution which, either as a part thereof or in an ordinance appended thereto, shall define the future relations of the United States with Cuba, substantially as follows:

"I. That the government of Cuba shall never enter into any treaty or other compact with any foreign power or powers which will impair or tend to impair the independence of Cuba, nor in any

SOURCE: Charles I. Bevans, comp., *Treaties and Other International Agreements of the United States of America: 1776–1949* (Washington, 1968 –), VI, pp. 1116–19.

manner authorize or permit any foreign power or powers to obtain by colonization or for military or naval purposes or otherwise, lodgement in or control over any portion of said island."

"II. That said government shall not assume or contract any public debt, to pay the interest upon which, and to make reasonable sinking fund provision for the ultimate discharge of which, the ordinary revenues of the island, after defraying the current expenses of government shall be inadequate."

"III. That the government of Cuba consents that the United States may exercise the right to intervene for the preservation of Cuban independence, the maintenance of a government adequate for the protection of life, property, and individual liberty, and for discharging the obligations with respect to Cuba imposed by the treaty of Paris on the United States, now to be assumed and undertaken by the government of Cuba."

"IV. That all Acts of the United States in Cuba during its military occupancy thereof are ratified and validated, and all lawful rights acquired thereunder shall be maintained and protected."

"V. That the government of Cuba will execute, and as far as necessary extend, the plans already devised or other plans to be mutually agreed upon, for the sanitation of the cities of the island, to the end that a recurrence of epidemic and infectious diseases may be prevented thereby assuring protection to the people and commerce of Cuba, as well as to the commerce of the southern ports of the United States and the people residing therein."

"VI. That the Isle of Pines shall be omitted from the proposed constitutional boundaries of Cuba, the title thereto being left to future adjustment by treaty."

"VII. That to enable the United States to maintain the independence of Cuba, and to protect the people thereof, as well as for its own defense, the government of Cuba will sell or lease to the United States lands necessary for coaling or naval stations at certain specified points to be agreed upon with the President of the United States.

"VIII. That by way of further assurance the government of Cuba will embody the foregoing provisions in a permanent treaty with the United States."

Whereas the Constitutional Convention of Cuba, on June twelfth, 1901, adopted a Resolution adding to the Constitution of the Republic of Cuba which was adopted on the twenty-first of

February 1901, an appendix in the words and letters of the eight enumerated articles of the above cited act of the Congress of the United States;

And whereas, by the establishment of the independent and sovereign government of the Republic of Cuba, under the constitution promulgated on the 20th of May, 1902, which embraced the foregoing conditions, and by the withdrawal of the Government of the United States as an intervening power, on the same date, it becomes necessary to embody the above cited provisions in a permanent treaty between the United States of America and the Republic of Cuba;

The United States of America and the Republic of Cuba, being desirous to carry out the foregoing conditions, have for that purpose appointed as their plenipotentiaries to conclude a treaty to that end,

The President of the United States of America, Herbert G. Squiers, Envoy Extraordinary and Minister Plenipotentiary at Havana,

And the President of the Republic of Cuba, Carlos de Zaldo y Beurmann, Secretary of State and Justice,—who after communicating to each other their full powers found in good and due form, have agreed upon the following articles: [There followed the first seven points of the Platt Amendment, as above enumerated.]

ARTICLE VIII.

The present Convention shall be ratified by each party in conformity with the respective Constitutions of the two countries, and the ratifications shall be exchanged in the City of Washington within eight months from this date.

B. REVOLUTION IN PANAMA

A BIG black mark on the escutcheon of the United States—so Samuel Flagg Bemis has described the acquisition of the Panama Canal Zone by the United States in 1903. Properly speaking, or formally speaking, the American government did not take Panama; the Panamanians separated themselves from Colombia, and within days offered a canal

SOURCE: William M. Malloy, comp., *Treaties, Conventions, International Acts* . . . (2 vols., Washington, D.C., 1910), II, pp. 1349–52, 1354–56.

treaty upon terms which the United States eagerly accepted, terms that also made Panama a protectorate.

The negotiations prior to acquisition of the Canal Zone were nothing if not complicated. The Clayton-Bulwer Treaty of 1850 with Great Britain had accorded the two signatories the right jointly to construct a canal, if they could make suitable arrangements with the local people, whether for the Panama route or the Nicaragua route. In 1901 the so-called second Hay-Pauncefote Treaty (the first failed in the Senate because it expressly forbade the United States to fortify any future canal) abrogated the treaty of 1850 and gave the United States the unilateral right to make local arrangements, so far as Britain was concerned. The Roosevelt administration opted for the Panama route perhaps partly out of feeling that there was danger of volcanic eruption in Nicaragua, mainly because Panama seemed the better route from an engineering point of view. When the Colombian government tried to hold out for more money than Secretary of State Hay proved willing to offer, and than President Roosevelt felt was correct to offer, revolution broke out in Panama. The New Panama Canal Company, which had obtained the rights of the old French company that had gone bankrupt some years before, was behind the Panamanian revolt, as it feared that its contract with Colombia might come to an end in 1904, or else the Roosevelt administration would tire of the delay with the Colombians and turn to Nicaragua. In either event it would not get the $40,000,000 it was asking for its rights.

Professor Bemis, of course, feels that the American government should have turned to Nicaragua, or paid what the Colombians wished, and if necessary let the New Company go down the drain.

One of the prime instigators of the Panama revolution, the Frenchman Philippe Bunau-Varilla, commissioned as minister of Panama to the United States, signed with Secretary Hay on November 18, 1903, just fifteen days after the revolution.

Article I.

. . . The United States guarantees and will maintain the independence of the Republic of Panama.

Article II.

The Republic of Panama grants to the United States in perpetuity the use, occupation and control of a zone of land and land under water for the construction, maintenance, operation, sanitation and protection of said Canal of the width of ten miles extending to the distance of five miles on each side of the center line of the route of the Canal to be constructed; the said zone beginning in the Caribbean Sea three marine miles from mean low water mark and extending to and across the Isthmus of Panama into the

Pacific ocean to a distance of three marine miles from mean low water mark with the proviso that the cities of Panama and Colon and the harbors adjacent to said cities, which are included within the boundaries of the zone above described, shall not be included within this grant. The Republic of Panama further grants to the United States in perpetuity the use, occupation and control of any other lands and waters outside of the zone above described which may be necessary and convenient for the construction, maintenance, operation, sanitation and protection of the said Canal or of any auxiliary canals or other works necessary and convenient for the construction, maintenance, operation, sanitation and protection of the said enterprise. . . .

ARTICLE III.

The Republic of Panama grants to the United States all the rights, power and authority within the zone mentioned and described in Article II of this agreement and within the limits of all auxiliary lands and waters mentioned and described in said Article II which the United States would possess and exercise if it were the sovereign of the territory within which said lands and waters are located to the entire exclusion of the exercise by the Republic of Panama of any such sovereign rights, power or authority. . . .

ARTICLE VI.

The grants herein contained shall in no manner invalidate the titles or rights of private land holders or owners of private property in the said zone or in or to any of the lands or waters granted to the United States by the provisions of any Article of this treaty, nor shall they interfere with the rights of way over the public roads passing through the said zone or over any of the said lands or waters unless said rights of way or private rights shall conflict with rights herein granted to the United States in which case the rights of the United States shall be superior. All damages caused to the owners of private lands or private property of any kind by reason of the grants contained in this treaty or by reason of the operations of the United States, its agents or employees, or by reason of the construction, maintenance, operation, sanitation and protection of the said Canal or of the works of sanitation and protection herein provided for, shall be appraised and settled by a joint Commission appointed by the Governments of the United States and the

Republic of Panama, whose decisions as to such damages shall be final and whose awards as to such damages shall be paid solely by the United States. No part of the work on said Canal or the Panama railroad or on any auxiliary works relating thereto and authorized by the terms of this treaty shall be prevented, delayed or impeded by or pending such proceedings to ascertain such damages. The appraisal of said private lands and private property and the assessment of damages to them shall be based upon their value before the date of this convention.

ARTICLE VII.

The Republic of Panama grants to the United States within the limits of the cities of Panama and Colon and their adjacent harbors and within the territory adjacent thereto the right to acquire by purchase or by the exercise of the right of eminent domain, any lands, buildings, water rights or other properties necessary and convenient for the construction, maintenance, operation and protection of the Canal and of any works of sanitation, such as the collection and disposition of sewage and the distribution of water in the said cities of Panama and Colon, which, in the discretion of the United States may be necessary and convenient for the construction, maintenance, operation, sanitation and protection of the said Canal and railroad. All such works of sanitation, collection and disposition of sewage and distribution of water in the cities of Panama and Colon shall be made at the expense of the United States, and the Government of the United States, its agents or nominees shall be authorized to impose and collect water rates and sewerage rates which shall be sufficient to provide for the payment of interest and the amortization of the principal of the cost of said works within a period of fifty years and upon the expiration of said term of fifty years the system of sewers and water works shall revert to and become the properties of the cities of Panama and Colon respectively, and the use of the water shall be free to the inhabitants of Panama and Colon, except to the extent that water rates may be necessary for the operation and maintenance of said system of sewers and water.

The Republic of Panama agrees that the cities of Panama and Colon shall comply in perpetuity with the sanitary ordinances whether of a preventive or curative character prescribed by the United States and in case the Government of Panama is unable or fails in its duty to enforce this compliance by the cities of Panama and Colon with the sanitary ordinances of the United States the Republic of Panama grants to the United States the right and authority to enforce the same.

The same right and authority are granted to the United States for the maintenance of public order in the cities of Panama and Colon and the territories and harbors adjacent thereto in case the Republic of Panama should not be, in the judgment of the United States, able to maintain such order. . . .

ARTICLE XIV.

As the price or compensation for the rights, powers and privileges granted in this convention by the Republic of Panama to the United States, the Government of the United States agrees to pay to the Republic of Panama the sum of ten million dollars ($10,-000,000) in gold coin of the United States on the exchange of the ratification of this convention and also an annual payment during the life of this convention of two hundred and fifty thousand dollars ($250,000) in like gold coin, beginning nine years after the date aforesaid.

The provisions of this Article shall be in addition to all other benefits assured to the Republic of Panama under this convention.

But no delay or difference of opinion under this Article or any other provisions of this treaty shall affect or interrupt the full operation and effect of this convention in all other respects. . . .

ARTICLE XVIII.

The Canal, when constructed, and the entrances thereto shall be neutral in perpetuity, and shall be opened upon the terms provided for by Section I of Article three of, and in conformity with all the stipulations of, the treaty entered into by the Governments of the United States and Great Britain on November 18, 1901. . . .

ARTICLE XXIII.

If it should become necessary at any time to employ armed forces for the safety or protection of the Canal, or of the ships that make use of the same, or the railways and auxiliary works, the United States shall have the right, at all times and in its discretion, to use its police and its land and naval forces or to establish fortifications for these purposes. . . .

ARTICLE XXV.

For the better performance of the engagements of this convention and to the end of the efficient protection of the Canal and the preservation of its neutrality, the Government of the Republic of Panama will sell or lease to the United States lands adequate and necessary for naval or coaling stations on the Pacific coast and on the western Caribbean coast of the Republic at certain points to be agreed upon with the President of the United States. . . .

C. THE ROOSEVELT COROLLARY

THE BRITISH, German, and Italian governments intervened in Venezuela in 1901–02 to collect some debts owed their nationals, and early in 1904 the Hague tribunal handed down a decision that Venezuela must pay its debts and that the three intervening nations would have first claim on payment. This decision opened the way for naval demonstrations against all the small, defaulting Caribbean and Central American nations. When the Dominican Republic shortly thereafter drifted into fiscal chaos and its government asked President Roosevelt to intervene, he did so gladly, the more so because the call for intervention came in December, 1904, just after Roosevelt's countrymen had elected him to the presidency. TR apparently felt that he now had a freer hand than before. In his state of the union message of December 6, 1904, he announced what became known as the Roosevelt Corollary to the Monroe Doctrine.

. . . It is not true that the United States feels any land hunger or entertains any projects as regards the other nations of the Western Hemisphere save such as are for their welfare. All that this country desires is to see the neighboring countries stable, orderly, and prosperous. Any country whose people conduct themselves well can count upon our hearty friendship. If a nation shows that it knows how to act with reasonable efficiency and decency in social and political matters, if it keeps order and pays its obligations, it need fear no interference from the United States. Chronic wrongdoing, or an impotence which results in a general loosening of the ties of civilized society, may in America, as elsewhere, ultimately require intervention by some civilized nation, and in the Western Hemisphere the adherence of the United States to the Monroe Doctrine may force the United States, however reluc-

SOURCE: Fred L. Israel, ed., *The State of the Union Messages of the Presidents: 1790–1966* (3 vols., New York, 1966), II, pp. 2134–35.

tantly, in flagrant cases of such wrongdoing or impotence, to the exercise of an international police power. If every country washed by the Caribbean Sea would show the progress in stable and just civilization which with the aid of the Platt amendment Cuba has shown since our troops left the island, and which so many of the republics in both Americas are constantly and brilliantly showing, all question of interference by this Nation with their affairs would be at an end. Our interests and those of our southern neighbors are in reality identical. They have great natural riches, and if within their borders the reign of law and justice obtains, prosperity is sure to come to them. While they thus obey the primary laws of civilized society they may rest assured that they will be treated by us in a spirit of cordial and helpful sympathy. We would interfere with them only in the last resort, and then only if it became evident that their inability or unwillingness to do justice at home and abroad had violated the rights of the United States or had invited foreign aggression to the detriment of the entire body of American nations. It is a mere truism to say that every nation, whether in America or anywhere else, which desires to maintain its freedom, its independence, must ultimately realize that the right of such independence can not be separated from the responsibility of making good use of it.

In asserting the Monroe Doctrine, in taking such steps as we have taken in regard to Cuba, Venezuela, and Panama, and in endeavoring to circumscribe the theater of war in the Far East, and to secure the open door in China, we have acted in our own interest as well as in the interest of humanity at large. There are, however, cases in which, while our own interests are not greatly involved, strong appeal is made to our sympathies. Ordinarily it is very much wiser and more useful for us to concern ourselves with striving for our own moral and material betterment here at home than to concern ourselves with trying to better the condition of things in other nations. We have plenty of sins of our own to war against, and under ordinary circumstances we can do more for the general uplifting of humanity by striving with heart and soul to put a stop to civic corruption, to brutal lawlessness and violent race prejudices here at home than by passing resolutions about wrongdoing elsewhere. Nevertheless there are occasional crimes committed on so vast a scale and of such peculiar horror as to make us doubt whether it is not our manifest duty to endeavor at least to show our disapproval of the deed and our sympathy with those who have suffered by it. The cases must be extreme in which such a course is justifiable. There must be no effort made to remove the mote from our brother's eye if we refuse to remove the beam from our own. But in extreme cases action may be justifiable and proper. . . .

D. Customs in the Dominican Republic

THE PRESIDENT first sought to put the Dominican Republic in bond through an executive agreement, but when word of this proposed arrangement leaked out there was an uproar and he translated his purposes into a treaty. The Senate turned the treaty down. Roosevelt appointed a retired American colonel as Dominican collector of customs for two years until, in 1907, the Senate consented to a treaty. Meanwhile the President was proud of his handiwork, and told Congress about it in his state of the union message of December 5, 1905.

. . . Santo Domingo, in her turn, has now made an appeal to us to help her, and not only every principle of wisdom but every generous instinct within us bids us respond to the appeal. It is not of the slightest consequence whether we grant the aid needed by Santo Domingo as an incident to the wise development of the Monroe Doctrine or because we regard the case of Santo Domingo as standing wholly by itself, and to be treated as such, and not on general principles or with any reference to the Monroe Doctrine. The important point is to give the needed aid, and the case is certainly sufficiently peculiar to deserve to be judged purely on its own merits. The conditions in Santo Domingo have for a number of years grown from bad to worse until a year ago all society was on the verge of dissolution. Fortunately, just at this time a ruler sprang up in Santo Domingo, who, with his colleagues, saw the dangers threatening their country and appealed to the friendship of the only great and powerful neighbor who possessed the power, and as they hoped also the will to help them. There was imminent danger of foreign intervention. The previous rulers of Santo Domingo had recklessly incurred debts, and owing to her internal disorders she had ceased to be able to provide means of paying the debts. The patience of her foreign creditors had become exhausted, and at least two foreign nations were on the point of intervention,

SOURCE: Israel, *State of the Union* . . . , III, pp. 2167–68.

and were only prevented from intervening by the unofficial assurance of this Government that it would itself strive to help Santo Domingo in her hour of need. In the case of one of these nations, only the actual opening of negotiations to this end by our Government prevented the seizure of territory in Santo Domingo by a European power. Of the debts incurred some were just, while some were not of a character which really renders it obligatory on or proper for Santo Domingo to pay them in full. But she could not pay any of them unless some stability was assured her Government and people.

Accordingly, the Executive Department of our Government negotiated a treaty under which we are to try to help the Dominican people to straighten out their finances. This treaty is pending before the Senate. In the meantime a temporary arrangement has been made which will last until the Senate has had time to take action upon the treaty. Under this arrangement the Dominican Government has appointed Americans to all the important positions in the customs service, and they are seeing to the honest collection of the revenues, turning over 45 per cent. to the Government for running expenses and putting the other 55 per cent. into a safe depository for equitable division in case the treaty shall be ratified, among the various creditors, whether European or American.

The Custom Houses offer well-nigh the only sources of revenue in Santo Domingo, and the different revolutions usually have as their real aim the obtaining of these Custom Houses. The mere fact that the Collectors of Customs are Americans, that they are performing their duties with efficiency and honesty, and that the treaty is pending in the Senate gives a certain moral power to the Government of Santo Domingo which it has not had before. This has completely discouraged all revolutionary movement, while it has already produced such an increase in the revenues that the Government is actually getting more from the 45 per cent. that the American Collectors turn over to it than it got formerly when it took the entire revenue. . . .

16. Dollars, Friendship, Bullets

A. COMMERCIAL DIPLOMACY

IN THE Roosevelt era Cuba, Panama, and the Dominican Republic became protectorates of the United States, and the Taft administration established an unofficial protectorate over Nicaragua. But Roosevelt's successor, Taft, hoped that increasing trade between the United States and the Latin nations would allay the animosities and hurt feelings of the era of intervention. With the best of intentions—the genial Will Taft never had any other—he spoke for a trade policy by using an epigram that with a slight alteration turned out to be alliterative in all the major Western languages. Taft's ill luck with a good phrase perhaps justifies the belief of some political leaders that it is never advisable to say things in public in a sprightly way.

. . . The diplomacy of the present administration has sought to respond to modern ideas of commercial intercourse. This policy has been characterized as substituting dollars for bullets. It is one that appeals alike to idealistic humanitarian sentiments, to the dictates of sound policy and strategy, and to legitimate commercial aims. It is an effort frankly directed to the increase of American trade upon the axiomatic principle that the Government of the United States shall extend all proper support to every legitimate and beneficial American enterprise abroad. How great have been the results of this diplomacy, coupled with the maximum and minimum provision of the tariff law, will be seen by some consideration of the wonderful increase in the export trade of the United States. Because modern diplomacy is commercial, there has been a disposition in some quarters to attribute to it none but materialistic aims. How strikingly erroneous is such an impression may be seen from a study of the results by which the diplomacy of the United States can be judged. . . .

SOURCE: state of the union message of Dec. 3, 1912, Israel, *State of the Union* . . . , III, pp. 2490–91.

B. The Commerce of Ideas

Every new administration, even if of the same political party, deems itself a new broom, and President Wilson in 1913 was willing to sweep out all sorts of dusty ideas, to clean up the dark places of American foreign policy. With the marvelous rhetoric of which he was a master, he set out his new Latin American policy in a speech before the Southern Commercial Congress on October 27, 1913.

. . . It is with unaffected pleasure that I find myself here to-day. I once before had the pleasure, in another southern city, of addressing the Southern Commercial Congress. I then spoke of what the future seemed to hold in store for this region, which so many of us love and toward the future of which we all look forward with so much confidence and hope. But another theme directed me here this time. I do not need to speak of the South. She has, perhaps, acquired the gift of speaking for herself. I come because I want to speak of our present and prospective relations with our neighbors to the south. I deemed it a public duty, as well as a personal pleasure, to be here to express for myself and for the Government I represent the welcome we all feel to those who represent the Latin American States.

The future, ladies and gentlemen, is going to be very different for this hemisphere from the past. These States lying to the south of us, which have always been our neighbors, will now be drawn closer to us by innumerable ties, and I hope, chief of all, by the tie of a common understanding of each other. Interest does not tie nations together; it sometimes separates them. But sympathy and understanding does unite them, and I believe that by the new route that is just about to be opened, while we physically cut two continents asunder, we spiritually unite them. It is a spiritual union which we seek.

I wonder if you realize, I wonder if your imaginations have been filled with the significance of the tides of commerce. Your governor alluded in very fit and striking terms to the voyage of Columbus, but Columbus took his voyage under compulsion of circumstances. Constantinople had been captured by the Turks and all the routes of trade with the East had been suddenly closed. If there was not a

Source: 63d Cong., 2d Sess., Senate Document 440 (Washington, D.C., 1914), pp. 5–8.

way across the Atlantic to open those routes again, they were closed forever, and Columbus set out not to discover America, for he did not know that it existed, but to discover the eastern shores of Asia. He set sail for Cathay and stumbled upon America. With that change in the outlook of the world, what happened? England, that had been at the back of Europe, with an unknown sea behind her, found that all things had turned as if upon a pivot and she was at the front of Europe; and since then all the tides of energy and enterprise that have issued out of Europe have seemed to be turned westward across the Atlantic. But you will notice that they have turned westward chiefly north of the Equator and that it is the northern half of the globe that has seemed to be filled with the media of intercourse and of sympathy and of common understanding.

Do you not see now what is about to happen? These great tides which have been running along parallels of latitude will now swing southward athwart parallels of latitude, and that opening gate at the Isthmus of Panama will open the world to a commerce that she has not known before, a commerce of intelligence, of thought and sympathy between north and south. The Latin American States, which, to their disadvantage, have been off the main lines, will now be on the main lines. I feel that these gentlemen honoring us with their presence to-day will presently find that some part, at any rate, of the center of gravity of the world has shifted. Do you realize that New York, for example, will be nearer the western coast of South America than she is now to the eastern coast of South America? Do you realize that a line drawn northward parallel with the greater part of the western coast of South America will run only about 150 miles west of New York? The great bulk of South America, if you will look at your globes (not at your Mercator's projection), lies eastward of the continent of North America. You will realize that when you realize that the canal will run southeast, not southwest, and that when you get into the Pacific you will be farther east than you were when you left the Gulf of Mexico. These things are significant, therefore, of this, that we are closing one chapter in the history of the world and are opening another, of great, unimaginable significance.

There is one peculiarity about the history of the Latin American States which I am sure they are keenly aware of. You hear of "concessions" to foreign capitalists in Latin America. You do not hear of concessions to foreign capitalists in the United States. They are not granted concessions. They are invited to make investments. The work is ours, though they are welcome to invest in it. We do not ask them to supply the capital and do the work. It is an invitation, not a privilege; and States that are obliged, because their territory does not lie within the main field of modern enterprise and action, to grant concessions are in this condition—that foreign interests are apt to dominate their domestic affairs, a condition of affairs always dangerous and apt to become intolerable. What these States are going to see, therefore, is an emancipation from the subordination, which has been inevitable, to foreign enterprise, and an assertion of the splendid character which, in spite of these difficulties, they have again and again been able to demonstrate. The dignity, the courage, the self-possession, the self-respect of the Latin American States, their achievements in the face of all these adverse circumstances, deserve nothing but the admiration and applause of the world. They have had harder bargains driven with them in the matter of loans than any other peoples in the world. Interest has been exacted of them that was not exacted of anybody else, because the risk was said to be greater; and then securities were taken that destroyed the risk—an admirable arrangement for those who were forcing the terms! I rejoice in nothing so much as in the prospect that they will now be emancipated from these conditions, and we ought to be the first to take part in assisting in that emancipation. I think some of these gentlemen have already had occasion to bear witness that the Department of State in recent months has tried to serve them in that wise. In the future they will draw closer and closer to us because of circumstances of which I wish to speak with moderation and, I hope, without indiscretion.

We must prove ourselves their friends and champions upon terms of equality and honor. You can not be friends upon any other terms than upon the terms of equality. You can not be friends at all except upon the terms of honor. We must show ourselves friends by comprehending their interest, whether it squares with our own interest or not. It is a very perilous thing to determine the foreign policy of a nation in the terms of material interest. It not only is unfair to those with whom you are dealing, but it is degrading as regards your own actions.

Comprehension must be the soil in which shall grow all the

fruits of friendship, and there is a reason and a compulsion lying behind all this which is dearer than anything else to the thoughtful men of America. I mean the development of constitutional liberty in the world. Human rights, national integrity, and opportunity as against material interests—that, ladies and gentlemen, is the issue which we now have to face. I want to take this occasion to say that the United States will never again seek one additional foot of territory by conquest. She will devote herself to showing that she knows how to make honorable and fruitful use of the territory she has, and she must regard it as one of the duties of friendship to see that from no quarter are material interests made superior to human liberty and national opportunity. I say this, not with a single thought that anyone will gainsay it, but merely to fix in our consciousness what our real relationship with the rest of America is. It is the relationship of a family of mankind devoted to the development of true constitutional liberty. We know that that is the soil out of which the best enterprise springs. We know that this is a cause which we are making in common with our neighbors, because we have had to make it for ourselves.

Reference has been made here to-day to some of the national problems which confront us as a nation. What is at the heart of all our national problems? It is that we have seen the hand of material interest sometimes about to close upon our dearest rights and possessions. We have seen material interests threaten constitutional freedom in the United States. Therefore we will now know how to sympathize with those in the rest of America who have to contend with such powers, not only within their borders but from outside their borders also.

I know what the response of the thought and heart of America will be to the program I have outlined, because America was created to realize a program like that. This is not America because it is rich. This is not America because it has set up for a great population great opportunities of material prosperity. America is a name which sounds in the ears of men everywhere as a synonym with individual opportunity because a synonym of individual liberty. I would rather belong to a poor nation that was free than to a rich nation that had ceased to be in love with liberty. But we shall not be poor if we love liberty, because the nation that loves liberty truly sets every man free to do his best and be his best, and that means the release of all the splendid energies of a great people who think for themselves. A nation of employees can not be free any more than a nation of employers can be.

In emphasizing the points which must unite us in sympathy and in spiritual interest with the Latin American peoples we are only emphasizing the points of our own life, and we should prove ourselves untrue to our own traditions if we proved ourselves untrue friends to them. Do not think, therefore, gentlemen, that the questions of the day are mere questions of policy and diplomacy. They are shot through with the principles of life. We dare not turn from the principle that morality and not expediency is the thing that must guide us and that we will never condone iniquity because it is most convenient to do so. It seems to me that this is a day of infinite hope, of confidence in a future greater than the past has been, for I am fain to believe that in spite of all the things that we wish to correct the nineteenth century that now lies behind us has brought us a long stage toward the time when, slowly ascending the tedious climb that leads to the final uplands, we shall get our ultimate view of the duties of mankind. We have breasted a considerable part of that climb and shall presently—it may be in a generation or two—come out upon those great heights where there shines unobstructed the light of the justice of God.

C. Rebellion in Haiti

THE MOBILE speech did not prove of much avail for Wilson's Mexican policy. The President some months before, on March 11, 1913, had announced a policy of nonrecognition of improperly revolutionary governments in Latin America (see below, pp. 246–247), and this first step in his Mexican policy soon drew him into a morass, leading to intervention at Veracruz in 1914 and Brigadier General John J. Pershing's expedition into northern Mexico in 1916. Nor did the Mobile speech have any relevance to the dreadful events in Haiti in 1915, which again forced the government of the United States to intervene. Haiti had been in trouble for a generation and more; since 1886 there had been twelve presidents of Haiti, none of whom served out a full term of seven years. Several presidents had met violent deaths while in office—and one of them was blown up with the presidential palace in Port-au-Prince. General Vilbrun Guillaume Sam took the presidency in March, 1915,

SOURCE: Davis to Secretary of State Lansing, Jan. 12, 1916, *Foreign Relations of the United States: 1916* (Washington, D.C., 1925), p. 317.

and by July had so alienated his fellow citizens that a group of them tried to set fire to the presidential palace while he was inside. Foiling this attempt, President Sam ordered the execution of 167 political prisoners. With extreme brutality the President's man, General Oscar, dispatched them, many by his own hand. Afterward Oscar secreted himself in the Dominican legation, but a mob dragged him out and dispatched him. Meanwhile President Sam had fled to the French legation. Consul Robert B. Davis, Jr., who was chargé d'affaires of the American legation, afterward described what happened on July 28, 1915.

. . . Shortly before the arrival of the mob, a doctor had been at the Legation—in fact was there at the time the mob entered, making his escape as soon as he learned what was happening. He had just finished dressing the bullet wound which the President had received in his leg the previous day, and in the dressing had used iodoform. It was the odor of this drug that betrayed the hiding place of the President. The members of the mob knew that the President himself was the only wounded person within the Legation, and on entering the bed room of the French Minister and noticing the odor of this drug in the room, they began a more careful search there and discovered that there was a closed door behind the head of the bed, which had been moved so as to hide it. The President was found in the bath room into which this door opened. He was seized by the mob, stabbed two or three times in his face, knocked down and dragged by his heels down the stairs, through the drawing room and out into the grounds, vainly protesting that he was innocent of any connection with the massacre of the day before, and begging most piteously for his life. No attention was paid to his protestations, and before the eyes of his wife and children he was dragged down the long driveway which leads to the gates. As he was being dragged along he clutched the spokes of a wheel of a buggy which stood at one side of the driveway, attempting to free himself from his captors. A blow of a club broke his arm and loosened his grip.

While these events were transpiring within the Legation itself, another mob composed of the rabble of Port au Prince had collected in the street before the Legation. Arriving at the gates, which were locked, the President was thrown over to the mob that waited on the outside. No sooner had his body touched the ground than it was literally torn to pieces. . . .

D. INTERVENTION

CONSUL Davis was en route to the French legation when members of the mob ran past him carrying parts of the President's body. It was about this time that he noticed a ship coming over the horizon, and sensed that it was the U.S.S. Washington, flagship of Rear Admiral W. B. Caperton, which he had summoned to the scene. The admiral dropped anchor in Port-au-Prince that very afternoon, and sent marines into the town where chaos was reigning. Government had collapsed everywhere in Haiti, and it became necessary to occupy the entire country. After establishment of a new regime, Davis on September 16, 1915, signed a treaty with its foreign minister.

ARTICLE II

The President of Haiti shall appoint, upon nomination by the President of the United States, a General Receiver and such aids and employees as may be necessary, who shall collect, receive and apply all customs duties on imports and exports accruing at the several custom houses and ports of entry of the Republic of Haiti.

The President of Haiti shall appoint, upon nomination by the President of the United States, a Financial Adviser, who shall be an officer attached to the Ministry of Finance, to give effect to whose proposals and labors the Minister will lend efficient aid. . . .

ARTICLE VIII

The Republic of Haiti shall not increase its public debt except by previous agreement with the President of the United States, and shall not contract any debt or assume any financial obligation unless the ordinary revenues of the Republic available for that purpose, after defraying the expenses of the Government, shall be adequate to pay the interest and provide a sinking fund for the final discharge of such debt.

ARTICLE IX

The Republic of Haiti will not without a previous agreement with the President of the United States, modify the customs duties in a manner to reduce the revenues therefrom. . . .

ARTICLE X

The Haitian Government obligates itself, for the preservation of domestic peace, the security of individual rights and full observ-

SOURCE: Foreign Relations . . . : 1916, pp. 329–31.

ance of the provisions of this treaty, to create without delay an efficient constabulary, urban and rural, composed of native Haitians. This constabulary shall be organized and officered by Americans, appointed by the President of Haiti, upon nomination by the President of the United States. The Haitian Government shall clothe these officers with the proper and necessary authority and uphold them in the performance of their functions. These officers will be replaced by Haitians as they, by examination, conducted under direction of a board to be selected by the senior American officer of this constabulary and in the presence of a representative of the Haitian Government, are found to be qualified to assume such duties. . . .

ARTICLE XI

The Government of Haiti agrees not to surrender any of the territory of the Republic of Haiti by sale, lease, or otherwise, or jurisdiction over such territory, to any foreign government or power, nor to enter into any treaty or contract with any foreign power or powers that will impair or tend to impair the independence of Haiti. . . .

ARTICLE XIII

The Republic of Haiti, being desirous to further the development of its natural resources, agrees to undertake and execute such measures as in the opinion of the high contracting parties may be necessary for the sanitation and public improvement of the Republic, under the supervision and direction of an engineer or engineers, to be appointed by the President of Haiti upon nomination by the President of the United States, and authorized for that purpose by the Government of Haiti.

ARTICLE XIV

The high contracting parties shall have authority to take such steps as may be necessary to insure the complete attainment of any of the objects comprehended in this treaty; and, should the necessity occur, the United States will lend an efficient aid for the preservation of Haitian Independence and the maintenance of a government adequate for the protection of life, property and individual liberty. . . .

VI

World Politics

At the very end of the nineteenth century, at the time of the Spanish War, the people of the United States began to consider their country a great power actively at work for good in the world. They demanded that the major European governments recognize this fact. Long before, of course, perhaps even at the founding of the Republic in 1775, the United States was a great power in terms of population and economic strength. By the Civil War, assuredly on the occasion of the Geneva arbitration of 1872, no government of Europe could consider the American government one of the smaller regimes of the world. Nonetheless, and whatever the potential of the United States, or its proper place among the nations, it was not until the end of the nineteenth century that the country demanded a position of great power.

To put the case in the above verities is not to say everything, however, for even after the end of the century the United States government chose not to exercise its power where it most needed demonstration, namely, the continent of Europe. Americans showed their strength in Latin America, and even in the Far East, but not in Europe. This was a pity, for Europe was about to come apart in the war of 1914—18, and the United States did almost nothing to prevent the catastrophe.

17. The Hague Movement

A. Conference

In the era of McKinley and Roosevelt, Americans liked to believe that a codification of international law, and the advance of pacific means for settling disputes, would help ensure peace. The tsar of Russia called the First Hague Conference in 1899 in a fumbling effort to save the imperial treasury some money during what was becoming a heated armament race in Europe. The results of the conference were hardly spectacular. In a convention of July 29, 1899, it did set up a panel of jurists to which quarreling nations might resort for arbitrators of their disputes.

Article 20

With the object of facilitating an immediate recourse to arbitration for international differences, which it has not been possible to settle by diplomacy, the Signatory Powers undertake to organize a permanent Court of Arbitration, accessible at all times and operating, unless otherwise stipulated by the parties, in accordance with the Rules of Procedure inserted in the present Convention.

Article 21

The Permanent Court shall be competent for all arbitration cases, unless the parties agree to institute a special Tribunal.

Article 23

Within the three months following its ratification of the present Act, each Signatory Power shall select four persons at the most, of known competency in questions of international law, of the highest moral reputation, and disposed to accept the duties of Arbitrators.

The persons thus selected shall be inscribed, as members of the Court, in a list which shall be notified by the Bureau to all the Signatory Powers.

Any alteration in the list of Arbitrators is brought by the Bureau to the knowledge of the Signatory Powers.

Two or more Powers may agree on the selection in common of one or more Members.

Source: Charles I. Bevans, comp., *Treaties and Other International Agreements of the United States of America: 1776–1949* (Washington, 1968 –), I, pp. 237–239.

The same person can be selected by different Powers.

The Members of the Court are appointed for a term of six years. Their appointments can be renewed.

In case of the death or retirement of a member of the Court, his place shall be filled in accordance with the method of his appointment.

ARTICLE 24

When the Signatory Powers desire to have recourse to the Permanent Court for the settlement of a difference that has arisen between them, the Arbitrators called upon to form the competent Tribunal to decide this difference, must be chosen from the general list of members of the Court.

Failing the direct agreement of the parties on the composition of the Arbitration Tribunal, the following course shall be pursued:—

Each party appoints two Arbitrators, and these together choose an Umpire.

If the votes are equal, the choice of the Umpire is intrusted to a third Power, selected by the parties by common accord.

If an agreement is not arrived at on this subject, each party selects a different Power, and the choice of the Umpire is made in concert by the Powers thus selected.

The Tribunal being thus composed, the parties notify to the Bureau their determination to have recourse to the Court and the names of the Arbitrators.

The Tribunal of Arbitration assembles on the date fixed by the parties.

The Members of the Court, in the discharge of their duties and out of their own country, enjoy diplomatic privileges and immunities.

ARTICLE 25

The Tribunal of Arbitration has its ordinary seat at The Hague.

Except in cases of necessity, the place of session can only be altered by the Tribunal with the assent of the parties.

ARTICLE 27

The Signatory Powers consider it their duty, if a serious dispute threatens to break out between two or more of them, to remind these latter that the Permanent Court is open to them.

Consequently, they declare that the fact of reminding the conflicting parties of the provisions of the present Convention, and the advice given to them, in the highest interests of peace, to have recourse to the Permanent Court, can only be regarded as friendly actions.

B. Ground Rules

THE FIRST *Hague Conference rather quaintly arranged a convention, dated July 29th, prohibiting the launching of projectiles and explosives from balloons, for a period of five years. It also codified the behavior of belligerent ground forces in a detailed way, as indicated in the listing of chapters in an annex of another convention of the same date.*

ARTICLES.

I. Instructions to forces.
II. When binding.
III. Ratification.

IV. Nonsignatory powers.
V. Renunciation.

ANNEX.

Section I.—Belligerents.

Chapter I.—Qualifications of belligerents.

I. Application of laws of war.
II. Unorganized belligerents.

III. Combatants; noncombatants.

Chapter II.—Prisoners of war.

IV. Treatment.
V. Confinement.
VI. Employment.
VII. Maintenance.
VIII. Laws; regulations; recapture.
IX. False statements.
X. Parole.
XI. Parole voluntary.

XII. Recapture after parole.
XIII. Reporters, sutlers, etc.
XIV. Bureau of information.
XV. Relief society.
XVI. Postage; gifts.
XVII. Officer's pay.
XVIII. Religious freedom.
XIX. Wills.
XX. Repatriation.

Chapter III.—Sick and wounded.

XXI. Obligation of belligerents.

SOURCE: Malloy comp., *Treaties, Conventions, International Acts* . . . , pp. 2042–43.

Section II.—Hostilities.

Chapter I.—Means of injuring enemy; sieges; bombardments.

Chapter II.—Spies.

Chapter III.—Flags of truce.

Chapter IV.—Capitulation.

Chapter V.—Armistices.

Section III.—Military authority over hostile territory.

Section IV.—Internment of belligerents and care of wounded in neutral countries.

C. The Porter Resolution

The Second Hague Conference, meeting in 1907, was much less successful than the first. The powers were beginning to sense the approach of a great European war, and no one wished to take any large steps toward peace. President Roosevelt that same year was worrying about Japan, and sent the fleet around the world as a service (as he later put it in his Autobiography) to peace. In this climate, the United States sponsored at The Hague the Porter Resolution, concluded October 18, 1907, named for one of the American delegates and ambassador to France, General Horace Porter.

Article 1

The Contracting Powers agree not to have recourse to armed force for the recovery of contract debts claimed from the Government of one country by the Government of another country as being due to its nationals.

This undertaking is, however, not applicable when the debtor State refuses or neglects to reply to an offer of arbitration, or, after accepting the offer, prevents any compromise from being agreed on, or, after the arbitration, fails to submit to the award.

Article 2

It is further agreed that the arbitration mentioned in paragraph 2 of the foregoing Article shall be subject to the procedure laid down in Part IV, Chapter III, of The Hague Convention for the Pacific Settlement of International Disputes. The award shall determine, except where otherwise agreed between the parties, the validity of the claim, the amount of the debt, and the time and mode of payment.

It was the hope of many Americans and Europeans that the Hague movement might continue with a third conference, but the World War interrupted that possibility and afterward the Hague idea blended into the project for a League of Nations which itself sponsored a World Court. The latter was no simple panel of jurists for occasional arbitrations, but met regularly, heard cases, and gave decisions like an ordinary court. The American steel tycoon Andrew Carnegie had constructed a splendid Peace Palace for the old

Source: Bevans, comp., Treaties . . . : 1776–1949, I, p. 614.

Hague Court, and the World Court (and its successor sponsored by the United Nations) met there. The Hague Court passed into limbo.

18. Alaska

A. BOUNDARY DISPUTE

PRESIDENT Roosevelt exerted American power toward Europe in another oblique way when he forced the settlement of the Alaskan boundary in 1903, a settlement at the expense of Canada but indirectly at the expense of Great Britain. By 1903, the British were in embarrassing straits. They had just won the Boer War, after exhibiting their military incompetence to all the world. Despite their chagrin they decided to avoid the slightest antagonism with the newly assertive American nation, and not merely consented on January 24, 1903, to an Alaskan settlement but saw to it that the settlement went the way the American government and its President desired.

ARTICLE I.

A tribunal shall be immediately appointed to consider and decide the questions set forth in Article IV of this convention. The tribunal shall consist of six impartial jurists of repute who shall consider judicially the questions submitted to them, each of whom shall first subscribe an oath that he will impartially consider the arguments and evidence presented to the tribunal and will decide thereupon according to his true judgment. Three members of the tribunal shall be appointed by the President of the United States, and three by His Britannic Majesty. All questions considered by the tribunal, including the final award, shall be decided by a majority of all the members thereof. . . .

ARTICLE II.

Each of the High Contracting Parties shall also name one person to attend the tribunal as its agent.

The written or printed case of each of the two parties, accompanied by the documents, the official correspondence and all other

SOURCE: Malloy, comp., Treaties, Conventions, International Acts . . . , I, pp. 788–89, 791.

evidence in writing or print on which each party relies, shall be delivered in duplicate to each member of the tribunal and to the agent of the other party as soon as may be after the organization of the tribunal, but within a period not exceeding two months from the date of the exchange of ratifications of this convention.

Within two months after the delivery on both sides of the written or printed case, either party may, in like manner, deliver in duplicate to each member of the tribunal, and to the agent of the other party, a counter-case and additional documents, correspondence and evidence in reply to the case, documents, correspondence and evidence so presented by the other party. The tribunal may, however, extend this last mentioned period when in their judgment it becomes necessary by reason of special difficulties which may arise in the procuring of such additional papers and evidence.

If in the case submitted to the tribunal either party shall have specified or referred to any report or document in its own exclusive possession without annexing a copy, such party shall be bound, if the other party shall demand it, within thirty days after the delivery of the case, to furnish to the party applying for it a duly certified copy thereof; and either party may call upon the other, through the tribunal, to produce the original or certified copies of any papers adduced as evidence, giving in each instance such reasonable notice as the tribunal may require; and the original or copy so requested shall be delivered as soon as may be and within a period not exceeding forty days after receipt of notice.

Each party may present to the tribunal all pertinent evidence, documentary, historical, geographical, or topographical, including maps and charts, in its possession or control and applicable to the rightful decision of the questions submitted; and if it appears to the tribunal that there is evidence pertinent to the case in the possession of either party, and which has not been produced, the tribunal may in its discretion order the production of the same by the party having control thereof.

It shall be the duty of each party through its agent or counsel, within two months from the expiration of the time limited for the delivery of the counter-case on both sides, to deliver in duplicate to each member of the said tribunal and to the agent of the other party a written or printed argument showing the points and referring to the evidence upon which his Government relies, and either party may also support the same before the tribunal by oral argument of counsel. The tribunal may, if they shall deem further elucidation with regard to any point necessary, require from either party a written, printed, or oral statement or argument upon the point; but in such case the other party shall have the right to reply thereto.

ARTICLE III.

It is agreed by the High Contracting Parties that the tribunal shall consider in the settlement of the questions submitted to its decision the Treaties respectively concluded between His Britannic Majesty and the Emperor of All the Russias under date of 28/16 February, A. D. 1825, and between the United States of America and the Emperor of All the Russias concluded under date of March 30/18, A. D. 1867 . . . as follows:

ARTICLE V.

The tribunal shall assemble for their first meeting at London as soon as practicable after receiving their commissions; and shall themselves fix the times and places of all subsequent meetings.

The decision of the tribunal shall be made so soon as possible after the conclusion of the arguments in the case, and within three months thereafter, unless the President of the United States and His Britannic Majesty shall by common accord extend the time therefor. . . .

B. GOLD IN THE KLONDIKE

THEODORE Roosevelt had pronounced ideas about the Alaskan panhandle, the area in dispute in 1903. The dispute went back to the Anglo-Russian treaty of 1825 which (together with a Russo-American treaty of 1824) set the southern limit of the panhandle at the later famous line of 54°40'. The Anglo-Russian treaty failed to establish the Canadian-Alaskan boundary along the panhandle with any exactitude—although its intent was clear enough: Russia was seeking, and to this the British had agreed, to retain control of the coast down to 54°40'. When the United States bought Alaska in 1867 no one worried much about this boundary, not even the Canadians, until gold was discovered in the Canadian Klondike in August, 1896. The easiest access to the Klondike was through the panhandle. The Canadians in June, 1898, laid claim to some of this uncertain territory, hoping to take the dispute to arbitration

SOURCE: Morison, ed., Letters of Theodore Roosevelt, III, p. 635.

and get something as a result. Roosevelt considered this tactic highway robbery and would have none of it. He explained himself volubly in letters to friends and in White House conversations—so volubly that his humor evidently reached not merely the British government but the principal British member of the Alaskan tribunal, the lord chief justice, Lord Alverstone. When the time came, Alverstone did his duty, if not by the law then by the interests of the British government. When everything was over TR was elated, and in a letter of October 20, 1903, pointed out to his son Theodore, Jr., what had happened.

Dear Ted:

. . . I am very much pleased over what has just been accomplished in the Alaska Boundary award. I hestitated sometime before I would consent to a commission to decide the case and I declined absolutely to allow any arbitration of the matter. Finally I made up my mind I would appoint three men of such ability and such firmness that I could be certain there would be no possible outcome disadvantageous to us as a nation; and would trust to the absolute justice of our case, as well as to a straight-out declaration to certain high British officials that I meant business, and that if this commission did not decide the case at issue, I would decline all further negotiations and would have the line run on my own hook. I think that both factors were of importance in bringing about the result. That is, I think that the British Commissioner who voted with our men was entitled to great credit, and I also think that the clear understanding the British Government had as to what would follow a disagreement was very important and probably decisive. *Ever your loving father*

C. Arbitration

The President prided himself that in the boundary settlement the Americans had yielded the Canadians a couple of islands, even though legally it was unnecessary to give them away. He was sensitive as to whether his appointees as commissioners—Secretary of War Elihu Root (a member of the administration), Senator Henry Cabot Lodge of Massachusetts (a presidential confidant), and ex-Senator George Turner of Washington (a resident of a state where opinions on the Alaska boundary question were strong)—were "impartial jurists of repute," as stipulated in the treaty setting up the tribunal. He wrote about these matters on December 7, 1903, to his friend Arthur Lee, a highly placed Britisher who had been a tentmate during the Spanish-American War.

Source: Morison, ed., *Letters of Theodore Roosevelt*, III, pp. 665–66.

. . . Now as to Alaska: Have you seen the maps in the big red atlas prepared by the British commissioners, and on the outside printed "British Case"? If so, I want you to take what the British Commission—that is, the two Canadian Commissioners and Lord Alverstone—submitted in the way of maps, and note that every Canadian and British map thus officially submitted by the British and Canadian Commissioners, for sixty years after the signing of the treaty between the Russians and the British, in 1825, sustained the American case. Lord Alverstone could not have decided otherwise than he did, and the action of the Canadian Commissioners, in my view, was outrageous alike from the standpoint of ethics and of professional decency. There is nothing I should enjoy more than to write an article about Lord Alverstone, reproducing all these maps, so that even the least thoughtful could see that Lord Alverstone could not, as an honorable man, decide otherwise than he did; and that as a matter of fact, he got every inch of territory for the Canadians that could by any possibility be held to be theirs. The only reason I do not say something in public in the matter is that I am afraid it might do Lord Alverstone hurt instead of good; but you are very welcome to show him this letter if you see fit.

You speak of your regret that the Commission was not composed exclusively of judges. I asked two judges of our Supreme Court, whom I thought most fit for the positions, to serve. They both declined; and as I now think, wisely. On this Commission we needed to have jurists who were statesmen. If the decision had been rendered purely judicially, *the Canadians would not have received the two islands which they did receive at the mouth of the Portland Canal;* and one of the judges to whom I offered the appointment has told me that on that account he would have been unable to sign the award. He would have felt that he was sitting purely as a judge, and that judicially the case did not admit of a compromise. Personally, while I think the American case even as regards these islands was the stronger, I yet attach so great importance to having the case settled that I am glad that our commissioners yielded to Lord Alverstone and thus rendered it possible for a decision to be made. But my belief is that if you had had two of our Supreme Court judges on the American Commission, they would have stood out steadily for a decision on every point in favor of the American view—a determination which I think would have been technically proper, but in its results most unfortunate. . . .

19. Morocco

A. FRANCO-GERMAN CONFLICT

THE ONLY serious intervention by the United States in Europe's affair, during the years from 1898 to 1914 occurred over Morocco in 1905–06. In the year 1904, Secretary Hay had startled the Republican National Convention in Chicago by a ringing telegram, "THIS GOVERNMENT WANTS PERDICARIS ALIVE OR RAISULI DEAD"—all over the capture in Morocco of an American citizen, Ion Perdicaris, by a dreadful local bandit named Raisuli. This initial Moroccan intervention was more political than diplomatic, as it stirred the Chicago Republicans to nominate Roosevelt. Hay later discovered that Perdicaris may not have been an American citizen. But in the following year a first-class European crisis arose when the German government chose publicly to affirm the sovereignty of the sultan of Morocco, with the not-too-concealed purpose of frustrating the French government which was on the verge of taking over Morocco. The offending French foreign minister, Théophile Delcassé, had to resign. Roosevelt was sufficiently alarmed to take a large hand in the Moroccan affair, as he afterward related to Ambassador Whitelaw Reid in London, in an enormous forty-two-page letter (including documentary inserts) of April 28, 1906.

Now you are about to receive a quarto-volume from me and I hope it will not daunt you. But there has been so much that is amusing and interesting, and indeed so much that has been of importance, in the queer negotiations wherein I have been the medium between France and Germany during the past year that it is possibly worth your while to know of them a little in detail.

On March 6th, 1905, Sternberg [Speck von Sternberg, the German Ambassador] came to me with a message from the Kaiser to ask me to join with the Kaiser in informing the Sultan of Morocco that he ought to reform his government, and that if he would do so we would stand behind him for the open door and would support him in any opposition he might make to any particular nation (that is to France) which sought to obtain exclusive control of Morocco. On the following day he submitted to me a

SOURCE: Morison, ed., Letters of Theodore Roosevelt, V, pp. 230 234, 236, 240, 242, 249–50.

memorandum to the same effect, stating that the Emperor regarded France and Spain as "a political unity," who wished to
divide up Morocco between themselves and debar her markets to
the rest of the world, and that if Spain should occupy Tangiers and
France the Hinterland they would be able to dominate the roads to
the Near and Far East. I answered this by stating that I did not see
my way clear to interfere in the matter, for I did not think that our
interests were sufficiently great, but expressed my friendliness to
Germany generally and my expectation and belief that her policy
was one for peace. I had some further interviews with Speck, and
on April 5th he wrote me again. This time he maintained that
England and France were allies; that he must insist upon a conference of the powers to settle the fate of Morocco. In this memorandum he (the Emperor) stated that Germany asked for no gains
in Morocco; she simply defended her interests and stood for equal
rights to all nations there. He then added, in Speck's words: "Besides this she is bound to think of her national dignity. This makes
it necessary for her to point out to France that her national interests cannot be disposed of without asking her for her consent and
cooperation. . . .

At the end of May I came back to Washington, and found
Jusserand and Speck both greatly concerned lest there should be a
war between France and Germany. Both of them were sincerely
anxious to avert such a possibility, and·each thought that his own
Government ought to make concessions to avoid the war. Speck, I
firmly believe, did not approve of the action his Government was
taking, but of course was obliged loyally to back up its position.
Jusserand, on the other hand, sympathized absolutely with the
general French indignation with Germany, but felt that it was
better to yield so far as the conference was concerned, if it could be
done honorably, rather than have a war. I saw Sir Mortimer on the
matter, but could get very little out of him. He was bitter about
Germany, and so far as he represented the British Government it
would appear that they were anxious to see Germany humiliated by
France's refusal to enter a conference, and that they were quite
willing to face the possibility of war under such circumstances. I
did not think this showed much valor on their part, although from
their point of view it was sagacious, as of course in such a war,
where the British and French fleets would be united, the German
fleet could have done absolutely nothing; while on land, where

Germany was so powerful, it would be France alone that would stand, and would have to stand, the brunt of the battle. I desired to do anything I legitimately could for France; because I like France, and I thought her in this instance to be in the right; but I did not intend to take any position which I would not be willing at all costs to maintain. . . .

It really did look as if there might be a war, and I felt in honor bound to try to prevent the war if I could, in the first place, because I should have felt such a war to be a real calamity to civilization; and in the next place, as I was already trying to bring about peace between Russia and Japan, I felt that a new conflict might result in what would literally be a world conflagration; and finally for the sake of France. Accordingly, I took active hold of the matter with both Speck and Jusserand, and after a series of communications with the French Government, through Jusserand, got things temporarily straightened up. Jusserand repeated to his government substantially just what I said. I told him that as chief of state I could not let America do anything quixotic, but that I had a real sentiment for France; that I would not advise her to do anything humiliating or disgraceful; but that it was eminently wise to avoid a war if it could be done by adopting a course which would save the Emperor's self-esteem; that for such purpose it was wise to help him save his face. I urged upon the French Government, in the first place, the great danger of war to them, and the fact that British assistance could avail them very, very little in the event of such a war, because France would be in danger of invasion by land; and in the next place, I pointed out that if there were a conference of the powers France would have every reason to believe that the conference would not sanction any unjust attack by Germany upon French interests, and that if all the powers, or practically all the powers, in the conference took an attitude favorable to France on such a point it would make it well-nigh impossible for Germany to assail her. I explained that I would not accept the invitation of the conference unless France was willing, and that if I went in I would treat both sides with absolute justice, and would, if necessary, take very strong grounds against any attitude of Germany which seemed to me unjust and unfair. At last, the French Government informed me through Jusserand that it would agree to the conference. At this time I was having numerous interviews with both Jusserand and Speck. With Speck I was on close terms; with Jusserand, who is

one of the best men I have ever met, and whose country was in the
right on this issue, I was on even closer terms. . . . There was,
however, much higgling as to exactly what should be discussed at
the conference; and both Jusserand and Speck came to me to say
they were still on the verge of seeing the negotiations broken off.
Finally I made a pencil memorandum as follows: "The two Governments consent to go to the conference with no program, and to
discuss there all questions in regard to Morocco, save of course
where either is in honor bound by a previous agreement with
another power." I gave a copy of this memorandum to Jusserand
and the memorandum itself to Speck, and after they had transmitted it to their respective governments, I received the assent of
both governments to the proposition. I explained to both that I did
not care to appear in the matter, and that no publicity whatever
would be given by me, or by any of our representatives, to what I
had done, and I thought it far better that it should take the shape
of an agreement freely entered into by themselves. You may
remember that not a hint of any kind got out throughout the
whole of last summer as to my taking any part in this Morocco
business.

. . . The Kaiser got uneasy again, and for some time insisted
upon the conference being held in Morocco, and upon Révoil not
being sent by France as a delegate. Again I had to do some cabling
to both the French and German Governments, but finally the
Kaiser's objections were removed. I had urged Jusserand not to let
his people boast or be disagreeable and try to humiliate the Kaiser
in connection with the conference, because the important point
was for them to get the kernel of the nut, and they did not have to
consider the shell. On August 9th Jusserand wrote me expressing
the thanks of his Government for what I had done; the German
Foreign Office thanked me by cable.

After this, trouble ceased as far as I was concerned, until the
conference met at Algeciras. Soon after the conference opened I
began to have a succession of visits from Speck and from Jusserand.
Jusserand generally gave me his messages verbally, Speck submitted
them in writing. Loyal though Speck was to his Government, both
Root and I became convinced that down in his heart the honest,
brave little gentleman did not really believe Germany was acting as
she should act. The attitude of France, as represented by the
French representatives at Algeciras, seemed to be more reasonable;

but I was entirely sure of France only when I could act directly through Jusserand, who rang true under any and all circumstances. It would have been a good thing if I could have kept in touch with England through Durand [Sir Mortimer Durand, the British Ambassador]. But Root and I, and for the matter of that Jusserand and Speck also, have absolutely given up any effort to work with Durand at all. He seems to have a brain of about eight-guinea-pig power. Why, under Heaven the English keep him here I do not know! If they do not care for an Ambassador, then abolish the embassy; but it is useless to have a worthy creature of mutton-suet consistency like the good Sir Mortimer.

I call your attention to the last paragraph in this telegram of March 19th. I had previously informed Speck, in a verbal conversation, that if the Emperor persevered in rejecting our proposals and a breakup ensued, I should feel obliged to publish the entire correspondence, and that I believed that our people would feel a grave suspicion of Germany's justice and good faith; but that if the Emperor would yield to what seemed to me our very fair proposals, I should not publish any of the correspondence, and would endeavor in every way to give Germany full credit for what was done; and with that in view would take an early opportunity to have him (Speck) bring a delegation of German war veterans to see me, so that I might make a public statement in praise of the emperor's position and expressive of my appreciation thereof, and of my hope that the relations between France and Germany would become steadily more friendly. Two or three days after the Emperor sent his cable saying he had yielded to our request, Speck called upon me to say that the Emperor very earnestly desired that I would make such public utterance. Accordingly I arranged for him to bring the German veterans around, and I made them the following speech, which I had previously gone over not only with Speck but with Jusserand: . . .

There, this is a hideously long communication! . . .

B. THE ALGECIRAS CONFERENCE

THE GENERAL Act and Additional Protocol of the Algeciras Conference signed on April 7, 1906, established a complicated regime for Morocco that preserved French influence and mollified German pride. The Ameri-

SOURCE: Bevans, comp., Treaties . . . : 1776–1949, I, p. 464n.

can plenipotentiaries, realizing that behind the polite words of the conference lurked the European balance of power, signed their names with the following reservation.

The Government of the United States of America, having no political interest in Morocco and no desire or purpose having animated it to take part in this conference other than to secure for all peoples the widest equality of trade and privilege with Morocco and to facilitate the institution of reforms in that country tending to insure complete cordiality of intercourse without and stability of administration within for the common good, declares that, in acquiescing in the regulations and declarations of the conference, in becoming a signatory to the General Act of Algeciras and to the Additional Protocol, subject to ratification according to constitutional procedure, and in accepting the application of those regulations and declarations to American citizens and interests in Morocco, it does so without assuming obligation or responsibility for the enforcement thereof.

C. Preserving America's Distance

THE SENATE likewise measured its consent to the Algeciras General Act and Additional Protocol. The "treaty of 1880" refers to a Moroccan arrangement to which the United States had been a party, and which was the nominal reason for participating in the Algeciras Conference.

. . . the Senate understands that the participation of the United States in the Algeciras Conference, and in the formation and adoption of the General Act and Protocol which resulted therefrom, was with the sole purpose of preserving and increasing its commerce in Morocco, the protection as to life, liberty and property of its citizens residing or traveling therein, and of aiding by its friendly offices and efforts in removing friction and controversy which seemed to menace the peace between powers signatory with the United States to the treaty of 1880, all of which are in terms of amity with this government; and without purpose to depart from the traditional American foreign policy which forbids participation by the United States in the settlement of political questions which are entirely European in their scope.

SOURCE: Bevans, comp., *Treaties . . . : 1776–1949*, I, p. 464n.

20. Treaties of Peace

A. SENATE OPPOSITION

SUCCESSIVE American Presidents and Secretaries of State sought to preserve the peace of the world through bilateral treaties of arbitration and conciliation. The first of these efforts may well have been the most important, for its failure in the Senate anticipated the problems of the subsequent treaties. Secretary Richard Olney signed a model treaty of arbitration with Great Britain on January 11, 1897, and submitted it to the Senate. The treaty failed in the Senate after sixteen amendments, the most important of which was that the Senate demanded the right to pass on each and every arbitration: that is, there had to be two treaties, the one setting out an intention to arbitrate and the second defining, for a specific occasion, the terms.

Article I. The High Contracting Parties agree to submit to Arbitration in accordance with the provisions and subject to the limitations of this Treaty all questions in difference between them which they may fail to adjust by diplomatic negotiation.

Article II. All pecuniary claims or groups of pecuniary claims which do not in the aggregate exceed £100,000 in amount, and which do not involve the determination of territorial claims, shall be dealt with and decided by an Arbitral Tribunal constituted as provided in the next following Article. . . .

Article III. Each of the High Contracting Parties shall nominate one arbitrator who shall be a jurist of repute and the two arbitrators so nominated shall within two months of the date of their nomination select an umpire. . . .

The person so selected shall be the President of the Tribunal and the award of the majority of the Members thereof shall be final.

Article IV. All pecuniary claims or groups of pecuniary claims which shall exceed £100,000 in amount and all other matters in difference, in respect of which either of the High Contracting Parties shall have rights against the other under Treaty or other-

SOURCE: *Foreign Relations of the United States: 1896* (Washington, D.C., 1897), pp. 238–40.

wise, provided that such matters in difference do not involve the determination of territorial claims, shall be dealt with and decided by an Arbitral Tribunal, constituted as provided in the next following Article.

Article V. Any subject of Arbitration described in Article IV shall be submitted to the Tribunal provided for by Article III, the award of which Tribunal, if unanimous, shall be final. If not unanimous either of the High Contracting Parties may within six months from the date of the award demand a review thereof. In such case the matter in controversy shall be submitted to an Arbitral Tribunal consisting of five jurists of repute, no one of whom shall have been a member of the Tribunal whose award is to be reviewed and who shall be selected as follows, viz:—two by each of the High Contracting Parties and, one to act as umpire, by the four thus nominated and to be chosen within three months after the date of their nomination. . . .

The person so selected shall be the President of the Tribunal and the award of the majority of the members thereof shall be final.

Article VI. Any controversy which shall involve the determination of territorial claims shall be submitted to a Tribunal composed of six members three of whom (subject to the provisions of Article VIII) shall be Judges of the Supreme Court of the United States or Justices of the Circuit Courts to be nominated by the President of the United States, and the other three of whom, (subject to the provisions of Article VIII) shall be Judges of the British Supreme Court of Judicature or Members of the Judicial Committee of the Privy Council to be nominated by Her Britannic Majesty, whose award by a majority of not less than five to one shall be final. In case of an award made by less than the prescribed majority, the award shall also be final unless either Power shall, within three months after the award has been reported protest that the same is erroneous, in which case the award shall be of no validity.

In the event of an award made by less than the prescribed majority and protested as above provided, or if the members of the Arbitral Tribunal shall be equally divided, there shall be no recourse to hostile measures of any description until the mediation of one or more friendly Powers has been invited by one or both of the High Contracting Parties. . . .

Article VIII. In cases where the question involved is one which concerns a particular State or Territory of the United States, it shall be open to the President of the United States to appoint a judicial officer of such State or Territory to be one of the Arbitrators under Article III or Article V or Article VI.

In like manner in cases where the question involved is one which concerns a British Colony or possession, it shall be open to Her Britannic Majesty to appoint a judicial officer of such Colony or possession to be one of the Arbitrators under Article III or Article V or Article VI. . . .

Article XIV. This Treaty shall remain in force for five years from the date at which it shall come into operation, and further until the expiration of twelve months after either of the High Contracting Parties shall have given notice to the other of its wish to terminate the same.

B. UTILIZING THE HAGUE COURT

SECRETARY *Hay a decade later allowed negotiation of ten general arbitration treaties, signed between November, 1904, and January, 1905. The treaties contained involved stipulations, but one of them set out that the parties in dispute before appealing to the Hague Court were to conclude a "special agreement" defining the issue in dispute, the scope of the arbitrator's powers, and the procedure to be followed. The Senate by vote of 50 to 9 amended the treaty with France so as to substitute the word "treaty" for the word "agreement." The cause of arbitration in America thereupon lapsed until Hay's successor, Root, took it up and negotiated twenty-five treaties in 1908–09, of which the treaty with Austria-Hungary, signed January 15, 1909, was typical.*

ARTICLE I.

Differences which may arise of a legal nature, or relating to the interpretation of treaties existing between the High Contracting Parties, and which it may not have been possible to settle by diplomacy, shall be referred to the Permanent Court of Arbitration established at The Hague by the Convention of the 29th July, 1899; provided, nevertheless, that they do not affect the vital interests, the independence, or the honor of the High Contracting Parties, and do not concern the interests of third Parties.

ARTICLE II.

In each individual case the High Contracting Parties, before appealing to the Permanent Court of Arbitration, shall conclude a

SOURCE: *Foreign Relations . . . . : 1909*, pp. 33–4.

special Agreement defined clearly the matter in dispute, the scope of the powers of the Arbitrators, and the periods to be fixed for the formation of the Arbitral Tribunal and the several stages of the procedure.

It is understood that such special agreements on the part of the United States will be made by the President of the United States by and with the advice and consent of the Senate thereof.

Such agreements shall be binding only when confirmed by the governments of the High Contracting Parties by an exchange of notes.

C. The Joint High Commission of Inquiry

PRESIDENT Taft tried a new set of treaties, beginning with Great Britain and France on August 3, 1911. Their terms admittedly were complex, perhaps too much for the Senate which believed that the proposed Joint High Commission of Inquiry infringed the treatymaking power. The Senate amended the treaties unmercifully and voted for the result overwhelmingly, 76 to 3. A hurt Taft withdrew the treaties, or what was left of them.

Article I. All differences hereafter arising between the High Contracting Parties, which it has not been possible to adjust by diplomacy, relating to international matters in which the High Contracting Parties are concerned by virtue of a claim of right made by one against the other under treaty or otherwise, and which are justiciable in their nature by reason of being susceptible of decision by the application of the principles of law or equity, shall be submitted to the Permanent Court of Arbitration established at The Hague by the Convention of October 18, 1907, or to some other arbitral tribunal, as may be decided in each case by special agreement, which special agreement shall provide for the organization of such tribunal if necessary, define the scope of the powers of the arbitrators, the question or questions at issue, and settle the terms of reference and the procedure thereunder. . . .

The special agreement in each case shall be made on the part of the United States by the President of the United States, by and with the advice and consent of the Senate thereof. . . .

Article II. The High Contracting Parties further agree to institute as occasion arises, and as hereinafter provided, a Joint High

SOURCE: Sixty-second Congress, Second Session, Senate Document No. 476, pp. 2–6.

Commission of Inquiry to which, upon the request of either Party, shall be referred for impartial and conscientious investigation any controversy between the Parties within the scope of Article I, before such controversy has been submitted to arbitration, and also any other controversy hereafter arising between them even if they are not agreed that it falls within the scope of Article I. . . .

Article III. . . . It is further agreed, however, that in cases in which the Parties disagree as to whether or not a difference is subject to arbitration under Article I of this Treaty, that question shall be submitted to the Joint High Commission of Inquiry; and if all or all but one of the members of the Commission agree and report that such difference is within the scope of Article I, it shall be referred to arbitration in accordance with the provisions of this Treaty.

D. UNILATERAL ARBITRATION

SECRETARY *Bryan proposed his so-called "cooling-off treaties" in 1913, and signed thirty of them. First he had called together the diplomatic corps on April 24 and advised them of what he had in mind.*

I have called you together in order that I may present to you all, simultaneously, a plan for the promotion of peace which I am directed by the President to submit. It reads as follows:

> The parties herto agree that all questions of whatever character and nature, in dispute between them, shall, when diplomatic efforts fail, be submitted for investigation and report to an international commission (the composition to be agreed upon): and the contracting parties agree not to declare war or begin hostilities until such investigation is made and report submitted.
>
> The investigation shall be conducted as a matter of course upon the initiative of the commission, without the formality of a request from either party; the report shall be submitted within (time to be agreed upon) from the date of the submission of the dispute, but the parties hereto reserve the right to act independently on the subject matter in dispute after the report is submitted.

You will notice that it is very brief and deals only with the principles involved, not with the details which must be considered in embodying the principles in diplomatic form. The President's

SOURCE: *Foreign Relations of the United States: 1913* (Washington, D.C., 1920), pp. 8–9

object is to hasten universal peace. All arbitration treaties contain certain exceptions—that is, certain questions are not to be submitted to arbitration, and, as these questions are of the highest importance, they are likely to become themselves a cause of war.

The plan proposed by the President, through you, to the nations which you represent, is intended to supplement the arbitration treaties now in existence and those which may be hereafter made. It is intended to subject to investigation those disputes which have not up to this time been considered fit subjects for arbitration. It is based upon the belief that we have now reached a point in the progress of civilization when nations cannot afford to engage in war before the cause of the war is impartially investigated and openly declared to the world. It is believed that the period of investigation—a time to be fixed by agreement, and which may be different in different agreements—will enable the parties to the controversy to separate questions of fact from questions of national honor and reach some amicable adjustment of their differences. The period of investigation will also allow passion to subside and the great forces that work for peace to assert themselves. When men are excited they talk about what they can do; when they are calm and capable of deliberation they talk about what they ought to do. And this is true of nations as well as of individuals. Public opinion is an increasing force in the world, and the time provided for investigation permits the formation and expression of public opinion.

You will note that while the proposed plan provides for the investigation of all questions which do not yield to diplomatic treatment, it reserves to each of the contracting nations the right to act independently after the investigation is concluded. If, after the time specified elapses and after the results of the investigation are made known, the nations still desire war, they are at liberty to settle their differences with the sword, but it is believed that this will seldom be the case and it is hoped that this agreement when entered into will make war between the contracting parties a remote possibility.

The plan as outlined does not prescribe the method by which the commission will be created. This is a matter of detail which is left for discussion. It may differ in the different agreements entered into, but it is desired that the commission shall be permanent in character, in order that the investigation may be made by the commission, upon its own initiative, without the formality of a request from either party. This is suggested because of the fear that in times of excitement neither party might be willing to ask for investigation lest such a request be regarded as an evidence of weakness.

In the original draft, as presented to the Foreign Relations Committee of the Senate, a suggestion was made that the period of investigation should not be utilized for a change in the naval program of the contracting nations, but this is a detail which has been omitted from the plan as proposed because it was feared that different nations might look upon it from different standpoints.

The plan has been made as simple as possible and everything has been eliminated except the things which seem essential to its success, and this Government stands ready to discuss with those Governments which are willing to enter into such an agreement such details as it may be necessary to consider.

In conclusion, let me assure you that I am very much gratified to be the medium through which the President presents this plan to the nations represented here, and I esteem myself fortunate to occupy the office with which the President has honored me at the time when the step is taken in the interest of peace. Our nation desires to use its influence for the promotion of the world's peace, and this plan is offered by the President with the hope that its acceptance by the nations will exert a large influence in this direction.

I thank you for your courtesy in coming at this time and giving me your attention. I hand to each one of you a copy of the plan as outlined, and on behalf of the President, I respectfully invite your cooperation in putting it into effect.

In the latter 1920s, Secretary of State Frank B. Kellogg revived the panels of the Bryan conciliation treaties—in many cases the individuals originally appointed had died—and extended both those treaties and the Root treaties of arbitration, changing the formula of the latter to exclude only domestic questions. But Kellogg's treaties proved useless in the 1930s, just as the other treaties had been a waste of time in advancing the cause of peace before the World War of 1914–18. Nothing came of the enormous American effort to achieve peace through arbitration and conciliation. Again, one relates with sadness that for all the strength of the American nation, it was not put to use in the one place where it most needed application, the balance of power in Europe.

VII

Neutrality, 1914–1917

The World War broke out in 1914 with a suddenness that caught Americans completely by surprise, and for the next two and a half years they sought to recover their balance and to view affairs in Europe with as much dispassionate analysis as they could bring to bear. Neutrality was the immediate American watchword in August, 1914. But from the outset this attitude of previous times—the attitude of the Washington, Adams, Jefferson, and Madison administrations toward the wars of the French revolution and Napoleon—did not easily prevail. Something always happened to disturb American neutrality, to provoke the largest nation of the New World into anger over policies of the Old World's belligerents. This was especially the case with German submarine warfare, which threatened the foundation of American neutrality, namely, observance of the rights and duties of a neutral according to the law of nations. President Wilson did his best to keep the country out of war, and in 1916 the Democratic Party conducted its national campaign on that slogan ("He Kept Us Out of War," or "War in the East, Peace in the West, Thank God for Wilson"). By early 1917 it seemed apparent to the President that the nation had to go in. As he put the issue in his war message of April 2nd, the world had to be made safe for democracy.

21. Hope and Reality

A. Proclamation of Neutrality

THE HOPE of *Wilson and almost all Americans in August, 1914, was that the nation could remain at peace, even while Europeans turned civilization back to barbarism or savagery. Wilson on August 4, 1914, proclaimed American neutrality in the same manner as his predecessors of a century and more before.*

. . . Now, therefore, I, WOODROW WILSON, President of the United States of America, in order to preserve the neutrality of the United States and of its citizens and of persons within its territory and jurisdiction, and to enforce its laws and treaties, and in order that all persons, being warned of the general tenor of the laws and treaties of the United States in this behalf, and of the law of nations, may thus be prevented from any violation of the same, do hereby declare and proclaim that by certain provisions of the act approved on the 4th day of March, A. D. 1909, commonly known as the "Penal Code of the United States" the following acts are forbidden to be done, under severe penalties, within the territory and jurisdiction of the United States, to-wit:—

1. Accepting and exercising a commission to serve either of the said belligerents by land or by sea against the other belligerent.
2. Enlisting or entering into the service of either of the said belligerents as a soldier, or as a marine, or seaman on board of any vessel of war, letter of marque, or privateer.
3. Hiring or retaining another person to enlist or enter himself in the service of either of the said belligerents as a soldier, or as a marine, or seaman on board any vessel of war, letter of marque, or privateer.
4. Hiring another person to go beyond the limits or jurisdiction of the United States with intent to be enlisted as aforesaid.

SOURCE: Carlton Savage, ed., *Policy of the United States toward Maritime Commerce in War* (2 vols., Washington, D.C., 1934–36), II, pp. 180–81, 183.

5. Hiring another person to go beyond the limits of the United States with intent to be entered into service as aforesaid.
6. Retaining another person to go beyond the limits of the United States with intent to be enlisted as aforesaid.
7. Retaining another person to go beyond the limits of the United States with intent to be entered into service as aforesaid. . . .
8. Fitting out and arming, or attempting to fit out and arm, or procuring to be fitted out and armed, or knowingly being concerned in the furnishing, fitting out, or arming of any ship or vessel with intent that such ship or vessel shall be employed in the service of either of the said belligerents.
9. Issuing or delivering a commission within the territory or jurisdiction of the United States for any ship or vessel to the intent that she may be employed as aforesaid.
10. Increasing or augmenting, or procuring to be increased or augmented, or knowingly being concerned in increasing or augmenting, the force of any ship of war, cruiser, or other armed vessel, which at the time of her arrival within the United States was a ship of war, cruiser, or armed vessel in the service of either of the said belligerents, or belonging to the subjects of either, by adding to the number of guns of such vessels, or by changing those on board of her for guns of a larger calibre, or by the addition thereto of any equipment solely applicable to war.
11. Beginning or setting on foot or providing or preparing the means for any military expedition or enterprise to be carried on from the territory or jurisdiction of the United States against the territories or dominions of either of the said belligerents.

And I do hereby further declare and proclaim that any frequenting and use of the waters within the territorial jurisdiction of the United States by the armed vessels of a belligerent, whether public ships or privateers, for the purpose of preparing for hostile operations, or as posts of observation upon the ships of war or privateers or merchant vessels of a belligerent lying within or being about to enter the jurisdiction of the United States, must be regarded as unfriendly and offensive, and in violation of that neutrality which it is the determination of this government to observe; . . .

And I do hereby warn all citizens of the United States, and all persons residing or being within its territory or jurisdiction that, while the free and full expression of sympathies in public and private is not restricted by the laws of the United States, . . . while all persons may lawfully and without restriction by reason of the aforesaid state of war manufacture and sell within the United States arms and munitions of war, and other articles ordinarily known as "contraband of war," yet they cannot carry such articles upon the high seas for the use or service of a belligerent, nor can they transport soldiers and officers of a belligerent, or attempt to break any blockade which may be lawfully established and maintained during the said wars without incurring the risk of hostile capture and the penalties denounced by the law of nations in that behalf. . . .

B. Provocation

In the first two years of war the German navy did not have enough submarines to convince either the naval high command or the civil government that by using these vessels against Allied shipping the German nation could win the war. There nonetheless was an inclination to employ submarines as much as possible, to hurt if not destroy the commerce of Great Britain. In the spring of 1915 the inevitable incident occurred—the sinking of the huge Cunard liner Lusitania, largest and fastest ship on the Atlantic run, with loss of 1,198 lives including 128 Americans. The great ship went down off the coast of Ireland on May 7, 1915, and next day an investigation by the State Department was underway.

In response to Mr. Woolsey's request on the telephone this morning, that I obtain certain information from the Collector at New York in regard to the Cunard Liner Lusitania, I beg to report as follows:—

1. Whether she had any contraband or ammunition on board at the time she sailed from New York:

   Practically all of her cargo was contraband of some kind.

SOURCE: Assistant Secretary of the Treasury A. J. Peters to the Counselor of the Department of State, Robert Lansing, May 8, 1915, Savage, ed., Policy of the United States . . . , II, pp. 307–08.

2. The character or nature of such contraband and munitions:
Her cargo included:

Cotton goods, 32 cases
Raw furs, 313 cases
Sheet brass, 260,000 lbs.
Copper ingots and base, 111,000 lbs.
Insulated copper wire, 58,000 lbs.
Cheese, 217,000 lbs.
Beef, 342,000 lbs.
Butter, 43,000 lbs.
Lard, 40,000 lbs.
Bacon, 85,000 lbs.
31 packages of hardware, aluminum, brass, iron, old rubber
1271 packages ammunition consigned by Bethlehem Steel Co.,
    consisting of
        6 cases of fuses
        12 "   "   "
        1250 " " shrapnel
8 packages of motor cycles and parts
89 pieces of leather
4200 cases of metallic packages [cartridges] shipped by
    Remington Arms Company.
185 cases accoutrements

3. Whether the vessel had any guns mounted on board:
Neutrality men were on board every day. No guns at any time found mounted, nor, so far as they knew, on board.

4. And whether she had any ammunition for the same, and its character:
Answered above.

C. British Reaction

SENTIMENT in Great Britain was that the Lusitania's sinking might bring the United States into the war.

. . . A profound effect has been produced on English opinion in general regarding both the surprising efficiency of the German submarine work and the extreme recklessness of the Germans. The sinking of the Lusitania, following the use of poisonous gas and the poisoning of wells and the torpedoing of the Gulflight and other

SOURCE: Ambassador Walter Hines Page to Lansing, May 8, 1915, Savage, ed., Policy of the United States . . . , II, pp. 308–09.

plainly marked neutral ships the English regard as the complete abandonment of war regulations and of humanity in its conduct as well as of any consideration for neutrals. Sir Edward Grey said to me last night "They are running amuck." It is war under the black flag. Indignation in the aggregate reached a new pitch.

Official comment is of course reticent. The freely expressed unofficial feeling is that the United States must declare war or forfeit European respect. So far as I know this opinion is universal. If the United States come in, the moral and physical effect will be to bring peace quickly and to give the United States a great influence in ending the war and in so reorganizing the world as to prevent its recurrence. If the United States submits to German disregard of her citizens' lives and of her property and of her neutral rights on the sea, the United States will have no voice or influence in settling the war nor in what follows for a long time to come. This, so far as I can ascertain, is the practically unanimous opinion here. The Americans in London are outspoken to the same effect.

Much the profoundest depression is felt today that has been felt since the war began and British opinion is stirred to its depths. . . .

I have heard the opinion expressed today in several well-informed but unofficial quarters that warlike action by the United States would be a signal for other neutral nations whose rights Germany has disregarded especially the Scandinavian countries and possibly Holland. For the correctness of this view I cannot vouch but I know it is widely entertained.

D. Justification

In 1915 it was too early to expect the Wilson administration, especially the pacific-minded Wilson, to take the country into war, even over so signal an incident as the Lusitania sinking. To the intense disgust of former President Theodore Roosevelt, Wilson made a speech in Philadelphia on May 10, 1915, three days after the Lusitania went down, and said there was such a thing as a man being too proud to fight. The President was addressing a group of several thousand foreign-born citizens, after ceremonies of naturalization.

See, my friends, . . . Americans must have a consciousness different from the consciousness of every other nation in the world.

Source: Albert Shaw, ed., Messages and Papers of Woodrow Wilson (2 vols., New York, 1924), I, pp. 114–18.

I am not saying this with even the slightest thought of criticism of other nations. You know how it is with a family. A family gets centered on itself if it is not careful and is less interested in the neighbors than it is in its own members. So a nation that is not constantly renewed out of new sources is apt to have the narrowness and prejudice of a family; whereas, America must have this consciousness, that on all sides it touches elbows and touches hearts with all the nations of mankind. The example of America must be a special example. The example of America must be the example not merely of peace because it will not fight, but of peace because peace is the healing and elevating influence of the world and strife is not. There is such a thing as a man being too proud to fight. There is such a thing as a nation being so right that it does not need to convince others by force that it is right. . . .

When I was asked, therefore, by the Mayor and the committee that accompanied him to come up from Washington to meet this great company of newly admitted citizens, I could not decline the invitation. I ought not to be away from Washington, and yet I feel that it has renewed my spirit as an American to be here. In Washington men tell you so many things every day that are not so, and I like to come and stand in the presence of a great body of my fellow-citizens, whether they have been my fellow-citizens a long time or a short time, and drink, as it were, out of the common fountain with them and go back feeling what you have so generously given me—the sense of your support and of the living vitality in your hearts of the great ideals which have made America the hope of the world.

E. German Assurances

DESPITE his peacemindedness, Wilson pressed the Germans in 1915 so hard that Secretary of State William Jennings Bryan resigned in protest. At last the German ambassador, Johann von Bernstorff, gave Wilson an assurance that his government would be more careful about the rights of neutrals.

. . . With reference to our conversation of this morning I beg to inform you that my instructions concerning our answer to your last Lusitania note contain the following passage:

SOURCE: Bernstorff to Bryan's successor, Secretary Lansing, Sept. 1, 1915, Savage, ed., Policy of the United States . . . , II, p. 378.

"Liners will not be sunk by our submarines without warning and without safety of the lives of noncombatants, provided that the liners do not try to escape or offer resistance." . . .

I have no objection to your making any use you may please of the above information.

22. The "Sussex" Demand

A. INDECISION

ALL THE peculiar problems of German submarine warfare came to focus in the case of the French Channel packet Sussex, an unarmed passenger vessel that either was torpedoed or struck a mine in the Channel on March 24, 1916. Secretary Lansing urged strong action. Incidentally, it is a nice question as to whether the Sussex was sunk. Part of it was sunk (the ship broke up into two parts), and the other part stayed afloat. The floating part was salvaged, a new section added, and years later the Sussex, under a new name, was still in service in Asia Minor.

. . . All the information which we are receiving in regard to the sinking of the Sussex in the English Channel, by which several Americans were injured and some undoubtedly killed, indicates that the vessel was torpedoed by a German submarine. . . .

Every effort undoubtedly will be made by the Allies to prove that the vessel was torpedoed, and I believe that they will make a strong case, judging from the telegrams we have thus far received. On the other hand, I feel sure that the German Government will deny the charge and assert that a floating mine of English origin caused the disaster. There will be thus a flat contradiction of statements as to the facts.

I do not believe that the Government can remain inactive because of this contradictory evidence. There will be a strong demand that something should be done and, personally, I would be disposed to view such a demand as justifiable. . . .

Proceeding on the assumption that the Sussex was torpedoed the action which seems to me the most practicable would be to

SOURCE: Lansing to Wilson, Mar. 27, 1916, Savage, ed., *Policy of the United States* . . . , II, pp. 468–70.

demand the immediate recall of Count Bernstorff and the severance of diplomatic relations with Germany. This action might be made conditional upon the German Government unequivocally admitting the illegality of submarine warfare in general, paying a just indemnity for the Americans killed and injured, and guaranteeing that the present method of warfare will cease. Such a conditional admission would be in the nature of an ultimatum which could very properly include a time limit at the expiration of which, in case of failure to comply with the conditions, Count von Bernstorff could be given his passports. . . .

LANSING *this time did not move the President.*

. . . I have your letter of the twenty-seventh in which you state your preliminary impressions about the *Sussex* Case. My impressions are not quite the same. The proof that the disaster was caused by a torpedo seems to me by no means satisfactory or conclusive. And, if it was caused by a torpedo, there are many particulars to be considered about the course we should pursue as well as the principle of it. The steps we take and the way we take them will, it seems to me, be of the essence of the matter if we are to keep clearly and indisputably within the lines we have already set ourselves.

But in this, as in other matters referred to in the papers I am now sending back to you, a personal conference is much the best means of reaching conclusions. We must have one very soon.

B. WARNING TO GERMANY

ALTHOUGH *the torpedoing of the Sussex killed no Americans, it killed or injured some eighty passengers and thus exposed Americans to danger. The President waited until he had the testimony of Americans aboard the vessel that they had seen the wake of a torpedo. He then worked out a note to Germany, with the help of Secretary Lansing. It was necessary to frame the note with care, to avoid moot issues of international law.*

SOURCE: Wilson to Lansing, Mar. 30, 1916, Savage, ed., *Policy of the United States* . . . , II, pp. 470–71.
SOURCE: Lansing to Wilson, Apr. 15, 1916, Savage, ed., *Policy of the United States* . . . , II, p. 473.

. . . I have been going over the ending of the instruction to Gerard in the submarine matter and I am more and more convinced that the formula which you propose in your redraft, beginning—"Unless the Imperial Government should now, etc.", raises some serious objections.

In the first place, the phrase—"return to a scrupulous observance of the principles clearly prescribed by the law of nations"—offers an opportunity to raise the question as to what are the clearly prescribed principles. As you know, these are not very well defined except as to visit and search. In addition to this, the whole question of the treatment of armed and unarmed merchantmen will be raised. There is a decided difference of opinion as to the conversion of a merchant vessel into a warship. I am afraid if we employ that language that we will be involved, unavoidably, in a discussion of that question, which I assume we both wish to avoid. Any phrase which raises a reasonable difference of opinion invites discussion, and the word "immediately" would be nullified.

If we are to follow, substantially, the language of the redraft, I would suggest its amendment as follows:

> Unless the Imperial Government immediately declares that it abandons its present method of submarine warfare against passenger and freight-carrying vessels, the Government of the United States can have no choice but to sever diplomatic relations with the German Empire.

I am always at your service to discuss this matter, when you desire to do so.

THE Sussex *note went out on April 18, 1916.*

. . . On the 24th of March, 1916, at about 2.50 o'clock in the afternoon, the unarmed steamer *Sussex*, with 325 or more passengers on board, among whom were a number of American citizens, was torpedoed while crossing from Folkestone to Dieppe. The *Sussex* had never been armed; was a vessel known to be habitually used only for the conveyance of passengers across the

SOURCE: Lansing to the American ambassador in Berlin, James W. Gerard, Savage, ed., *Policy of the United States* . . . , II, pp. 477, 479–80.

English Channel; and was not following the route taken by troop ships or supply ships. About 80 of her passengers, non-combatants of all ages and sexes including citizens of the United States, were killed or injured.

(3) A careful, detailed, and scrupulously impartial investigation by naval and military officers of the United States has conclusively established the fact that the *Sussex* was torpedoed without warning or summons to surrender and that the torpedo by which she was struck was of German manufacture. In the view of the Government of the United States these facts from the first made the conclusion that the torpedo was fired by a German submarine unavoidable. . . .

(4) The Government of the United States, after having given careful consideration to the note of the Imperial Government of the 10th of April, regrets to state that the impression made upon it by the statements, and proposals contained in that note is that the Imperial Government has failed to appreciate the gravity of the situation which has resulted, not alone from the attack on the *Sussex*, but from the whole method and character of submarine warfare as disclosed by the unrestrained practice of the commanders of German undersea craft during the past twelvemonth and more in the indiscriminate destruction of merchant vessels of all sorts, nationalities, and destinations. If the sinking of the *Sussex* had been an isolated case, the Government of the United States might find it possible to hope that the officer who was responsible for that act had wilfully violated his orders or had been criminally negligent in taking none of the precautions they prescribed, and that the ends of justice might be satisfied by imposing upon him an adequate punishment, coupled with a formal disavowal of the act and payment of a suitable indemnity by the Imperial Government. But, though the attack upon the *Sussex* was manifestly indefensible and caused a loss of life so tragical as to make it stand forth as one of the most terrible examples of the inhumanity of submarine warfare as the commanders of German vessels are conducting it, it unhappily does not stand alone. . . .

(9) Vessels of neutral ownership, even vessels of neutral ownership bound from neutral port to neutral port, have been destroyed along with vessels of belligerent ownership in constantly increasing numbers. Sometimes the merchantmen attacked have been warned and summoned to surrender before being fired on or torpedoed;

sometimes their passengers and crews have been vouchsafed the poor security of being allowed to take to the ship's boats before the ship was sent to the bottom. But again and again no warning has been given, no escape even to the ship's boats allowed to those on board. Great liners like the *Lusitania* and *Arabic* and mere passenger boats like the *Sussex* have been attacked without a moment's warning, often before they have even become aware that they were in the presence of an armed ship of the enemy, and the lives of non-combatants, passengers and crew, have been destroyed wholesale and in a manner which the Government of the United States cannot but regard as wanton and without the slightest color of justification. No limit of any kind has in fact been set to their indiscriminate pursuit and destruction of merchantmen of all kinds and nationalities within the waters which the Imperial Government has chosen to designate as lying within the seat of war. The roll of Americans who have lost their lives upon ships thus attacked and destroyed has grown month by month until the ominous toll has mounted into the hundreds. . . .

(12) If it is still the purpose of the Imperial Government to prosecute relentless and indiscriminate warfare against vessels of commerce by the use of submarines without regard to what the Government of the United States must consider the sacred and indisputable rules of international law and the universally recognized dictates of humanity, the Government of the United States is at last forced to the conclusion that there is but one course it can pursue. Unless the Imperial Government should now immediately declare and effect an abandonment of its present methods of submarine warfare against passenger and freight-carrying vessels, the Government of the United States can have no choice but to sever diplomatic relations with the German Empire altogether. This action the Government of the United States contemplates with the greatest reluctance but feels constrained to take in behalf of humanity and the rights of neutral nations.

BERNSTORFF and Lansing talked freely about the Sussex affair.

SOURCE: memorandum by Lansing of a conversation with Bernstorff, April 20, 1916, Savage, ed., *Policy of the United States . . .*, II, pp. 480–84.

L.—Good morning.

B.—Good morning, Sir. You handed me a copy of the note yesterday, and in the present state of affairs of course my chief object is to find a way how this break can be avoided, because I hope it can be avoided. My idea is to find a way out of it, but of course I had to telegraph my Government that this Government seemed to offer little opportunity for settlement. If it means the entire stopping of the use of submarines, I am afraid that it cannot be arranged.

L.—You will recall that we said in the first *Lusitania* note that we thought it was impossible to use submarines in a really humane way and that later, in our note of July 21, we said that the way submarine warfare had been conducted for the past two months showed that it was possible and therefore we hoped that course would be pursued. Then we had the sinking of the *Arabic* right on top of that, which was another great disaster. Our position is that, if submarine warfare had been conducted in that way, that possibly there would have been no further question raised. But it has not. It has been conducted in the most indiscriminate way and we cannot help but believe that it is ruthless. In those conditions submarine warfare should stop against commercial vessels, unless visit and search is observed.

B.—That, of course, is impossible. Germany cannot abandon submarine warfare. No government could come out and say—"We give up the use of submarines." They would have to resign.

L.—What possible methods in the use of submarines, that are effective from a belligerent standpoint, can be suggested which will comply with the law?

B.—I had always supposed that warning was to be given.

L.—We do not consider that the people on board—the non-combatants on board the vessels—are in a place of safety when put into an open boat a hundred miles from land. It might be calm there, but in the two days it would take them to reach land there might be a severe storm. That is one of the grounds of complaint.

B.—That, of course, speaking of neutral vessels—

L.—The fact that we do not have Americans on these vessels does not remove the menace to American lives. The sinking of neutral vessels shows that Americans cannot travel with safety on neutral vessels even. That is the serious part of it and I do not know how your Government can modify submarine warfare and make it effective and at the same time obey the law and the dictates of humanity.

B.—Humanity. Of course war is never humane.

L.—"Humanity" is a relative expression when used with "war" but the whole tendency in the growth of international law in regard to warfare in the past 125 years has been to relieve noncombatants of needless suffering.

B.—Of course I think it would be an ideal state of affairs, but our enemies violate all the rules and you insist on their being applied to Germany.

L.—One deals with life; the other with property.

B.—Yes.

L.—The German method seems reckless to me. It is as if a man who has a very dim vision should go out on the street with a revolver in search of an enemy and should see the outline of a figure and should immediately fire on him and injure him seriously and then go up and apologize and say he made a mistake. I do not think that would excuse him. That seems to be the course pursued by your submarine commanders—they fire first and inquire afterwards.

B.—I myself cannot at all explain how it comes that so many neutral vessels have been attacked. I have not the slightest evidence. I do not know anything about it from our communications.

L.—Of course we are gradually collecting the evidence. We have not in all the cases but we have in certain ones. The *Tubantia*, for example, seems to have been torpedoed by a German torpedo—a Schwartz kopf.

B.—She was at anchor.

L.—No. I do not think she had let her anchor down but she was preparing to anchor. She was at rest.

B.—Yes, I know. And then there was a Spanish vessel which—

L.—Of course there is this, Mr. Ambassador, that any discussion of the submarine and its present method of attack cannot go on indefinitely.

B.—What was your idea to prevent the break—that we should for the time being stop?

L.—I think the only way is to declare an abandonment and then if the German Government desires to discuss a method of renewal—

B.—An absolute abandonment, to my mind, is impossible. It

might be possible to announce stopping for a time for discussion and giving the reason plainly for the purpose of quieting our public opinion, that might be possible.

L.—I understand you are speaking entirely without instructions.

B.—I am not at all instructed. I am speaking to you purely from my desire to prevent a break.

L.—In view of our note I would not want to say that that would be satisfactory, but if it was made—

B.—I am only trying to see what can be done because a declaration to my Government to absolutely abandon submarine warfare would make a break absolutely necessary. To abandon it would mean the overthrow of the Chancellor.

L.—Probably you would get a more radical man. I realize that.

B.—So the question is what we can do.

L.—There would have to be a complete abandonment first and then if the German Government desires to discuss the matter—

B.—I want to do what I can, because I am perfectly convinced they do not want to break; quite apart from the sentimental side I think they do not want a break. A break would prolong the war. It would last for years.

L.—We do not any of us want to prolong the war.

B.—That is exactly why I want to get out of this present difficulty. From the present state of affairs it looks as if the end is coming and if now there was a break and the United States was brought into the war it would prolong it. It would cause new complications.

L.—New complications?

B.—New economic difficulties.

L.—I think that would be Germany's problem. The only possible course is an abandonment of submarine warfare, whether limited or not would depend on the terms. I would want to see an abandonment first and then possibly a discussion could follow as to how submarine warfare can be conducted within the rules of international law and entire safety of non-combatants, because, of course, in my viewpoint that is the chief question of international law in regard to attacks by belligerents on enemy's commerce.

B.—Then I am to understand that you do not recognize the law of retaliation?

L.—We do not recognize retaliation when it affects the rights of neutrals.

B.—The British retaliate by stopping all commerce to Germany.

L.—It is a very different thing. The right to life is an inherent right, which man has from birth; the right of property is a purely legal right.

B.—Only in this case, England's methods affect the lives of non-combatants of Germany.

L.—Not neutrals.

B.—No, but it affects non-combatants.

L.—Does it affect their lives? I thought from the statements which have been made that Germany was not suffering from want of food.

B.—But they are trying to starve them. You do not stop England but insist we must stop our retaliation.

L.—But you must appreciate that we care more for the lives of our people than we do for the property.

B.—We have the same difficulty—our people are getting to care more for lives. That is the whole difficulty—we are dealing with a warlike population.

L.—I realize that. I appreciate that you have great difficulty with your public.

B.—If you and I were to have the say in settling the case it would be an easy matter, because one can discuss the matter without heat.

L.—I realize that. It makes it very difficult, but I do not think there is any other course. That certainly may be an impossible course for your Government to pursue, yet I see no other way, and I think I am as anxious to preserve peace as anyone.

B.—I wanted to find out what I could do, because I do not see how they can do it though they might do it temporarily. I am sure that in the first place they would say they believed in the submarine entirely and that secondly the rules of international law must be modified by conditions. Your idea is that the submarine cannot be used if it does comply with the rules.

L.—That is true. My view is that certain instruments of war are not proper to use under certain conditions, and that is the viewpoint that has largely been held in regard to the submarine as a commerce destroyer. You can not and do not know the nationality of the boat attacking. It attacks without being seen and so avoids responsibility. It gives every opportunity to kill indiscriminately and recklessly.

B.—I perfectly agree with you that sinking without warning would have to stop entirely, sinking without warning is an international offense, and that is why I thought possibly my Government might give up the retaliation, but I do not think it would be possible to say we would give up submarine warfare. I do not think we would do it.

L.—And if they should now sink another vessel it would be very serious—that is the way I look at the situation.

B.—And if they continue the submarine warfare and an instance should happen directly after the break of diplomatic relations, if that should come, it would be still more serious.

L.—That is logical.

B.—That is why I look at it so seriously.

L.—I do not feel that breaking off of diplomatic relations necessarily means war.

B.—I do not say it myself but I do not see how it can be avoided. If we refuse it will be because we are to continue submarine warfare and then something might happen which would mean war. I came to see if something could not be done.

L.—I am very much obliged to you for coming in, sir.

B.—Good bye, Mr. Secretary.

L.—Good bye.

The German government gave in on the Sussex issue on May 4, 1916, promising to treat merchant vessels only according to the rules of cruiser warfare, but sought to make its promise contingent upon British good behavior. President Wilson accepted the German announcement, but said that he accepted it absolutely, not conditionally. In this somewhat uncertain state German-American relations continued for the rest of the year.

23. Decision for War

A. SEVERING DIPLOMATIC RELATIONS

EARLY in 1917 the German high command, which by this time dominated the civil government in Berlin, believed that it possessed enough submarines to win the war, if the submarines could employ so-called unrestricted warfare against Allied and neutral commerce. That meant sinking ships on sight, without observing the punctilios of international law that required an attacking vessel to halt its suspect, examine the nature of the cargo, and if the vessel then was subject to destruction to provide for the safety of passengers and crew. To this list of requirements upon Germany by the United States, President Wilson had added the need for German submarines to respect the right of Americans to travel aboard belligerent passenger ships. In going over to unrestricted warfare the Germans therefore were directly challenging the American President and people, and upon announcement of this tactic by Ambassador Bernstorff on January 31, 1917, Wilson handed him his passports. The question then became whether the Germans would carry out their announced policy. In the weeks after Bernstorff departed they did just that. Meanwhile, the British government had intercepted an extraordinary instruction from the German foreign minister, Arthur Zimmermann, to the German minister in Mexico City. The Zimmermann Telegram appeared in American newspapers on March 1, 1917.

130	(number of		18222	stop(.)	stop(.)
	telegram)	—	21560	Wir	We
13042	(code identifica-		10247	beabsichtigen	intend
	tion number)	—	11518	am	from the
13401	Auswärtiges		23677	ersten	first
	Amt	Foreign Office	13605	Februar	February
8501	telegraphiert	telegraphs	3494	un-	un-
115	Januar 16	January 16	14963	eingeschränkt	restricted
3528	colon(:)	colon(:)	98092	U-boot	U-boat
416	number 1	no. 1	5905	Krieg	war
17214	ganz geheim	strictly secret	11311	zu	to
6491	selbst	yourself	10392	beginnen	begin
11310	zu	to	10371	stop(.)	stop(.)
18147	entziffern	decipher	4458	Gemeinsam	Together

SOURCE: Barbara W. Tuchman, *The Zimmermann Telegram* (New York, 1958), pp. 201–02.*

* For permission to use Mrs. Tuchman's translation of the decode made by the American embassy in London, I am indebted to her publisher. Reprinted by permission of the Macmillan Company from *The Zimmerman Telegram* by Barbara Tuchman. Copyright © 1958, 1966 by Barbara W. Tuchman.

5905	Krieg	war		20420	mit	with
17166	führen	make		39689	Vereinigten	
13851	stop(.)	stop(.)			Staaten	United States
4458	Gemeinsam	Together		13732	fest	certain
17149	Friedenschluss	peace		20667	steht	is
14471	stop(.)	stop(.)		0302	Es wird	It will
6706	Reichlich	Generous		21290	versucht	attempted
13850	finanzielle	financial		5161	werden	be
12224	unterstützung	support		39695	Vereinigten	
6929	und	and			Staaten	United States
14991	einverständnis	understanding		23571	trotzdem	nevertheless
7382	unserer seits	our part		17504	neutral	neutral
15857	dass	that		11269	zu	to
67893	Mexico	Mexico		18276	erhalten	keep
14218	in	in		18101	stop(.)	stop(.)
36477	Texas	Texas		0217	Für den Fall	In the event
5870	comma(,)	comma (,)		0228	dass dies	that this
17553	New	New		17694	nicht	not
67893	Mexico	Mexico		4473	gelingen	succeed
5870	comma(,)	comma(,)		22284	sollte	should
5454	AR	AR		22200	comma(,)	comma(,)
16102	IZ	IZ		19452	schlagen	offer
15217	ON	ON		21589	wir	we
22801	A	A		67893	Mexico	Mexico
17138	früher	former		5569	auf	on
21001	verloren	lost		13918	folgender	following
17388	Gebiet	territory		8958	Grundlage	terms
7446	zurück	back		12137	Bündnis	alliance
23638	erobern	conquer		1333	vor	(prefix of verb
18222	stop(.)	stop(.)				vorschlagen—
6719	Regelung	Settlement				to offer)
14331	im	in the				
15021	Einzelnen	details		4725	stop(.)	stop(.)
23845	Euer Hoch-	Your Excel-		6929	und	and
	wohlgeboren	lency		5275	Anregung	suggestion
3156	überlassen	to be left		18507	hinzufügen	add
23552	stop(.)	stop(.)		52262	Japan	Japan
22096	Sie	You		1340	von	by
21604	wollen	will		22049	sich	himself
4797	vorstehendes	of the fore-		13339	aus	from
9497	dem	going		11265	zu	to
		the		22295	sofortig	immediately
22464	Präsident	President		10439	beitretung	join
20855	streng	in strictest		14814	einladen	invite
4377	geheim	secrecy		4178	(setze infinitiv	(form the infin-
23610	eröffnen	inform			mit zu—i.e.,	itive—i.e., to
18140	comma(,)	comma(,)			einzuladen)	invite)
22260	sobald	as soon as		6992	und	and
5905	Kriegs	war's		8784	gleichzeitig	at the same
13347	Ausbruch	outbreak				time
				7632	zwischen	between

7357	uns	us	9350	bietet	offers
6926	und	and	9220	comma(,)	comma(,)
52262	Japan	Japan	76036	England	England
11267	zu	to	14219	in	in
21100	vermitteln	mediate	5144	wenigen	few
21272	stop(.)	stop(.)	2831	Monat-	month-
9346	Bitte	Please	17920	en	s
9559	den	the	11347	zum	to
22464	Präsident	President	17142	Frieden	peace
15874	darauf	of this	11264	zu	be
18502	hinweisen	point to	7667	zwingen	compelled
18500	comma(,)	comma(,)	7762	stop(.)	stop(.)
15857	dass	that	15099	Empfang	Receipt
2188	rücksichtslos	ruthless	9110	bestahigen	acknowledge
5376	Anwendung	employment	10482	stop(.)	stop(.)
7381	unserer	our	97556	Zimmermann	Zimmermann
98092	U-boote	U-boats	3569	stop(.)	stop(.)
16127	jetzt	now	3670	Schluss der	End of dis-
13486	Aussich	prospect		Depesche	patch
				BERNSTORFF	

B. IN DEFENSE OF NEUTRAL RIGHTS

PRESIDENT Wilson in his message to Congress of April 2, 1917, brought together the issues and arguments that impelled him to ask the nation to go to war. It is interesting that he did not mention propaganda, or economic involvement, or the ties of language and culture between Britain and the United States. In regard to economic involvement, especially, the fact that American wartime trade with the Allies had grown to huge proportions, that there were large amounts of Allied bonds held in the United States, and that the Allies were facing an acute dollar shortage in the first months of 1917 and soon might have to appeal to the American Treasury to back up their bond issues or else make available United States government funds—in regard to such economic involvement it is interesting that Wilson said nothing to his country-men on April 2, not even a bow and a scrape to the influence of inter-national bankers or Wall Street bankers. Is it not then possible to conclude (and this is the present writer's conclusion) that it was the toils of neutral rights, the defense of those rights by the President and administration, not least the President's desire to ensure the safety of Americans traveling aboard belligerent ships, that took the nation to war in 1917 when the German government wilfully violated such rights and challenged the President's position as set out so clearly after the sinking of the Sussex the year before? It is possible to argue, of course, that behind the contentions of neutral rights were "silent" arguments, naturally not mentioned by the President, not often discussed even by

SOURCE: Carlton Savage, ed., Policy of the United States toward Maritime Commerce in War, II, pp. 587–94.

*his supporters. Still, this makes a weak argument in view of the clear
documentary steps by which the defense of neutral rights, and therein
(so Wilson believed) of democracy and civilization itself, forced the
nation's involvement.*

. . . I have called the Congress into extraordinary session because there are serious, very serious, choices of policy to be made,
and made immediately, which it was neither right nor constitu-
tionally permissible that I should assume the responsibility of
making.

On the third of February last I officially laid before you the
extraordinary announcement of the Imperial German Government
that on and after the first day of February it was its purpose to put
aside all restraints of law or of humanity and use its submarines to
sink every vessel that sought to approach either the ports of Great
Britain and Ireland or the western coasts of Europe or any of the
ports controlled by the enemies of Germany within the Mediterranean. That had seemed to be the object of the German submarine warfare earlier in the war, but since April of last year the
Imperial Government had somewhat restrained the commanders
of its undersea craft in conformity with its promise then given to us
that passenger boats should not be sunk and that due warning
would be given to all other vessels which its submarines might seek
to destroy, when no resistance was offered or escape attempted, and
care taken that their crews were given at least a fair chance to save
their lives in their open boats. The precautions taken were meagre
and haphazard enough, as was proved in distressing instance after
instance in the progress of the cruel and unmanly business, but a
certain degree of restraint was observed. The new policy has swept
every restriction aside. Vessels of every kind, whatever their flag,
their character, their cargo, their destination, their errand, have
been ruthlessly sent to the bottom without warning and without
thought of help or mercy for those on board, the vessels of friendly
neutrals along with those of belligerents. Even hospital ships and
ships carrying relief to the sorely bereaved and stricken people of
Belgium, though the latter were provided with safe conduct through
the proscribed areas by the German Government itself and were
distinguished by unmistakable marks of identity, have been sunk
with the same reckless lack of compassion or of principle.

I was for a little while unable to believe that such things would
in fact be done by any government that had hitherto subscribed to

the humane practices of civilized nations. International law had its origin in the attempt to set up some law which would be respected and observed upon the seas, where no nation had right of dominion and where lay the free highways of the world. By painful stage after stage has that law been built up, with meagre enough results, indeed, after all was accomplished that could be accomplished, but always with a clear view, at least, of what the heart and conscience of mankind demanded. This minimum of right the German Government has swept aside under the plea of retaliation and necessity and because it had no weapons which it could use at sea except these which it is impossible to employ as it is employing them without throwing to the winds all scruples of humanity or of respect for the understandings that were supposed to underlie the intercourse of the world. I am not now thinking of the loss of property involved, immense and serious as that is, but only of the wanton and wholesale destruction of the lives of noncombatants, men, women, and children, engaged in pursuits which have always, even in the darkest periods of modern history, been deemed innocent and legitimate. Property can be paid for; the lives of peaceful and innocent people cannot be. The present German submarine warfare against commerce is a warfare against mankind.

It is a war against all nations. American ships have been sunk, American lives taken, in ways which it has stirred us very deeply to learn of, but the ships and people of other neutral and friendly nations have been sunk and overwhelmed in the waters in the same way. There has been no discrimination. The challenge is to all mankind. Each nation must decide for itself how it will meet it. The choice we make for ourselves must be made with a moderation of counsel and a temperateness of judgment benefitting our character and our motives as a nation. We must put excited feeling away. Our motive will not be revenge or the victorious assertion of the physical might of the nation, but only the vindication of right, of human right, of which we are only a single champion.

When I addressed the Congress on the twenty-sixth of February last I thought that it would suffice to assert our neutral rights with arms, our right to use the seas against unlawful interference, our right to keep our people safe against unlawful violence. But armed neutrality, it now appears, is impracticable. Because submarines are in effect outlaws when used as the German submarines have been used against merchant shipping, it is impossible to defend ships against their attacks as the law of nations has assumed that merchantmen would defend themselves against privateers or cruisers, visible craft giving chase upon the open sea. It is common prudence in such circumstances, grim necessity indeed, to endeavour to destroy them before they have shown their own intention. They must be dealt with upon sight, if dealt with at all. The German Government denies the right of neutrals to use arms at all within the areas of the sea which it has proscribed, even in the defense of rights which no modern publicist has ever before questioned their right to defend. The intimation is conveyed that the armed guards which we have placed on our merchant ships will be treated as beyond the pale of law and subject to be dealt with as pirates would be. Armed neutrality is ineffectual enough at best; in such circumstances and in the face of such pretensions it is worse than ineffectual: it is likely only to produce what it was meant to prevent; it is practically certain to draw us into the war without either the rights or the effectiveness of belligerents. There is one choice we cannot make, we are incapable of making: we will not choose the path of submission and suffer the most sacred rights of our nation and our people to be ignored or violated. The wrongs against which we now array ourselves are no common wrongs; they cut to the very roots of human life.

With a profound sense of the solemn and even tragical character of the step I am taking and of the grave responsibilities which it involves, but in unhesitating obedience to what I deem my constitutional duty, I advise that the Congress declare the recent course of the Imperial German Government to be in fact nothing less than war against the government and people of the United States; that it formally accept the status of belligerent which has thus been thrust upon it; and that it take immediate steps not only to put the country in a more thorough state of defense but also to exert all its power and employ all its resources to bring the Government of the German Empire to terms and end the war. . . .

While we do these things, these deeply momentous things, let us be very clear, and make very clear to all the world what our motives and our objects are. My own thought has not been driven from its habitual and normal course by the unhappy events of the last two months, and I do not believe that the thought of the nation has been altered or clouded by them. . . . Our object now, as then, is to vindicate the principles of peace and justice in the life of the world as against selfish and autocratic power and to set up amongst the really free and self-governed peoples of the world such a concert of purpose and of action as will henceforth ensure the observance of those principles. Neutrality is no longer feasible or desirable where the peace of the world is involved and the freedom of its peoples, and the menace to that peace and freedom lies in the existence of autocratic governments backed by organized force which is controlled wholly by their will, not by the will of their people. We have seen the last of neutrality in such circumstances. We are at the beginning of an age in which it will be insisted that the same standards of conduct and of responsibility for wrong done shall be observed among nations and their governments that are observed among the individual citizens of civilized states.

We have no quarrel with the German people. We have no feeling towards them but one of sympathy and friendship. It was not upon their impulse that their government acted in entering this war. It was not with their previous knowledge or approval. It was a war determined upon as wars used to be determined upon in the old, unhappy days when peoples were nowhere consulted by their rulers and wars were provoked and waged in the interest of dynasties or of little groups of ambitious men who were accustomed to use their fellow men as pawns and tools. Self-governed nations do not fill their neighbour states with spies or set the course of intrigue to bring about some critical posture of affairs which will give them an opportunity to strike and make conquest. Such designs can be successfully worked out only under cover and where no one has the right to ask questions. Cunningly contrived plans of deception or aggression, carried, it may be, from generation to generation, can be worked out and kept from the light only within the privacy of courts or behind the carefully guarded confidences of a narrow and privileged class. They are happily impossible where public opinion commands and insists upon full information concerning all the nation's affairs.

A steadfast concert for peace can never be maintained except by a partnership of democratic nations. No autocratic government could be trusted to keep faith within it or observe its convenants. It must be a league of honour, a partnership of opinion. . . .

Does not every American feel that assurance has been added to our hope for the future peace of the world by the wonderful and heartening things that have been happening within the last few weeks in Russia? Russia was known by those who knew it best to have been always in fact democratic at heart, in all the vital habits of her thought, in all the intimate relationships of her people that spoke their natural instinct, their habitual attitude towards life. The autocracy that crowned the summit of her political structure, long as it had stood and terrible as was the reality of its power, was not in fact Russian in origin, character, or purpose; and now it has been shaken off and the great, generous Russian people have been added in all their naive majesty and might to the forces that are fighting for freedom in the world, for justice, and for peace. Here is a fit partner for a League of Honour.

One of the things that has served to convince us that the Prussian autocracy was not and could never be our friend is that from the very outset of the present war it has filled our unsuspecting communities and even our offices of government with spies and set criminal intrigues everywhere afoot against our national unity of counsel, our peace within and without, our industries and our commerce. . . . That it means to stir up enemies against us at our very doors the intercepted note to the German Minister at Mexico City is eloquent evidence.

We are accepting this challenge of hostile purpose because we know that in such a government, following such methods, we can never have a friend; and that in the presence of its organized power, always lying in wait to accomplish we know not what purpose, there can be no assured security for the democratic governments of the world. We are now about to accept gauge of battle with this natural foe to liberty and shall, if necessary, spend the whole force of the nation to check and nullify its pretensions and its power. We are glad, now that we see the facts with no veil of false pretence about them, to fight thus for the ultimate peace of the world and for the liberation of its peoples, the German peoples included: for the rights of nations great and small and the privilege of men everywhere to choose their way of life and of obedience. The world must be made safe for democracy. . . .

It is a distressing and oppressive duty, Gentlemen of the Congress, which I have performed in thus addressing you. There are, it may be, many months of fiery trial and sacrifice ahead of us. It is a fearful thing to lead this great peaceful people into war, into the most terrible and disastrous of all wars, civilization itself seeming to be in the balance. But the right is more precious than peace, and we shall fight for the things which we have always carried nearest our hearts,—for democracy, for the right of those who submit to authority to have a voice in their own governments, for the rights and liberties of small nations, for a universal dominion of right by such a concert of free peoples as shall bring peace and safety to all nations and make the world itself at last free. To such a task we can dedicate our lives and our fortunes, everything that we are and everything that we have, with the pride of those who know that the day has come when America is privileged to spend her blood and her might for the principles that gave her birth and happiness and the peace which she has treasured. God helping her, she can do no other.

VIII

War and Peace

Outbreak of the World War in Europe in 1914 caught Americans wholly by surprise, and the ensuing months of argument over neutral rights tended to reduce American observations about the war to legalities; so that after the United States entered the conflict there was a sudden need to take a second look at the war and decide what sort of world the postwar world should be. President Wilson already had made statements about Latin America, notably the Mobile address of 1913, and it is entirely possible that his desire for democracy and cooperation in the Western Hemisphere translated easily into his program for Europe and the world. But one must hasten to add that Wilson by nature, and by long practice both as a professor and as a government man, was interested in principle and theory, and his new work as leader of the Allied and Associated powers (the President merely associated the United States with the Allies, and did not sign the Treaty of London of 1914 which bound the European powers) was for him a natural undertaking.

24. Making the Peace

A. THE FOURTEEN POINTS

THE EUROPEAN powers had been fighting so many months by April, 1917, that they almost had forgotten what they were fighting for, beyond such general propositions as places in the sun, or a fight against autocracy. When in November, 1917, a new group, the Bolsheviks, came into power in Russia and not merely published the Allied secret treaties, from the archives of the old Tsarist government, but engaged—during peace talks with the German government at Brest-Litovsk—in a virtual campaign for peace in Europe, it was utterly necessary that there be a detailed peace program. The time had come, and Wilson seized it on January 8, 1918, when he announced to Congress the Fourteen Points as the American and presumably the Allied peace program. By taking the initiative from the jaded Allied governments in Europe, the President of the United States showed a considerable diplomatic cleverness.

. . . Once more, as repeatedly before, the spokesmen of the Central Empires have indicated their desire to discuss the objects of the war and the possible bases of a general peace. Parleys have been in progress at Brest-Litovsk between Russian representatives and representatives of the Central Powers to which the attention of all the belligerents has been invited for the purpose of ascertaining whether it may be possible to extend these parleys into a general conference with regard to terms of peace and settlement. . . .

Within the last week Mr. Lloyd George has spoken with admirable candor and in admirable spirit for the people and Government of Great Britain. There is no confusion of counsel among the adversaries of the Central Powers, no uncertainty of principle, no vagueness of detail. The only secrecy of counsel, the only lack of fearless frankness, the only failure to make definite statement of the objects of the war, lies with Germany and her allies. The issues of life and death hang upon these definitions. No statesman who has the least conception of his responsibility ought for a moment to permit himself to continue this tragical and appalling outpouring of blood and treasure unless he is sure beyond a peradventure that the objects of the vital sacrifice are part and parcel of the very

SOURCE: *Foreign Relations of the United States: 1918, Supplement 1* (Washington, D.C., 1933), pp. 12–17.

life of society and that the people for whom he speaks think them right and imperative as he does. . . .

It will be our wish and purpose that the processes of peace, when they are begun, shall be absolutely open and that they shall involve and permit henceforth no secret understandings of any kind. The day of conquest and aggrandizement is gone by; so is also the day of secret covenants entered into in the interest of particular governments and likely at some unlooked-for moment to upset the peace of the world. It is this happy fact, now clear to the view of every public man whose thoughts do not still linger in an age that is dead and gone, which makes it possible for every nation whose purposes are consistent with justice and the peace of the world to avow now or at any other time the objects it has in view.

We entered this war because violations of right had occurred which touched us to the quick and made the life of our own people impossible unless they were corrected and the world secured once for all against their recurrence. What we demand in this war, therefore, is nothing peculiar to ourselves. It is that the world be made fit and safe to live in; and particularly that it be made safe for every peace-loving nation which, like our own, wishes to live its own life, determine its own institutions, be assured of justice and fair dealing by the other peoples of the world as against force and selfish aggression. All the peoples of the world are in effect partners in this interest, and for our own part we see very clearly that unless justice be done to others it will not be done to us. The programme of the world's peace, therefore, is our programme; and that programme, the only possible programme, as we see it, is this:

I. Open covenants of peace, openly arrived at, after which there shall be no private international understandings of any kind but diplomacy shall proceed always frankly and in the public view.

II. Absolute freedom of navigation upon the seas, outside territorial waters, alike in peace and in war, except as the seas may be closed in whole or in part by international action for the enforcement of international covenants.

III. The removal, so far as possible, of all economic barriers and the establishment of an equality of trade conditions among all the nations consenting to the peace and associating themselves for its maintenance.

IV. Adequate guarantees given and taken that national armaments will be reduced to the lowest point consistent with domestic safety.

V. A free, open-minded, and absolutely impartial adjustment of all colonial claims, based upon a strict observance of the principle that in determining all such questions of sovereignty the interests of the populations concerned must have equal weight with the equitable claims of the government whose title is to be determined.

VI. The evacuation of all Russian territory and such a settlement of all questions affecting Russia as will secure the best and freest cooperation of the other nations of the world in obtaining for her an unhampered and unembarrassed opportunity for the independent determination of her own political development and national policy and assure her of a sincere welcome into the society of free nations under institutions of her own choosing; and, more than a welcome, assistance also of every kind that she may need and may herself desire. The treatment accorded Russia by her sister nations in the months to come will be the acid test of their good will, of their comprehension of her needs as distinguished from their own interests, and of their intelligent and unselfish sympathy.

VII. Belgium, the whole world will agree, must be evacuated and restored, without any attempt to limit the sovereignty which she enjoys in common with all other free nations. No other single act will serve as this will serve to restore confidence among the nations in the laws which they have themselves set and determined for the government of their relations with one another. Without this healing act the whole structure and validity of international law is forever impaired.

VIII. All French territory should be freed and the invaded portions restored, and the wrong done to France by Prussia in 1871 in the matter of Alsace-Lorraine, which has unsettled the peace of the world for nearly fifty years, should be righted, in order that peace may once more be made secure in the interest of all.

IX. A readjustment of the frontiers of Italy should be effected along clearly recognizable lines of nationality.

X. The peoples of Austria-Hungary, whose place among the nations we wish to see safeguarded and assured, should be accorded the freest opportunity of autonomous development.

XI. Rumania, Serbia, and Montenegro should be evacuated; occupied territories restored; Serbia accorded free and secure access to the sea; and the relations of the several Balkan states to one another determined by friendly counsel along historically established lines of allegiance and nationality; and international guarantees of the political and economic independence and territorial integrity of the several Balkan states should be entered into.

XII. The Turkish portions of the present Ottoman Empire should be assured a secure sovereignty, but the other nationalities which are now under Turkish rule should be assured an undoubted security of life and an absolutely unmolested opportunity of autonomous development, and the Dardanelles should be permanently opened as a free passage to the ships and commerce of all nations under international guarantees.

XIII. An independent Polish state should be erected which should include the territories inhabited by indisputably Polish populations, which should be assured a free and secure access to the sea, and whose political and economic independence and territorial integrity should be guaranteed by international covenant.

XIV. A general association of nations must be formed under specific covenants for the purpose of affording mutual guarantees of political independence and territorial integrity to great and small states alike. . . .

. . . We have spoken now, surely, in terms too concrete to admit of any further doubt or question. An evident principle runs through the whole programme I have outlined. It is the principle of justice to all peoples and nationalities, and their right to live on equal terms of liberty and safety with one another, whether they be strong or weak. Unless this principle be made its foundation no part of the structure of international justice can stand. The people of the United States could act upon no other principle; and to the vindication of this principle they are ready to devote their lives, their honor, and everything that they possess. The moral climax of this the culminating and final war for human liberty has come, and they are ready to put their own strength, their own highest purpose, their own integrity and devotion to the test.

B. Explanations and Compromise

It was one thing to make a statement of principles, and quite another to get those principles recognized as the basis of peace after the war, and in subsequent months Wilson devoted himself to this task and managed to accomplish it just before the signing of the armistice on

Source: Charles Seymour, ed., *The Intimate Papers of Colonel House* (4 vols., Boston, 1926–28), IV, pp. 193–95, 197–200.

November 11, 1918. In the autumn the Germans had sued for peace, and negotiated first with Wilson on the basis of the Fourteen Points. Obtaining German agreement on them, Wilson instructed his confidential adviser, Colonel Edward M. House, present at sessions of the Supreme War Council in Paris, to obtain the consent of the Allies. House accomplished this (with Anglo-French reservation of two points, freedom of the seas and reparations) after obliquely threatening a separate American peace with Germany and also after allowing the Allies to see a long exegesis of the Fourteen Points that in some places qualified them considerably. As House's biographer, the late Charles Seymour once wrote, House at all times during the arguments in Paris had the so-called Cobb-Lippmann memorandum available, and frequently read from it. Two of House's assistants, the newspapermen Frank I. Cobb and Walter Lippmann, had drawn up this memorandum, which House had cabled to Wilson for approval. Although the President cagily had cabled back that the commentary was a satisfactory interpretation but that its details should be regarded merely as illustrative suggestions, the memorandum as used in Paris became the official interpretation.

[Interpretation of Point I] . . . The purpose is clearly to prohibit treaties, sections of treaties or understandings that are secret, such as the Triple Alliance, etc.

The phrase 'openly arrived at' need not cause difficulty. In fact, the President explained to the Senate last winter that the phrase was not meant to exclude confidential diplomatic negotiations involving delicate matters. The intention is that nothing which occurs in the course of such confidential negotiations shall be binding unless it appears in the final covenant made public to the world. . . .

[Point IV] "Domestic safety" clearly implies not only internal policing, but the protection of territory against invasion. The accumulation of armaments above this level would be a violation of the intention of the proposal.

What guarantees should be given and taken, or what are to be the standards of judgment have never been determined. It will be necessary to adopt the general principle and then institute some kind of international commission of investigation to prepare detailed projects for its execution. . . .

[Point VI] The first question is whether Russian territory is synonymous with territory belonging to the former Russian Empire. This is clearly not so, because Proposition XIII stipulates an independent Poland, a proposal which excludes the territorial reestablishment of the Empire. What is recognized as valid for the Poles will certainly have to be recognized for the Finns, the Lithuanians, the Letts, and perhaps also for the Ukrainians. Since the formulation of this condition, these subject nationalities have emerged, and there can be no doubt that they will have to be given an opportunity of free development. . . .

[Point VIII] Attention is called to the strong current of French opinion which claims 'the boundaries of 1814' rather than of 1871. The territory claimed is the Valley of the Saar with its coal fields. No claim on grounds of nationality can be established, but the argument leans on the possibility of taking this territory in lieu of indemnity. It would seem to be a clear violation of the President's proposal. . . .

[Point IX] This proposal is less than the Italian claim, less of course, than the territory allotted by the Treaty of London, less than the arrangement made between the Italian Government and the Jugo-Slav State.

In the region of Trent the Italians claim a strategic rather than an ethnic frontier. It should be noted in this connection that Italy and Germany will become neighbors if German Austria joins the German Empire. And if Italy obtains the best geographical frontier she will assume sovereignty over a large number of Germans. This is a violation of principle. But, it may be argued that by drawing a sharp line along the crest of the Alps, Italy's security will be enormously enhanced and the necessity of heavy armaments reduced. It might, therefore, be provided that Italy should have her claim in the Trentino, but that the northern part, inhabited by Germans, should be completely autonomous, and that the population should not be liable to military service in the Italian army. Italy could thus occupy the uninhabited Alpine peaks for military purposes, but would not govern the cultural life of the alien population to the south of her frontier.

The other problems of the frontier are questions between Italy and Jugo-Slavia, Italy and the Balkans, Italy and Greece. . . .

[Point X] This proposition no longer holds. Instead we have to-day the following elements:

1. CzECHO-SLOVAKIA. Its territories include at least a million Germans, for whom some provision must be made.

The independence of Slovakia means the dismemberment of the northwestern counties of Hungary.

2. GALICIA. Western Galicia is clearly Polish. Eastern Galicia is in large measure Ukrainian, (or Ruthenian,) and does not of right belong to Poland.

There also are several hundred thousand Ukrainians along the north and northeastern borders of Hungary, and in parts of Buko-wina (which belonged to Austria).

3. GERMAN AUSTRIA. This territory should of right be permitted to join Germany, but there is strong objection in France because of the increase of population involved.

4. JUGO-SLAVIA. It faces the following problems:

a. Frontier questions with Italy in Istria and the Dalmatian Coast; with Rumania in the Banat.

b. An internal problem arises out of the refusal of the Croats to accept the domination of the Serbs of the Serbian Kingdom.

c. A problem of the Mohammedan Serbs of Bosnia who are said to be loyal to the Hapsburgs. They constitute a little less than one third of the population.

5. TRANSYLVANIA. Will undoubtedly join Roumania, but provision must be made for the protection of the Magyars, Szeklers and Germans who constitute a large minority.

6. HUNGARY. Now independent, and very democratic in form, but governed by Magyars whose aim is to prevent the detachment of the territory of the nationalities on the fringe.

The United States is clearly committed to the programme of national unity and independence. It must stipulate, however, for the protection of national minorities, for freedom of access to the Adriatic and the Black Sea, and it supports a programme aiming at a Confederation of Southeastern Europe. . . .

[Point XII] The same difficulty arises here, as in the case of Austria-Hungary, concerning the word 'autonomous.'

It is clear that the Straits and Constantinople, while they may remain nominally Turkish, should be under international control. This control may be collective or be in the hands of one Power as mandatory of the League.

Anatolia should be reserved for the Turks. The coast lands, where Greeks predominate, should be under special international control, perhaps with Greece as mandatory.

Armenia must be given a port on the Mediterranean, and a protecting power established. France may claim it, but the Armenians would prefer Great Britain.

Syria has already been allotted to France by agreement with Great Britain.

Britain is clearly the best mandatory for Palestine, Mesopotamia and Arabia. . . .

[Point XIII] The chief problem is whether Poland is to obtain territory west of the Vistula which would cut off the Germans of East Prussia from the Empire, or whether Danzig can be made a free port and the Vistula internationalized.

On the east, Poland should receive no territory in which Lithuanians or Ukrainians predominate.

If Posen and Silesia go to Poland rigid protection must be afforded the minorities of Germans and Jews living there, as well as in other parts of the Polish state.

The principle on which frontiers will be delimited is contained in the President's words 'indisputably.' This may imply the taking of an impartial census before frontiers are marked. . . .

[Point XIV] The question of a League of Nations as the primary essential of a permanent peace has been so clearly presented by President Wilson in his speech of September 27, 1918 [not printed], that no further elucidation is required. It is the foundation of the whole diplomatic structure of a permanent peace.

25. Defending the League

A. THE COVENANT

THE LEAGUE of Nations was preeminently a Wilsonian proposition. It was no accident that the constitution of the League, hammered out in long committee meetings in Paris during the spring of 1919, took the name of a Calvinist agreement. Had Wilson not gone to Paris as head of the American peace delegation it is probable that no world organization would have emerged from the conference. The Covenant became the first twenty-six articles of all the treaties of peace signed at special ceremonies in the suburbs of Paris—Versailles with Germany, Trianon with Hungary, Neuilly with Bulgaria, St. Germain with Austria.

SOURCE: *Foreign Relations of the United States: The Paris Peace Conference, 1919* (13 vols., Washington, D.C., 1942–47), XIII, pp. 73–105.

Article 1. . . . . Any Member of the League may, after two years' notice of its intention to do so, withdraw from the League, provided that all its international obligations and all its obligations under this Covenant shall have been fulfilled at the time of its withdrawal.

Article 2. The action of the League under this Covenant shall be effected through the instrumentality of an Assembly and of a Council, with a permanent Secretariat.

Article 3. The Assembly shall consist of Representatives of the Members of the League.

The Assembly shall meet at stated intervals and from time to time as occasion may require at the Seat of the League or at such other place as may be decided upon.

The Assembly may deal at its meetings with any matter within the sphere of action of the League or affecting the peace of the world.

At meetings of the Assembly each Member of the League shall have one vote, and may have not more than three Representatives.

Article 4. The Council shall consist of Representatives of the Principal Allied and Associated Powers, together with Representatives of four other Members of the League. These four Members of the League shall be selected by the Assembly from time to time in its discretion. . . .

Article 5. Except where otherwise expressly provided in this Covenant or by the terms of the present Treaty, decisions at any meeting of the Assembly or of the Council shall require the agreement of all the Members of the League represented at the meeting.

All matters of procedure at meetings of the Assembly or of the Council, including the appointment of Committees to investigate particular matters, shall be regulated by the Assembly or by the Council and may be decided by a majority of the Members of the League represented at the meeting.

The first meeting of the Assembly and the first meeting of the Council shall be summoned by the President of the United States of America.

Article 6. The permanent Secretariat shall be established at the Seat of the League. The Secretariat shall comprise a Secretary General and such secretaries and staff as may be required. . . .

Article 7. The Seat of the League is established at Geneva. . . .

Article 8. The Members of the League recognise that the maintenance of peace requires the reduction of national armaments to the lowest point consistent with national safety and the enforcement by common action of international obligations.

The Council, taking account of the geographical situation and circumstances of each State, shall formulate plans for such reduction for the consideration and action of the several Governments. . . .

The Members of the League agree that the manufacture by private enterprise of munitions and implements of war is open to grave objections. The Council shall advise how the evil effects attendant upon such manufacture can be prevented, due regard being had to the necessities of those Members of the League which are not able to manufacture the munitions and implements of war necessary for their safety.

The Members of the League undertake to interchange full and frank information as to the scale of their armaments, their military, naval and air programmes and the condition of such of their industries as are adaptable to war-like purposes.

Article 9. A permanent Commission shall be constituted to advise the Council on the execution of the provisions of Articles 1 and 8 and on military, naval and air questions generally.

Article 10. The Members of the League undertake to respect and preserve as against external aggression the territorial integrity and existing political independence of all Members of the League. In case of any such aggression or in case of any threat or danger of such aggression the Council shall advise upon the means by which this obligation shall be fulfilled.

Article 11. Any war or threat of war, whether immediately affecting any of the Members of the League or not, is hereby declared a matter of concern to the whole League, and the League shall take any action that may be deemed wise and effectual to safeguard the peace of nations. . . .

Article 12. The Members of the League agree that if there should arise between them any dispute likely to lead to a rupture, they will submit the matter either to arbitration or to inquiry by the Council, and they agree in no case to resort to war until three months after the award by the arbitrators or the report by the Council. . . .

Article 13. The Members of the League agree that whenever any dispute shall arise between them which they recognise to be suitable for submission to arbitration and which cannot be satisfactorily settled by diplomacy, they will submit the whole subject-matter to arbitration.

Disputes as to the interpretation of a treaty, as to any question of international law, as to the existence of any fact which if established would constitute a breach of any international obligation, or as to the extent and nature of the reparation to be made for any such breach, are declared to be among those which are generally suitable for submission to arbitration. . . .

Article 14. The Council shall formulate and submit to the Members of the League for adoption plans for the establishment of a Permanent Court of International Justice. The Court shall be competent to hear and determine any dispute of an international character which the parties thereto submit to it. The Court may also give an advisory opinion upon any dispute or question referred to it by the Council or by the Assembly.

Article 15. If there should arise between Members of the League any dispute likely to lead to a rupture, which is not submitted to arbitration in accordance with Article 13, the Members of the League agree that they will submit the matter to the Council. . . .

If a report by the Council is unanimously agreed to by the members thereof other than the Representatives of one or more of the parties to the dispute, the Members of the League agree that they will not go to war with any party to the dispute which complies with the recommendations of the report. . . .

If the dispute between the parties is claimed by one of them, and is found by the Council, to arise out of a matter which by international law is solely within the domestic jurisdiction of that party, the Council shall so report, and shall make no recommendation as to its settlement. . . .

Article 16. Should any Member of the League resort to war in disregard of its covenants under Articles 12, 13 or 15, it shall *ipso facto* be deemed to have committed an act of war against all other Members of the League, which hereby undertake immediately to subject it to the severance of all trade or financial relations, the prohibition of all intercourse between their nationals and the nationals of the covenant-breaking State, and the prevention of all financial, commercial or personal intercourse between the nationals of the covenant-breaking State and the nationals of any other State, whether a Member of the League or not.

It shall be the duty of the Council in such case to recommend to the several Governments concerned what effective military, naval or air force the Members of the League shall severally contribute to the armed forces to be used to protect the covenants of the League.

The Members of the League agree, further, that they will mutually support one another in the financial and economic measures which are taken under this Article, in order to minimise the loss and inconvenience resulting from the above measures, and that they will mutually support one another in resisting any special measures aimed at one of their number by the covenant-breaking State, and that they will take the necessary steps to afford passage through their territory to the forces of any of the Members of the League which are co-operating to protect the covenants of the League.

Any Member of the League which has violated any covenant of the League may be declared to be no longer a Member of the League by a vote of the Council concurred in by the Representatives of all the other Members of the League represented thereon.

Article 17. In the event of a dispute between a Member of the League and a State which is not a Member of the League, or between States not Members of the League, the State or States not Members of the League shall be invited to accept the obligations of membership in the League for the purposes of such dispute, upon such conditions as the Council may deem just. . . .

Article 18. Every treaty or international engagement entered into hereafter by any Member of the League shall be forthwith registered with the Secretariat and shall as soon as possible be published by it. No such treaty or international engagement shall be binding until so registered.

Article 19. The Assembly may from time to time advise the reconsideration by Members of the League of treaties which have become inapplicable and the consideration of international conditions whose continuance might endanger the peace of the world.

Article 20. The Members of the League severally agree that this Covenant is accepted as abrogating all obligations or understandings *inter se* which are inconsistent with the terms thereof, and solemnly undertake that they will not hereafter enter into any engagements inconsistent with the terms thereof.

In case any Member of the League shall, before becoming a Member of the League, have undertaken any obligations inconsistent with the terms of this Covenant, it shall be the duty of such

Member to take immediate steps to procure its release from such obligations.

Article 21. Nothing in this Covenant shall be deemed to affect the validity of international engagements, such as treaties of arbitration or regional understandings like the Monroe doctrine, for securing the maintenance of peace.

Article 22. To those colonies and territories which as a consequence of the late war have ceased to be under the sovereignty of the States which formerly governed them and which are inhabited by peoples not yet able to stand by themselves under the strenuous conditions of the modern world, there should be applied the principle that the well-being and development of such peoples form a sacred trust of civilization and that securities for the performance of this trust should be embodied in this Covenant.

The best method of giving practical effect to this principle is that the tutelage of such peoples should be entrusted to advanced nations who by reason of their resources, their experience or their geographical position can best undertake this responsibility, and who are willing to accept it, and that this tutelage should be exercised by them as Mandatories on behalf of the League. . . .

In every case of mandate, the Mandatory shall render to the Council an annual report in reference to the territory committed to its charge. . . .

Article 23. Subject to and in accordance with the provisions of international conventions existing or hereafter to be agreed upon, the Members of the League:

(a) will endeavour to secure and maintain fair and humane conditions of labour for men, women, and children, both in their own countries and in all countries to which their commercial and industrial relations extend, and for that purpose will establish and maintain the necessary international organizations;

(b) undertake to secure just treatment of the native inhabitants of territories under their control;

(c) will entrust the League with the general supervision over the execution of agreements with regard to the traffic in women and children, and the traffic in opium and other dangerous drugs;

(d) will entrust the League with the general supervision of the trade in arms and ammunition with the countries in which the control of this traffic is necessary in the common interest;

(e) will make provision to secure and maintain freedom of

communications and of transit and equitable treatment for the commerce of all Members of the League. In this connection, the special necessities of the regions devastated during the war of 1914–18 shall be borne in mind;

(f) will endeavor to take steps in matters of international concern for the prevention and control of disease.

Article 24. There shall be placed under the direction of the League all international bureaux already established by general treaties if the parties to such treaties consent. . . .

Article 25. The Members of the League agree to encourage and promote the establishment and co-operation of duly authorised voluntary national Red Cross organizations having as purposes the improvement of health, the prevention of disease and the mitigation of suffering throughout the world.

Article 26. Amendments to this Covenant will take effect when ratified by the Members of the League whose Representatives compose the Council and by a majority of the Members of the League whose Representatives compose the Assembly.

No such amendment shall bind any Member of the League which signifies its dissent therefrom, but in that case it shall cease to be a Member of the League.

B. Article 10

IN THE tortuous progress of the Covenant from the committee of the peace conference in Paris to the floor of the United States Senate, a notable occasion was the meeting of Wilson with members of the Committee on Foreign Relations at the White House, on August 19, 1919, in which the harassed President, knowing that the Covenant and Treaty of Versailles was in trouble, sought to defend his handiwork. Tension was not far from the surface, and Wilson was in a bristling mood.

The committee met at the White House at 10 o'clock A.M., pursuant to the invitation of the President, and proceeded to the East Room, where the conference was held.

Present: Hon. Woodrow Wilson, President of the United States, and the following members of the committee: Senators

SOURCE: 66th Cong., 1st Sess., *Hearings before the Committee on Foreign Relations, United States Senate Doc. 106* (Washington, D.C., 1919), pp. 499, 502, 517, 524–26, 552.

Lodge (chairman), McCumber, Borah, Brandegee, Fall, Knox, Harding, Johnson of California, New, Moses, Hitchcock, Williams, Swanson, Pomerene, Smith, and Pittman.

   . . . The PRESIDENT. Mr. Chairman, I have taken the liberty of writing out a little statement in the hope that it might facilitate discussion by speaking directly on some points that I know have been points of controversy and upon which I thought an expression of opinion would not be unwelcome. . . .

Article 10 is in no respect of doubtful meaning when read in the light of the covenant as a whole. The council of the league can only "advise upon" the means by which the obligations of that great article are to be given effect to. Unless the United States is a party to the policy or action in question, her own affirmative vote in the council is necessary before any advice can be given, for a unanimous vote of the council is required. If she is a party, the trouble is hers anyhow. And the unanimous vote of the council is only advice in any case. Each Government is free to reject it if it pleases. Nothing could have been made more clear to the conference than the right of our Congress under our Constitution to exercise its independent judgment in all matters of peace and war. No attempt was made to question or limit that right. The United States will, indeed, undertake under article 10 to "respect and preserve as against external aggression the territorial integrity and existing political independence of all members of the league," and that engagement constitutes a very grave and solemn moral obligation. But it is a moral, not a legal, obligation, and leaves our Congress absolutely free to put its own interpretation upon it in all cases that call for action. It is binding in conscience only, not in law.

Article 10 seems to me to constitute the very backbone of the whole covenant. Without it the league would be hardly more than an influential debating society. . . .

Senator McCUMBER. Mr. President, I think, due to my own fault, I do not fully comprehend your distinction between a moral and a legal obligation in a treaty. If we enter into a treaty with France to defend her against aggression from Germany for any length of time, that is a legal obligation, is it not?

The PRESIDENT. Legal in the sense that a treaty is of binding force; yes.

Senator McCUMBER. Yes; that is what I meant. It is as legal as any treaty could be made legal, and there is also a moral obligation to keep that treaty, is there not?

The PRESIDENT. Yes, sir. I happened to hear Senator Knox say what I am glad to adopt. It is a legal obligation with a moral sanction.

Senator BORAH. That is true generally, is it not?

The PRESIDENT. Yes, Senator; but I have already defined in what special sense I use the world "legal." . . .

Senator JOHNSON of California. I think you answered to Senator Borah the question I am about to ask, so pardon me if it is repetitive. It is this: Was the United States Government officially informed, at any time between the rupture of diplomatic relations with Germany and the signing of the armistice, of agreements made by the allied Governments in regard to the settlement of the war?

The PRESIDENT. No; not so far as I know.

Senator JOHNSON of California. So far as you are aware, was it unofficially informed during that period?

The PRESIDENT. I would be more clear in my answer, Senator, if I knew just what you were referring to.

Senator JOHNSON of California. I am referring to the so-called secret treaties which disposed of territory among the belligerents.

The PRESIDENT. You mean like the treaty of London?

Senator JOHNSON of California. Yes; like the London pact.

The PRESIDENT. No; no, sir. . . .

. . . Senator JOHNSON of California. When our Government through you, Mr. President, in January, 1918, made the 14 points as the basis for peace, were those points made with the knowledge of the existence of the secret agreements?

The PRESIDENT. No; oh, no.

Senator JOHNSON of California. It was not intended, then, by the expression of these 14 points, to supplant the aims contained in the secret treaties?

The PRESIDENT. Since I knew nothing of them, necessarily not.

. . . Senator JOHNSON of California. Do you know, Mr. President, whether or not our Government stated to China that if China would enter the war we would protect her interests at the peace conference?

The PRESIDENT. We made no promises.

Senator JOHNSON of California. No representations of that sort?

The PRESIDENT. No. She knew that we would as well as we could. She had every reason to know that.

Senator JOHNSON of California. Pardon me a further question: You did make the attempt to do it, too; did you not?

The PRESIDENT. Oh, indeed I did; very seriously.

Senator JOHNSON of California. And the decision ultimately reached at the peace conference was a disappointment to you?

The PRESIDENT. Yes, sir; I may frankly say that it was.

Senator JOHNSON of California. You would have preferred, as I think most of us would, that there had been a different conclusion of the Shantung provision, or the Shantung difficulty or controversy, at the Paris peace conference?

The PRESIDENT. Senator, do you think I ought to redebate here the fundamental questions that we debated at Paris? I think that would be a mistake, sir.

Senator JOHNSON of California. Mr. President, it is on that very theory that I refrained from asking many of those things, the thoughts of which crowd one's mind, and which one would like to ask.

The PRESIDENT. Of course. You see, you are going into the method by which the treaty was negotiated. Now, with all respect, sir, I think that is a territory that we ought not to enter.

Senator NEW. Of course, if there is any reason why it should not be answered, I will withdraw it. Is there objection to answering this, Mr. President: What was France's solution proposed for administration of the Saar Basin?

The PRESIDENT. I do not think I ought to answer those questions, Senator, because of course they affect the policy and urgency of other Governments. I am not at liberty to go into that.

Senator NEW. Mr. President, would our position in the War of 1812 and the Spanish-American War have been secure under the league covenant?

The PRESIDENT. Oh, Senator, you can judge of that as well as I could. I have tried to be a historical student, but I could not quite get the league back into those days clearly enough in my mind to form a judgment.

Senator NEW. What would have been the procedure under the covenant in those two cases, in your opinion?

The PRESIDENT. Why, Senator, I could figure that out if you gave me half a day, because I would have to refresh my mind as to the circumstances that brought on the wars; but that has not been regarded as a profitable historical exercise—hypothetically to reconstruct history.

. . . The CHAIRMAN. Mr. President, I do not wish to interfere in any way, but the conference has now lasted about three hours and a half, and it is half an hour after the lunch hour.

The PRESIDENT. Will not you gentlemen take luncheon with me? It will be very delightful.

C. WILSON ASKS THE PEOPLE

CONTRARY to the advice of his physician, Wilson decided to take his case to the people in a speaking tour. The eight-thousand-mile trip out to the Pacific coast and back, in twenty-two days, involved thirty-six speeches averaging about an hour in length. All this before the heyday of speechwriters—so that as the train swayed from mile to mile the President pecked away at his little portable typewriter, barely preparing a speech before the occasion was upon him to give it. Moreover, it was all before the day of voice amplifiers—the President often had to shout to make himself heard in the great halls before thousands of people. And it was all before the time of air-conditioners; the air was so bad in the Mormon tabernacle in Salt Lake City that Wilson could hardly breathe. Sixty-two years old, worn out, the President at Pueblo, Colorado, on the night of September 25, 1919, barely got through his evening address. Throbbing headaches, inadequately diagnosed, forced cancellation of further speeches, and the train took the President back to Washington. There, a few days later, he suffered a paralytic stroke that turned him into a physical wreck. The Pueblo speech follows.

. . . When you come to the heart of the covenant, my fellow citizens, you will find it in article 10, and I am very much interested to know that the other things have been blown away like bubbles. There is nothing in the other contentions with regard to the league of nations, but there is something in article 10 that you ought to realize and ought to accept or reject. Article 10 is the heart of the whole matter. What is article 10? I never am certain that I can from memory give a literal repetition of its language, but I am sure that I can give an exact interpretation of its meaning. Article 10

SOURCE: 66th Cong., 1st Sess., *Congressional Record*, LVIII (1919), Pt. 7, pp. 6425–427.

provides that every member of the league covenants to respect and preserve the territorial integrity and existing political independence of every other member of the league as against external aggression. Not against internal disturbance. There was not a man at that table who did not admit the sacredness of the right of self-determination. . . .

But you will say, "What is the second sentence of article 10? That is what gives very disturbing thoughts." The second sentence is that the council of the league shall advise what steps, if any, are necessary to carry out the guaranty of the first sentence, namely, that the members will respect and preserve the territorial integrity and political independence of the other members. I do not know any other meaning for the word "advise" except "advise." The council advises, and it can not advise without the vote of the United States. Why gentlemen should fear that the Congress of the United States would be advised to do something that it did not want to do I frankly can not imagine. . . .

Yet article 10 strikes at the taproot of war. Article 10 is a statement that the very things that have always been sought in imperialistic wars are henceforth forgone by every ambitious nation in the world. . . .

You will say, "Is the league an absolute guaranty against war?" No; I do not know any absolute guaranty against the errors of human judgment or the violence of human passion, but I tell you this: With a cooling space of nine months for human passion, not much of it will keep hot. I had a couple of friends who were in the habit of losing their tempers, and when they lost their tempers they were in the habit of using very unparliamentary language. Some of their friends induced them to make a promise that they never would swear inside the town limits. When the impulse next came upon them, they took a street car to go out of town to swear, and by the time they got out of town they did not want to swear. They came back convinced that they were just what they were, a couple of unspeakable fools, and the habit of getting angry and of swearing' suffered great inroads upon it by that experience. Now, illustrating the great by the small, that is true of the passions of nations. It is true of the passions of men however you combine them. Give them space to cool off. I ask you this: If it is not an absolute insurance against war, do you want no insurance at all? Do you want nothing? Do you want not only no probability that war will not recur, but the probability that it will recur? The arrangements of justice do not stand of themselves my fellow citizens. The arrangements of this treaty are just, but they need the support of the combined power of the great nations of the world. And they will have that support. Now that the mists of this great question have cleared away, I believe that men will see the truth, eye to eye and face to face. There is one thing that the American people always rise to and extend their hand to, and that is the truth of justice and of liberty and of peace. We have accepted that truth and we are going to be led by it, and it is going to lead us, and through us the world, out into pastures of quietness and peace such as the world never dreamed of before.

26. Against the League

WILSON *instructed his supporters in the Senate to vote against any reservations to the Covenant, and this instruction assured the League's defeat. The President's opponents acted out of a multitude of purposes —to preserve the unity of the Republican Party (some anti-Leaguers led by Senator William E. Borah of Idaho threatened to leave the party), out of pique that the President had dominated the government during the war, out of knowledge of the President's views of hostile senators (he believed they had "bungalow minds"), out of honest feeling that the United States should maintain a free hand in world affairs and not join a body whose major interests would probably lie in Europe. Whatever the reasoning, the student of the present day, reading the yellowing pages of the Congressional Record for November 19, 1919, cannot conclude that the debate over the Covenant was the Senate's finest hour.*

    . . . The Chaplain, Rev. Forrest J. Prettyman, D. D., offered the following prayer:

Almighty God, we come before Thee as we face the tremendous responsibilities of this hour. The welfare of millions is dependent upon the action of the Senate. We would seek the guidance of the God of our fathers in the performance of our duty. We pray for Thy spirit, the spirit of wisdom and counsel, the spirit of a sound mind, that we may do our duty as in God's sight, and so well

SOURCE: 66th Cong., 1st Sess., *Congressional Record*, LVIII (1919), Pt. 9, pp. 8767, 8777–78, 8791–92.

perform it as that it may have Thy approval. We ask for Jesus' sake. Amen.

[After some debate there followed the Lodge reservations to the Covenant:]

1. The United States so understands and construes article 1 that in case of notice of withdrawal from the league of nations, as provided in said article, the United States shall be the sole judge as to whether all its international obligations and all its obligations under the said covenant have been fulfilled, and notice of withdrawal by the United States may be given by a concurrent resolution of the Congress of the United States.

2. The United States assumes no obligation to preserve the territorial integrity or political independence of any other country or to interfere in controversies between nations—whether members of the league or not—under the provisions of article 10, or to employ the military or naval forces of the United States under any article of the treaty for any purpose, unless in any particular case the Congress, which, under the Constitution, has the sole power to declare war or authorize the employment of the military or naval forces of the United States, shall by act or joint resolution so provide.

3. No mandate shall be accepted by the United States under article 22, part 1, or any other provision of the treaty of peace with Germany, except by action of the Congress of the United States.

4. The United States reserves to itself exclusively the right to decide what questions are within its domestic jurisdiction and declares that all domestic and political questions relating wholly or in part to its internal affairs, including immigration, labor, coastwise traffic, the tariff, commerce, the suppression of traffic in women and children, and in opium and other dangerous drugs, and all other domestic questions, are solely within the jurisdiction of the United States and are not under this treaty to be submitted in any way either to arbitration or to the consideration of the council or of the assembly of the league of nations, or any agency thereof, or to the decision or recommendation of any other power.

5. The United States will not submit to arbitration or to inquiry by the assembly or by the council of the league of nations, provided for in said treaty of peace, any questions which in the judgment of the United States depend upon or relate to its long-established policy, commonly known as the Monroe doctrine; said doctrine is

to be interpreted by the United States alone and is hereby declared to be wholly outside the jurisdiction of said league of nations and entirely unaffected by any provision contained in the said treaty of peace with Germany.

6. The United States withholds its assent to articles 156, 157, and 158, and reserves full liberty of action with respect to any controversy which may arise under said articles between the Republic of China and the Empire of Japan.

7. The Congress of the United States will provide by law for the appointment of the representatives of the United States in the assembly and the council of the league of nations, and may in its discretion provide for the participation of the United States in any commission, committee, tribunal, court, council, or conference, or in the selection of any members thereof and for the appointment of members of said commissions, committees, tribunals, courts, councils, or conferences, or any other representatives under the treaty of peace, or in carrying out its provisions, and until such participation and appointment have been so provided for and the powers and duties of such representatives have been defined by law, no person shall represent the United States under either said league of nations or the treaty of peace with Germany or be authorized to perform any act for or on behalf of the United States thereunder, and no citizen of the United States shall be selected or appointed as a member of said commissions, committees, tribunals, courts, councils, or conferences except with the approval of the Senate of the United States.

8. The United States understands that the reparation commission will regulate or interfere with exports from the United States to Germany, or from Germany to the United States, only when the United States by act or joint resolution of Congress approves such regulation or interference.

9. The United States shall not be obligated to contribute to any expenses of the league of nations, or of the secretariat, or of any commission, or committee, or conference, or other agency, organized under the league of nations or under the treaty or for the purpose of carrying out the treaty provisions, unless and until an appropriation of funds available for such expenses shall have been made by the Congress of the United States.

10. If the United States shall at any time adopt any plan for the limitation of armaments proposed by the council of the league of

nations under the provisions of article 8, it reserves the right to increase such armaments without the consent of the council whenever the United States is threatened with invasion or engaged in war.

11. The United States reserves the right to permit, in its discretion, the nationals of a covenant-breaking State, as defined in article 16 of the covenant of the league of nations, residing within the United States or in countries other than that violating said article 16, to continue their commercial, financial, and personal relations with the nationals of the United States.

12. Nothing in articles 296, 297, or in any of the annexes thereto or in any other article, section, or annex of the treaty of peace with Germany shall, as against citizens of the United States, be taken to mean any confirmation, ratification, or approval of any act otherwise illegal or in contravention of the rights of citizens of the United States.

13. The United States withholds its assent to Part XIII (articles 387 to 427, inclusive) unless Congress by act or joint resolution shall hereafter make provision for representation in the organization established by said Part XIII, and in such event the participation of the United States will be governed and conditioned by the provisions of such act or joint resolution.

14. The United States assumes no obligation to be bound by any election, decision, report, or finding of the council or assembly in which any member of the league and its self-governing dominions, colonies, or parts of empire, in the aggregate have cast more than one vote, and assumes no obligation to be bound by any decision, report, or finding of the council or assembly arising out of any dispute between the United States and any member of the league if such member, or any self-governing dominion, colony, empire, or part of empire united with it politically has voted. . . .

[In the subsequent discussion, prior to defeat of the treaty, Senator Warren G. Harding of Ohio distinguished himself.]

Mr. HARDING. Mr. President, I have been content to allow the final disposition of the pending measure without any further remarks, but I could not well be content to permit the statement of the Senator from Alabama [Mr. UNDERWOOD] to go unchallenged. I quite agree with him that no one can fool the country; and, in order that we may make the situation clear to the country to-night, when all of the United States is watching the action of this body no less intently than are those who honor us with their presence, and when all the world is watching to see what this great Republic will do, I am in favor of doing what may be expressed in a well-understood sporting term as "laying all the cards on the table, face up." . . .

I have not liked this treaty; I think, as originally negotiated, it is the colossal blunder of all time; but, recognizing the aspirations of our own people and the people of the world to do something toward international cooperation for the promotion and preservation of peace and a more intimate and better understanding between nations, I have wished to make it possible to accept this covenant. I could, however, no more vote to ratify this treaty without reservations which make sure America's independence of action, which make sure the preservation of American traditions, which make sure and certain our freedom in choosing our course of action, than I could participate in a knowing betrayal of this Republic.

Mr. President, in letting the public understand let us review the situation. In the Senate there are four distinct schools of thought in dealing with this treaty: One is the unconditional-ratification school, those who either through their own conscientious convictions or the lash of the Executive—choose as you will—want this treaty ratified without a single modification or reservation. That is group No. 1. In direct opposition is the so-called irreconcilable group, those who are unalterably opposed to any ratification. That is group 2. The third is the group, to which I choose to belong, if I may, who are agreed to bring about the ratification of this treaty if they are convinced that reservations have been adopted which are sufficient to safeguard the interests of the United States of America. There still remains another group—or, rather, a group within a group—popularly known as the "mild reservationists," those who are anxious to ratify, who are anxious to safeguard the interests of this Republic, but at the same time desire to make the reservations as little offensive as possible to those who assumed to negotiate the treaty in contempt of the Senate.

We have had the four groups to deal with; and in the progress of the debate and after much discussion we have finally come to an understanding on this side alone—because on the other side there were those who took the position that there could be no reservations at all—and have accommodated our differences to the extent that the majority has agreed upon a program of reservations.

The Senator from Alabama, Mr. President, who is himself, if I

remember correctly, an advocate of cloture and a strong advocate
of the policy of the majority doing business, makes a rather doubtful statement when he challenges the ability of the majority to do
business in this Chamber, because again and again the majority has
demonstrated its determination to support the reservations reported to this body. That is why they are added to the resolution.
If a man is the advocate of the majority in a legislative body performing its functions, he must accept the dictum of the majority of
this body.

That leads me, if you please, to indulge in a little reflection. The
whole trouble with the treaty, Senators, is that it was negotiated
upon a misunderstanding upon the part of the Executive. No one
doubts for a moment that the President, in that disregard for the
Senate which grew out of war conditions, in that little consideration for this body which followed a state of submergence, undertook to negotiate a treaty, which was his towering ambition,
notwithstanding he knew the opposition of a majority and in
defiance of the expressed wish or the expressed opinion of a
sufficient number to defeat ratification, under the Executive impression that no modification or alteration could be effected except
by a two-thirds majority vote of the Senate.

Mr. McCORMICK. And he so stated.

Mr. HARDING. He himself not only so stated, but those who
have been students of the whole negotiation and the aftermath
have clearly seen that the Executive proceeded on that theory. But
it develops, Mr. President, that there is still a United States Senate
and a majority, of course, in the Senate which is determined to
reassert itself.

It was all right, Senators, to submerge ourselves as members of
the Government commissioned by the people, as we did submerge
ourselves during the period of the war; I was a participant in the
submergence; but when the war ended and the greatest document
in importance ever negotiated in the world came to this body for
consideration, then it was becoming, indeed, for the United States
Senate again to assume its constitutional authority.

. . . I know, Mr. President, that in this covenant we have
originally bartered American independence in order to create a
league. We have traded away America's freedom of action in order
to establish a supergovernment of the world, and it was never
intended to be any less. I speak for one who is old-fashioned

enough to believe that the Government of the United States of America is good enough for me. In speaking my reverence for the Government of the United States of America, Senators, I want the preservation of those coordinate branches of government which were conceived and instituted by the fathers; and if there is nothing else significant in the action of this day, you can tell to the people of the United States of America and to the world that the Senate of the United States has once more reasserted its authority, and representative government abides.

IX

The Twenties

The 1920s, an era bounded on the one side by the end of the
World War, and on the other by the beginning of the Great Depression, constituted a sort of last chance for international relations
to organize for peace and justice, prior to the troubles of the
1930s—Hitler, Mussolini, Japan—which brought on the Second
World War and the troubles of the postwar years, our own time. If
only the 1920s had gone differently. If people during that brief
period of quiet, perhaps a tired quiet, after the exertions in what
they then called the Great War, could somehow have possessed
the foresight that the times demanded, some sense of the extraordinary confusions of the world's affairs that shortly, because of
failure to organize the peace, were to begin.

27. The Washington Conference

A. THE FOUR-POWER PACT

THE UNITED States stood on the sidelines of world affairs in the 1920s. The American government sought to arrange naval armaments, on the theory that the fewer weapons in the world the more peaceful it would be; and also tried to "freeze over" the Pacific, at long last to contain Japanese aggressiveness and ensure peaceful development of the Chinese nation. The first order of business at the Washington Conference of 1921–22, which opened on the day after Armistice Day, 1921, was to get rid of the Anglo-Japanese Alliance, which in its successive renewals had seemed a threat to American interests. The resultant Four-Power Pact was what Elihu Root, one of the American delegates, described as a splendid facade. "I doubt," he declared, "if any formal treaty ever accomplished so much by doing so little."

I

The High Contracting Parties agree as between themselves to respect their rights in relation to their insular possessions and insular dominions in the region of the Pacific Ocean.

If there should develop between any of the High Contracting Parties a controversy arising out of any Pacific question and involving their said rights which is not satisfactorily settled by diplomacy and is likely to affect the harmonious accord now happily subsisting between them, they shall invite the other High Contracting Parties to a joint conference to which the whole subject will be referred for consideration and adjustment.

II

If the said rights are threatened by the aggressive action of any other Power, the High Contracting Parties shall communicate with one another fully and frankly in order to arrive at an understanding as to the most efficient measures to be taken, jointly or separately, to meet the exigencies of the particular situation.

SOURCE: *Foreign Relations of the United States: 1922* (2 vols., Washington, D.C., 1938), I, p. 35.

III

This Treaty shall remain in force for ten years from the time it shall take effect, and after the expiration of said period it shall continue to be in force subject to the right of any of the High Contracting Parties to terminate it upon twelve months' notice.

IV

This Treaty shall be ratified as soon as possible in accordance with the constitutional methods of the High Contracting Parties and shall take effect on the deposit of ratifications, which shall take place at Washington, and thereupon the agreement between Great Britain and Japan, which was concluded at London on July 13, 1911, shall terminate. . . .

JAPANESE concern that the treaty might seem to apply to Japan's home islands produced a curious supplementary declaration of December 13, 1921.

In signing the Treaty this day between The United States of America, The British Empire, France and Japan, it is declared to be the understanding and intent of the Signatory Powers:
1. That the Treaty shall apply to the Mandated Islands in the Pacific Ocean; provided, however, that the making of the Treaty shall not be deemed to be an assent on the part of The United States of America to the mandates and shall not preclude agreements between The United States of America and the Mandatory Powers respectively in relation to the mandated islands.
2. That the controversies to which the second paragraph of Article I refers shall not be taken to embrace questions which according to principles of international law lie exclusively within the domestic jurisdiction of the respective Powers. . . .

B. BALANCING NAVAL POWER

NEGOTIATION of a naval treaty among the naval powers, chiefly the United States, Britain, and Japan, proved more difficult, as the French

SOURCE: *Foreign Relations* . . . : 1922, I, pp. 36–37.
SOURCE: *Foreign Relations* . . . : 1922, I, pp. 249–53, 265.

and Italians also would have to be brought in and the latter two nations were so jealous of each other that they were bound to complicate the calculations of the great naval powers. If, for example, the British felt that building by the French and Italians would threaten the British traditional two-power standard (maintenance of a navy equal to the forces of Europe's two largest naval powers), the British would build; and if the British went up, the Americans would go up, and the Japanese. Moreover, in the naval calculations of the 1920s there was a subtle argument constantly running between the British and French, for the French did not trust the British to continue the entente cordiale into the postwar era and wished to maintain the threat of a large French navy, so as to keep the British in line. There were subtleties within subtleties. The Americans, led by Secretary of State Charles Evans Hughes, moved ahead, and on February 6, 1922, managed to secure a limitation of capital ships and aircraft carriers represented by the numerical ratios for the United States, Britain, and Japan, of 5:5:3. The French and Italians followed with 1.67:1.67. It was necessary to limit aircraft carriers because the powers otherwise might convert excess battleship tonnage to carriers. The treaty did nothing to limit smaller naval craft, other than define as a battleship any vessel displacing more than 10,000 tons and carrying more than 8-inch guns. In the latter 1920s, a rivalry in cruisers of the so-called heavy type, with maximum tonnage and guns permitted under the treaty of 1922, led to the London Naval Conference of 1930, which limited cruisers, destroyers, and submarines. The effort to secure peace through disarmament ended with failure of a second London conference in 1935–36.

Article I

The Contracting Powers agree to limit their respective naval armament as provided in the present Treaty.

Article II

The Contracting Powers may retain respectively the capital ships which are specified in Chapter II, Part 1. On the coming into force of the present Treaty, but subject to the following provisions of this Article, all other capital ships, built or building, of the United States, the British Empire and Japan shall be disposed of as prescribed in Chapter II, Part 2.

In addition to the capital ships specified in Chapter II, Part 1, the United States may complete and retain two ships of the West Virginia class now under construction. On the completion of these two ships the North Dakota and Delaware shall be disposed of as prescribed in Chapter II, Part 2.

The British Empire may, in accordance with the replacement

table in Chapter II, Part 3, construct two new capital ships not exceeding 35,000 tons (35,560 metric tons) standard displacement each. On the completion of the said two ships the *Thunderer*, *King George V*, *Ajax* and *Centurion* shall be disposed of as prescribed in Chapter II, Part 2.

Article III

Subject to the provisions of Article II, the Contracting Powers shall abandon their respective capital ship building programs, and no new capital ships shall be constructed or acquired by any of the Contracting Powers except replacement tonnage which may be constructed or acquired as specified in Chapter II, Part 3.

Ships which are replaced in accordance with Chapter II, Part 3, shall be disposed of as prescribed in Part 2 of that Chapter.

Article IV

The total capital ship replacement tonnage of each of the Contracting Powers shall not exceed in standard displacement, for the United States 525,000 tons (533,400 metric tons); for the British Empire 525,000 tons (533,400 metric tons); for France 175,000 tons (177,800 metric tons); for Italy 175,000 tons (177,800 metric tons); for Japan 315,000 tons (320,040 metric tons).

Article V

No capital ship exceeding 35,000 tons (35,560 metric tons) standard displacement shall be acquired by, or constructed by, for, or within the jurisdiction of, any of the Contracting Powers.

Article VI

No capital ship of any of the Contracting Powers shall carry a gun with a calibre in excess of 16 inches (406 millimetres).

Article VII

The total tonnage for aircraft carriers of each of the Contracting Powers shall not exceed in standard displacement, for the United States 135,000 tons (137,160 metric tons); for the British Empire 135,000 tons (137,160 metric tons); for France 60,000 tons (60,960 metric tons); for Italy 60,000 tons (60,960 metric tons); for Japan 81,000 tons (82,296 metric tons).

Article VIII

The replacement of aircraft carriers shall be effected only as prescribed in Chapter II, Part 3, provided, however, that all aircraft carrier tonnage in existence or building on November 12, 1921, shall be considered experimental, and may be replaced, within the total tonnage limit prescribed in Article VII, without regard to its age.

Article IX

No aircraft carrier exceeding 27,000 tons (27,432 metric tons) standard displacement shall be acquired by, or constructed by, for or within the jurisdiction of, any of the Contracting Powers.

However, any of the Contracting Powers may, provided that its total tonnage allowance of aircraft carriers is not thereby exceeded, build not more than two aircraft carriers, each of a tonnage of not more than 33,000 tons (33,528 metric tons) standard displacement, and in order to effect economy any of the Contracting Powers may use for this purpose any two of their ships, whether constructed or in course of construction, which would otherwise be scrapped under the provisions of Article II. The armament of any aircraft carriers exceeding 27,000 tons (27,432 metric tons) standard displacement shall be in accordance with the requirements of Article X, except that the total number of guns to be carried in case any of such guns be of a calibre exceeding 6 inches (152 millimetres), except anti-aircraft guns and guns not exceeding 5 inches (127 millimetres), shall not exceed eight.

Article X

No aircraft carrier of any of the Contracting Powers shall carry a gun with a calibre in excess of 8 inches (203 millimetres). Without prejudice to the provisions of Article IX, if the armament carried includes guns exceeding 6 inches (152 millimetres) in calibre the total number of guns carried, except anti-aircraft guns and guns not exceeding 5 inches (127 millimetres), shall not exceed ten. If alternatively the armament contains no guns exceeding 6 inches (152 millimetres) in calibre, the number of guns is not limited. In either case the number of anti-aircraft guns and of guns not exceeding 5 inches (127 millimetres) is not limited.

Article XI

No vessel of war exceeding 10,000 tons (10,160 metric tons) standard displacement, other than a capital ship or aircraft carrier, shall be acquired by, or constructed by, for, or within the jurisdiction of, any of the Contracting Powers. Vessels not specifically built as fighting ships nor taken in time of peace under government control for fighting purposes, which are employed on fleet duties or as troop transports or in some other way for the purpose of assisting in the prosecution of hostilities otherwise than as fighting ships, shall not be within the limitations of this Article.

Article XII

No vessel of war of any of the Contracting Powers, hereafter laid down, other than a capital ship, shall carry a gun with a calibre in excess of 8 inches (203 millimetres). . . .

Article XIX

The United States, the British Empire and Japan agree that the *status quo* at the time of the signing of the present Treaty, with regard to fortifications and naval bases, shall be maintained in their respective territories and possessions specified hereunder:

(1) The insular possessions which the United States now holds or may hereafter acquire in the Pacific Ocean, except (a) those adjacent to the coast of the United States, Alaska and the Panama Canal Zone, not including the Aleutian Islands, and (b) the Hawaiian Islands;

(2) Hongkong and the insular possessions which the British Empire now holds or may hereafter acquire in the Pacific Ocean, east of the meridian of 110° east longitude, except (a) those adjacent to the coast of Canada, (b) the Commonwealth of Australia and its Territories, and (c) New Zealand;

(3) The following insular territories and possessions of Japan in the Pacific Ocean, to wit: the Kurile Islands, the Bonin Islands, Amami-Oshima, the Loochoo Islands, Formosa and the Pescadores, and any insular territories or possessions in the Pacific Ocean which Japan may hereafter acquire.

The maintenance of the *status quo* under the foregoing provisions implies that no new fortifications or naval bases shall be established in the territories and possessions specified; that no measures shall be taken to increase the existing naval facilities for the repair and maintenance of naval forces, and that no increase shall be made in the coast defences of the territories and possessions above specified. This restriction, however, does not preclude such repair and replacement of worn-out weapons and equipment as is customary in naval and military establishments in time of peace. . . .

Article XXIII

The present Treaty shall remain in force until December 31st, 1936, and in case none of the Contracting Powers shall have given notice two years before that date of its intention to terminate the Treaty, it shall continue in force until the expiration of two years from the date on which notice of termination shall be given by one of the Contracting Powers, whereupon the Treaty shall terminate as regards all the Contracting Powers. . . .

C. The Nine-Power Treaty

A PRECEDING chapter has mentioned that the secret protocol of the Lansing-Ishii agreement appeared without identification in the Nine-Power Treaty of Washington of February 6, 1922, but the more important result of that treaty was that it bound the signatories—the five naval powers together with China and the European small powers having territorial or economic interests in China (Belgium, Portugal, and the Netherlands)—to observe the open door in China. The first open door note had never really gained adherence of the powers, and the second was a circular stating American policy that required no promises by anyone.

Article I. The Contracting Powers, other than China, agree:

(1) To respect the sovereignty, the independence, and the territorial and administrative integrity of China;

(2) To provide the fullest and most unembarrassed opportunity to China to develop and maintain for herself an effective and stable government;

(3) To use their influence for the purpose of effectually establishing and maintaining the principle of equal opportunity for the commerce and industry of all nations throughout the territory of China;

(4) To refrain from taking advantage of conditions in China in order to seek special rights or privileges which would abridge the

SOURCE: Foreign Relations . . . : 1922, I, pp. 278–80.

rights of subjects or citizens of friendly States, and from countenancing action inimical to the security of such States.

Article II. The Contracting Powers agree not to enter into any treaty, agreement, arrangement, or understanding, either with one another, or, individually or collectively, with any Power or Powers, which would infringe or impair the principles stated in Article I.

Article III. With a view to applying more effectually the principles of the Open Door or equality of opportunity in China for the trade and industry of all nations, the Contracting Powers, other than China, agree that they will not seek, nor support their respective nationals in seeking—

(a) any arrangement which might purport to establish in favour of their interests any general superiority of rights with respect to commercial or economic development in any designated region of China;

(b) any such monopoly or preference as would deprive the nationals of any other Power of the right of undertaking any legitimate trade or industry in China, or of participating with the Chinese Government, or with any local authority, in any category of public enterprise, or which by reason of its scope, duration or geographical extent is calculated to frustrate the practical application of the principle of equal opportunity.

It is understood that the foregoing stipulations of this Article are not to be so construed as to prohibit the acquisition of such properties or rights as may be necessary to the conduct of a particular commercial, industrial, or financial undertaking or to the encouragement of invention and research.

China undertakes to be guided by the principles stated in the foregoing stipulations of this Article in dealing with applications for economic rights and privileges from Governments and nationals of all foreign countries, whether parties to the present Treaty or not.

Article IV. The Contracting Powers agree not to support any agreements by their respective nationals with each other designed to create Spheres of Influence or to provide for the enjoyment of mutually exclusive opportunities in designated parts of Chinese territory.

Article V. China agrees that, throughout the whole of the railways in China, she will not exercise or permit unfair discrimination of any kind. In particular there shall be no discrimination whatever, direct or indirect, in respect of charges or of facilities on the ground of the nationality of passengers or the countries from which or to which they are proceeding, or the origin or ownership of goods or the country from which or to which they are consigned, or the nationality or ownership of the ship or other means of conveying such passengers or goods before or after their transport on the Chinese Railways.

The Contracting Powers, other than China, assume a corresponding obligation in respect of any of the aforesaid railways over which they or their nationals are in a position to exercise any control in virtue of any concession, special agreement or otherwise.

Article VI. The Contracting Powers, other than China, agree fully to respect China's rights as a neutral in time of war to which China is not a party; and China declares that when she is a neutral she will observe the obligations of neutrality.

Article VII. The Contracting Powers agree that, whenever a situation arises which in the opinion of any one of them involves the application of the stipulations of the present Treaty, and renders desirable discussion of such application, there shall be full and frank communication between the Contracting Powers concerned.

28. The World Court

IF AN American diplomat of the decade once described the World Court as an issue of extraordinary unimportance, during the years after the World War more attention focused on it, in particular on what might happen if the United States joined it, than almost any other single issue of American foreign relations. In that respect, then, there is value in looking at the Senate debate of January 27, 1926, over American membership in the court, to see the pride and prejudice, the intense extrapolation that accompanied any discussion of this petty institution of the League of Nations. It is of interest that after the Second World War the United States by joining the United Nations automatically joined the UN court. There seems to have been no serious result.

SOURCE: *Congressional Record,* LXVII (1924), pp. 2795–96, 2810–11, 2813–15, 2817–20, 2824–25.

. . . Mr. MOSES. Mr. President, I ask that the question which was pending at the moment of recess yesterday may be stated.

The VICE PRESIDENT. The clerk will read.

The CHIEF CLERK. On page 3, after line 10, the Senator from New Hampshire [Mr. MOSES] moves to insert:

> 6. That the adherence of the United States to the statute of the World Court is conditioned upon the understanding and agreement that the judgments, decrees, and/or advisory opinions of the court shall not be enforced by war under any name or in any form whatever.

Mr. MOSES. . . . Thousands of people who have addressed Senators by letter, by telegram, or by petition, urging the adherence of the United States to the League of Nations court, have equally stressed the point of their belief that the court is an agency to prevent war.

I hold, Mr. President, that those Senators who expressed these opinions and that those citizens who have addressed us in these terms are wholly misguided. It has been my opinion from the first that as we trace the lineage of the protocol back to its origin in the covenant of the League of Nations we shall be sure to find the court as an essential element in the mechanism of the League of Nations and that the League of Nations is designed as a military alliance and in no sense whatever as a peace machine. . . .

Mr. President, I have offered the reservation now pending with the view to making the court, into which I suppose we soon shall enter, a real instrument of peace to the extent at least that it shall not be made an instrument of war. I want all Senators who are intending to vote to adhere to the court, because they believe, or have been led to believe, that in some fashion it is an instrument for the outlawry of war, and I want all the people of the country who approach the subject from that viewpoint to understand that by the adoption of the reservation which I have presented and which is now pending, we shall make it certain that the court can not in any case be made use of as an excuse or as an instrument for the bringing on of war . . .

. . . Mr. BORAH. . . . let us get back to the real proposition which we are discussing, and that is whether we are going to rely on the power of public opinion to enforce the judgments of the court or whether we are simply going to take the judgment of the court and resort to war, precisely as we are doing now. What is the difference between a war which is carried on prior to the judgment and a war which is carried on after the judgment is rendered? It is war, and we are asked to enter into a combination which, according to their argument as they now produce it, is to be carried on and executed through the members, to wit, that of war.

I say, as was said in the debates in the convention in 1787, that the time has come when we must rely upon the power of public opinion. As John Marshall said in the debates in 1787 for the ratification of the Constitution, What are courts for if not to avoid conflicts and the employment of war for the purpose of executing our rights? Those men were willing to rely upon the power of public opinion; and had they not been willing to do so, in my opinion this blessed American Union would have disappeared in the first 20 years of its existence. It was their great wisdom and sublime faith which enabled them to avoid that pitfall. They took the risk and saved the Republic.

. . . Of course, all nations profess peace and sanction peace; and as soon as this is out of the way, heavy bills for the purpose of enlarging the Army and enlarging the Navy, probably, in the name of peace, will be presented to us. I have no doubt. I am not challenging the sincerity of any Senator who says he is in favor of peace, or who believes in peace, and still votes for a large Army and a large Navy for the sake of peace, but we believe we can accomplish it in different ways, that is all. Some believe that we rely too much upon force. Others believe we rely too little upon force, and that we have too small an Army and too small a Navy. I believe that we rely entirely too little upon the power of public opinion. I do not agree with those who think that public opinion can not operate upon these questions and can not effectuate great purposes in regard to these matters. I believe that the power of public opinion is infinitely stronger, nine times out of ten, for the purpose of accomplishing peace, than either an army or a navy. Peace is never accomplished, except temporarily, unless the matter is settled right, and it is seldom settled right when it is settled by sheer force.

Mr. WALSH. Mr. President, I can not believe that if this reservation now pending is understood by this body, it can possibly have its approval.

It is agreed upon all hands, it has been repeatedly asserted here upon the floor, and as far as I know never disputed, that there is no provision in the statute appended to the protocol providing for the enforcement of any judgment or any opinion the court may render. If any provision is found for the enforcement of any judgment this court may render, it must be found in some other instrument. The other instrument suggested is the covenant of the League of Nations. Of course, then, the reservation now offered is a proposal to amend and revise the covenant of the League of Nations. I wonder who is prepared to undertake that task here at this time? . . . Would the Senator like to propose a reservation that the United States accept compulsory jurisdiction?

Mr. BORAH. I will answer that. Mr. President, if we could secure a code of international law to which the United States should have agreed I would unhesitatingly vote that we become a member of a court which had compulsory jurisdiction over controversies arising under such international law. It is the only court that is worthy of the name.

Mr. WALSH. How long does the Senator think it would take to get a complete codification of international law?

Mr. BORAH. I do not know how long it would take, but the Senator and his class of advocates of peace, have been trying for 2,000 years to get peace by this scheme of employing force, and where are we to-day? I think we could get a code of international law inside of 2,000 years. . . .

Mr. SHORTRIDGE. Mr. President, may I ask the Senator a question?

The VICE PRESIDENT. Does the Senator from Idaho yield to the Senator from California?

Mr. BORAH. I do.

Mr. SHORTRIDGE. Does the Senator from Idaho think that all wars are unrighteous and wicked?

Mr. BORAH. On one side they are. [Laughter.]

Mr. SHORTRIDGE. If that be the answer, does the Senator think that all wars in the past have been unrighteous? Is there not such a thing as a righteous war by the aggressor?

Mr. BORAH. Will the Senator name one?

Mr. SHORTRIDGE. The Revolutionary War.

Mr. BORAH. Well, yes; that was righteous on our side, but does the Senator think it was on the side of Great Britain?

Mr. SHORTRIDGE. I think it was righteous on our side.

Mr. BORAH. Exactly; but does the Senator think it was righteous on the side of Great Britain?

Mr. SHORTRIDGE. It was not.

Mr. BORAH. No. [Laughter.]

Mr. REED of Missouri. Mr. President, I wish to take about five minutes in discussing this particular question, and I want to say by way of parenthesis that my ears have been shocked more this afternoon than in my entire life. I have heard the lips that have been singing nothing but peace on earth and good will to men; that have told us the League of Nations would produce peace, and that if it did not the court certainly would; that there would be no more war; that the lion and the lamb would lie down together—and each of those gentlemen came out leading his particular lamb [laughter]—I have heard gentlemen who have been proclaiming on the platform and in this Chamber the doctrine that all the United States needed to do to stop war and devastation was to take the moral leadership of the world and that peace would result talk of nothing but war, become the advocates of war, and assert its necessity and its justice upon this floor for the last two hours. So I think it is about time to pull the mask of hypocrisy from the face of pretenders and to get down to the real merits of this question.

It has been admitted here this afternoon that the League of Nations is a military compact. It has been admitted that the League of Nations is a contract between the various nations of the earth belonging to it by which they do agree to apply force and to make war, and that that contract is of such binding force and of such specific nature in favor of war that if we ask the members of the league to sign a contract that they will not make war to enforce the decisions of the court we thereby run counter to the contract already signed.

So I want it understood now that all of these advocates of peace are now standing here the advocates of war, and of its necessity, and of its righteousness; and I want another thing understood, and that is that the compact of the League of Nations was a compact so much for war that the respective parties to that compact can not sign an agreement not to make war without violating the agreement which they made when they signed the League of Nations covenant.

When we understand that we begin to understand that the pretense that this court will end war, the pretense that this court will usher in the millennium, the pretense that this court will bring peace and eternal good will, is all froth and fustian, and that it is a bunco game that is being played on the American Republic.

We now have arrived at the statement, I repeat, that the League of Nations is a military compact for the purpose of making war, and so much a compact of that kind that we can not ask the members to sign an agreement not to go to war without amending this bloody document that has been proclaimed the charter of peace and good will. It is an admission of what I have contended from the first—that the League of Nations is nothing and never was anything but a combination of 55 nations at the present time, or perhaps 57, that they will make war, a great trust of power which somebody will control or some combination of the representatives of great nations will control, and that that power exists to-day with its armies and its navies. . . .

Mr. President, this court is the vermiform appendix of the League of Nations. The vitality it has comes from the League of Nations. The little blood that circulates through it comes from the body of the League of Nations. . . .

Mr. FERNALD. That is a matter of law. The Senator understands that. I am not discussing the technicalities of law. But I say that the United States of America, with 110,000,000 of the best people on the face of God's earth, ought to have, if we are going to discuss these measures in a court of justice, the same representation numerically, based on numerical strength, that any possession of Great Britain has. Of course, we can not change this now. Lloyd-George, for years and years, has been arranging for our coming into the World Court. They have 7 votes to our 1.

My genial friend from New York, think of your great State of New York, with 10,400,000 people, the great Empire State—and I speak of it in the right way, because it is an empire State, because it is the center of the finances of the world; it has a great harbor, a great port, which is one of the questions proposed to be taken up by the World Court—ports, waterways, and naturalization. So, of course, the port of New York might become a matter for consideration by the World Court. But think of the State of New York, with more than 10,000,000 people, representing one forty-eighth as much power or right numerically as the little country of Liberia! Think of a representative of the United States, with 48 States, going to this great temple of justice with one forty-eighth the power or right that Siam has!

Think of Pennsylvania, the State of my genial friend [Mr. PEP-PER], with 8,300,000 people, the finest people on God's earth, with its institutions of learning, with its great manufacturing establishments, with all that it possesses, having but one forty-eighth the numerical strength in this court that the little country of Liberia has! Think of the representative of the United States walking up to this great assembly of justice side by side with a little colored gentleman and depositing his vote! Think of the States of Illinois, Ohio, and Texas, with 13,000,000 people, as fine as there are in the whole Nation, having a representation in this court of one forty-eighth as many as a little country of 1,000,000 people!

Mr. BRUCE. Mr. President—

The VICE PRESIDENT. Does the Senator from Maine yield to the Senator from Maryland?

Mr. FERNALD. I yield.

Mr. BRUCE. I will ask the Senator from Maine whether there is anything more anomalous in that than in the fact that the little State of Rhode Island and the little State of Delaware have as many Senators in this body as have the great States of New York and Pennsylvania?

Mr. FERNALD. My dear Senator, that is very proper, for that was forecast when the Constitution of the United States was framed. That was one of the best things that was adopted in our Constitution, so that the little States should have the same representation as have the big States.

Mr. BRUCE. If that is such a good thing, should we not follow that example, and the sooner the better?

Mr. FERNALD. It is quite a different thing when we go in with 110,000,000 people as against 1,600,000,000 foreigners. . . .

Mr. BLEASE. Mr. President, I had not intended to have anything further to say about this matter, but it has been called to my attention that there is no provision in the pending resolution for each State of this Union to have a vote in the election of judges. I offered a reservation to that effect, and I can not see why it should not be adopted. I notice that Haiti has a voice in the election of the judges. I call the attention of Senators from the South, while they are voting on this reservation, to the fact that they are voting for a court where we are to sit side by side with a full-blooded "nigger" [laughter], who has as much right as we have in the election of the judges of this court. I ask them if they realize the fact that there may be and very probably will be a representative of Haiti as a judge on this court, so that the southern Senators are voting to throw the destinies of southern women and southern men into the lap of a black man? Haiti has joined the League of Nations and has a representative in the assembly of the league who will vote for the judges of the court.

Mr. REED of Missouri. So has Liberia. . . .

Mr. BLEASE. . . . Something has been said to-day about the Catholics. I am not a Catholic, and I am not here to defend the Catholics or the Catholic religion. They need no defense. But they are a great denomination, and they are a great people, and they have done a great deal for this country. If it had not been for the Catholics, and if it were not for the Catholics in the days to come, the Democratic Party never would have had and never will have a President of the United States.

Then these Ku-Klux members. I do not belong to their organization either, but I know some parts of this country where they have done good. I know it to be a fact. While personally I am not a member of their organization, I have not any special objection to what they do or what they want to do. Some people have slurred them to-day. I am no apologist for them. They need none. But they can vote, and I imagine that when the Catholics go to the ballot box and the Ku-Klux members go to the ballot box they will stop and remember some things that have been said, and they will remember some criticisms that have been made, and they will stop and consider the fact that when they protested their protests were disregarded. . . .

One other point on this league business. Here is an article that appeared in yesterday's Washington Post. This is in the newspapers or I would not read it:

GIRL IN PAJAMAS HALTS PROCEDURE OF COURT—TRIAL AFTER AUTO COLLISION IS POSTPONED WHEN JUDGE VIEWS ATTIRE—END OF TWO-DAY PARTY

A reported two-day "endurance party" participated in by Miss Benita Kennison, 19 years old, of Toledo, Ohio, ended abruptly in the snowstorm yesterday afternoon when the automobile which she was driving crashed against a lamp-post at Eleventh and S Streets NW.

When arraigned in police court late yesterday afternoon before Judge George H. Macdonald on charges of driving while drunk and failing to show an operator's permit, she stopped the wheels of justice when it was discovered she was clad in a flaming red bathing suit, a pair of silk pajamas, high-heeled silver evening slippers, and silver hose to match.

Judge Macdonald took one look and decided to postpone her trial until this morning, in the meantime ordering that she be taken care of at the house of detention.

Miss Kennison was arrested after the crash by Policemen Heide and Schultz, members of Captain Burlingame's "flying squadron," after a chase of several blocks. . . .

Heide said his suspicions were aroused when the machine driven by her passed him on S Street at a fast rate of speed. The girl told police she crashed into the lamp-post when she tried to avert striking the police car that had caught up with her.

Miss Kennison, according to the story told police, came from Toledo three days ago to visit her sister, Miss Velma Kennison, 21 years old, at 1465 Columbia Road NW. Her sister is declared to have tendered her a "welcome party" that police say lasted until the crash yesterday.

Here is the part I want especially to call your attention to:

Her sister is alleged to have told police that they had been celebrating on "embassy refreshments."

There you are, Mr. President. There is part of your vote. There is part of your league court. In your own country, right under your nose, right under your own eyes, right in your own face, almost within calling distance of the White House of this Nation, you are allowing foreigners to violate the law day by day. You are letting them transport whisky day by day. You are letting them use it if they see fit to use it in their homes day by day. There is nobody to protest against it. There is nobody to stop it; and yet we are standing here to-night saying that we are willing to go into a court, into an alliance with people who are represented in this country by that class of people, representing people whom you say to the American people you should go in with; you should have an alliance with them; you would let them say whether Japs shall come over into California or not; you are saying that if there should be any question in the United States about any place or boundary of the United States, we should allow these people to settle the dispute as to where that boundary line shall be. You say to these people: "Come on." . . .

Mr. JOHNSON. . . . Some Senator said to-day that the President was to be commended for finally altering the traditional policy of the United States. Maybe he is, and maybe we are wrong, these few who have kept the faith in our position; but the Senator who made the statement said what was exactly accurate: The traditional policy of the United States is about to be altered now—

altered by the great Republican Party, God help it! Altered by men upon this side who stood their ground in days gone by, perhaps, in behalf of that traditional policy; but altered it is about to be, and we are to go upon this uncharted sea, and we are to become a part of the European system finally.

Those of us who fought the fight will fight just as hard in the future, my friends, for our common country and its preservation. But before this vote is taken I want no man to labor under any delusion, none to forget the days of March, 1920, and every man on the Republican side hereafter to know just what his vote means not only to the United States of America but to the Republican Party. . . .

By vote of 76 to 17, the Senate then consented to adherence of the United States to the protocol of the World Court, with the following reservations:

1. That such adherence shall not be taken to involve any legal relation on the part of the United States to the League of Nations or the assumption of any obligations by the United States under the treaty of Versailles.

2. That the United States shall be permitted to participate, through representatives designated for the purpose and upon an equality with the other states, members, respectively, of the Council and Assembly of the League of Nations, in any and all proceedings of either the council or the assembly for the election of judges or deputy judges of the Permanent Court of International Justice or for the filling of vacancies.

3. That the United States will pay a fair share of the expenses of the court as determined and appropriated from time to time by the Congress of the United States.

4. That the United States may at any time withdraw its adherence to the said protocol and that the statute for the Permanent Court of International Justice adjoined to the protocol shall not be amended without the consent of the United States.

5. That the court shall not render any advisory opinion except publicly after due notice to all states adhering to the court and to all interested states and after public hearing or opportunity for hearing given to any state concerned; nor shall it, without the consent of the United States, entertain any request for an advisory

opinion touching any dispute or question in which the United States has or claims an interest.

The signature of the United States to the said protocol shall not be affixed until the powers signatory to such protocol shall have indicated, through an exchange of notes, their acceptance of the foregoing reservations and understandings as a part and a condition of adherence by the United States to the said protocol.

Resolved further, As a part of this act of ratification that the United States approve the protocol and statute hereinabove mentioned, with the understanding that recourse to the Permanent Court of International Justice for the settlement of differences between the United States and any other state or states can be had only by agreement thereto through general or special treaties concluded between the parties in dispute; and

Resolved further, That adherence to the said protocol and statute hereby approved shall not be so construed as to require the United States to depart from its traditional policy of not intruding upon, interfering with, or entangling itself in the political questions of policy or internal administration of any foreign state; nor shall adherence to the said protocol and statute be construed to imply a relinquishment by the United States of its traditional attitude toward purely American questions.

These qualifications proved sufficient to prevent adherence of the United States to the protocol. Elihu Root went to Europe in 1929 to seek a compromise with the member states of the World Court, and this compromise languished in the Senate until 1935 when it failed.

29. The Kellogg-Briand Pact

A. Renunciation of War

As the years went by and the Washington Naval Conference receded from public memory, and the battle over the World Court turned into obscurantism, many people in the United States began to think that their government should do something for world peace, although

Source: Foreign Relations of the United States: 1927 (3 vols., Washington, D.C., 1942), II, pp. 611–13.

clearly the Republican administrations of the 1920s would not touch the League of Nations and, otherwise, it was rather difficult to know what the United States should do. By organization, and pressure, a Chicago corporation lawyer named Salmon O. Levinson by this time had begun to din into the public mind the notion that it would be a good move for peace to outlaw war. Levinson enlisted a group of individuals, including Senator Borah and the philosopher John Dewey (if people would not think of war, Dewey said, there would be no war), and in 1926–27 the forces of the "outlawrists"—Levinson had coined the word "outlawry"—were joined by the president of the Carnegie Endowment for International Peace, President Nicholas Murray Butler of Columbia University, who had hit upon a somewhat similar phrase of his own, renunciation of war as an instrument of national policy. Butler, one should add, had little regard for Levinson, and there was not an open alliance, but the two ideas and their champions looked in the same direction. At this juncture, early in 1927, the foreign minister of France learned from President Butler's assistant in the Carnegie Endowment, Professor James T. Shotwell of Columbia, that it might be a good proposal for France and the United States mutually to renounce war in their relations, the more so because the tenth anniversary of American entrance into the World War, April 6, 1927, was approaching. Shotwell suggested that Briand might use the occasion. Shotwell wrote up a newspaper "message to the American people" which Briand duly released for the papers of April 6th.

The discussions over disarmament . . . have served at least to make clear, politically, the common inspiration and identity of aims which exist between France and the United States. . . . If there were any need between these two great democracies to testify more convincingly in favor of peace and to present to the peoples a more solemn example, France would be ready publicly to subscribe, with the United States, to any mutual engagement tending, as between those two countries, to "outlaw war," to use an American expression. The renunciation of war as an instrument of national policy is a conception already familiar to the signatories of the Covenant of the League of Nations and of the Treaties of Locarno. Any engagement subscribed to in the same spirit by the United States with another nation such as France would greatly contribute in the eyes of the world to broaden and strengthen the foundation upon which the international policy of peace is being raised. Thus two great friendly nations, equally devoted to the cause of peace, would give the world the best illustrations of this truth, that the accomplishment most immediately to be attained is not so much disarmament as the practice of peace. . . .

FOLLOWING *Charles A. Lindbergh's epochal transatlantic flight from New York to Paris, which at least momentarily strengthened the ties of Franco-American friendship, Briand proposed a treaty dated June 20, 1927.*

Article 1. The high contracting power solemnly declare in the name of the French people and the people of the United States of America that they condemn recourse to war and renounce it, respectively, as an instrument of their national policy towards each other.

Article 2. The settlement or the solution af all disputes or conflicts of whatever nature or of whatever origin they may be which may arise between France and the United States of America shall never be sought by either side except by pacific means.

B. THE PACT OF PARIS

THE CHIEF *of the division of Western European affairs of the Department of State, J. Theodore Marriner, prepared a memorandum on Briand's proposal, dated June 24, 1927, which set the course of the Department away from the French bilateral proposition, toward what became the great multilateral Pact of Paris of August, 1928.*

The text of Mr. Briand's proposals for a Treaty . . . should be carefully considered from every point of view.

Mr. Briand's insistence that negotiations should begin at once without awaiting the arrival in this country of M. Claudel [the French ambassador] would seem to indicate that he was most anxious to keep this topic in the public eye most prominently during the meeting of the Naval Conference at Geneva [a three-power conference which failed] in order to draw attention away from the fact that France is not there represented in a constructive step towards World Peace.

The vague wording and lack of precision in the draft seems also intended to give the effect of a kind of perpetual alliance between the United States and France, which would certainly serve to disturb the other great European Powers,—England, Germany and Italy. This would be particularly true as it would make the neutral position of the United States during any European war in which

SOURCE: *Foreign Relations . . . . : 1927*, II, p. 616.
SOURCE: *Foreign Relations . . . . : 1927*, II, pp. 617–18.

France might be engaged extremely difficult, since France might deem it necessary to infringe upon our rights as a neutral under this guaranty of non-aggression. A further point which Mr. Briand has not touched on is the question of France's obligations under the Covenant of the League of Nations to aid the League in the punishment of an aggressor state. It might likewise be used internally in France to postpone the ratification of the Debt Settlement and to create a feeling that payment was unnecessary [the Mellon-Béranger proposal to refund France's war debt to the United States].

In order to avoid this interpretation, it would be incumbent on the United States at once to offer a treaty in the same terms to England and Japan, more especially as we are negotiating with them at the present moment [at the Geneva Naval Conference] and could hardly wish them to feel that we were entering into an alliance at the same time with another Power.

Certainly a single treaty of this nature, and, according to press despatches, France desires that it be an absolutely unique instrument, would raise the question of an alliance with a country outside the American hemisphere. A series of such agreements, unless it were absolutely world wide, would raise the same objections. All this tends to indicate that it would be best to keep the subject in abeyance at least until the conclusion of some agreement in Geneva. However, when the time comes actually to negotiate, it would seem that the only answer to the French proposition would be that, as far as our relations with France were concerned, adequate guarantees were contained in the Bryan Treaty, and that if any step further than this were required, it should be in the form of a universal undertaking not to resort to war, to which the United States would at any time be most happy to become a party. Before such a time, treaties of the nature which France suggests become practically negative military alliances. . . .

C. PEACE WITH RESERVATIONS

SECRETARY of State Frank B. Kellogg sat on Briand's proposal until December, 1927, when public pressure had mounted to such a height that it appeared as if Kellogg would have to do something to meet it. The result was a proposal to Briand that all the nations of the world

SOURCE: Foreign Relations of the United States: 1928 (3 vols., Washington, D.C., 1942–43), I, p. 68.

sign a treaty not to go to war. The trick had been turned, as one of Kellogg's closest associates put the situation; there was really a problem about such a general treaty, as it would have deranged all of Briand's alliances with the anti-German nations of Europe, alliances that rested on the possibility of war. Briand tried to squirm out of the new proposition—to no avail because Kellogg pressed him unmercifully. At last the American Secretary of State began to admit the need for reservations to any multilateral peace treaty. The introduction of these caveats—which, incidentally, were not made formal reservations but had the same effect (for in international law the correspondence of the parties qualifies the result)—made it possible for the French government to join what now had become an American démarche. Kellogg reserved questions of self-defense. The British government, however, cut the largest hole in the antiwar pledge. Foreign Secretary Sir Austen Chamberlain wrote Kellogg on May 19, 1928.

. . . I should remind Your Excellency that there are certain regions of the world the welfare and integrity of which constitute the special and vital interest for our peace and safety. His Majesty's Government had been at pains to make it clear in the past that interference with these regions cannot be suffered. Their protection against attack is to the British Empire a measure of self-defense. It must be clearly understood that His Majesty's Government in Great Britain accept the new treaty upon the distinct understanding that it does not prejudice their freedom of action in this respect.

KELLOGG went to Paris for a ceremony of signature of the Kellogg-Briand Pact, on August 27, 1928. The major powers signed at that time, and other nations adhered, until altogether most of the nations of the world had signed or adhered.

ARTICLE I
The High Contracting Parties solemnly declare in the names of their respective peoples that they condemn recourse to war for the solution of international controversies, and renounce it as an instrument of national policy in their relations with one another.

ARTICLE II
The High Contracting Parties agree that the settlement or solution of all disputes or conflicts of whatever nature or of whatever origin they may be, which may arise among them, shall never be sought except by pacific means.

SOURCE: Foreign Relations . . . . : 1928, I, p. 155.

X

The Great Depression

When the Great Depression began in 1929 the bloom came off the Golden Twenties, and the world entered a period of stark economic want. For a few years there was merely a sort of politics of survival, and then, beginning in 1933, a new regime in Germany lent urgency to the great problems of peace and war. Already, in 1931–33, the American government under President Herbert Hoover and his doughty Secretary of State, Henry L. Stimson, had spoken out against aggression in the Far East, the attack of Japan upon Chinese Manchuria. The European nations did not take large notice of this affair until Adolf Hitler's rise to power worried them into measures in support of peace. By that time the United States under President Franklin D. Roosevelt had become isolationist, more so than in the memory of men then living. The American government in the crucial period 1935–37, when the politics of Europe were turning downward with a vengeance, proclaimed its neutrality in unmistakable fashion.

30. Words of Warning

A. THE STIMSON DOCTRINE

THE DEPRESSION was nearly two years old when on September 18, 1931, the Japanese army in Manchuria, the 10,000 troops of the so-called Kwantung Army, moved against the ill-led hordes of the Chinese warlord Chang Hsueh-liang, who had allied with the Nationalist leader in Nanking, Chiang Kai-shek. There followed an uncertain period of a few months when it seemed as if the Japanese troops might cease their forward movements, presumably coming under control of the civil government in Tokyo. Nothing persuaded them to stop, including the prospect of an investigation by the League of Nations—the Lytton Commission was appointed in December, 1931, and was to spend most of the following year in the Far East before its report appeared in the autumn of 1932. When Japanese troops moved into the town of Chinchow in Manchuria, it became evident to Secretary Stimson that Japanese appetite had improved with eating. The result was the Stimson Doctrine of January 7, 1932.

. . . With the recent military operations about Chinchow, the last remaining administrative authority of the Government of the Chinese Republic in South Manchuria, as it existed prior to September 18th, 1931, has been destroyed. The American Government continues confident that the work of the neutral commission recently authorized by the Council of the League of Nations will facilitate an ultimate solution of the difficulties now existing between China and Japan. But in view of the present situation and of its own rights and obligations therein, the American Government deems it to be its duty to notify both the Imperial Japanese Government and the Government of the Chinese Republic that it cannot admit the legality of any situation de facto nor does it intend to recognize any treaty or agreement entered into between those Governments, or agents thereof, which may impair the treaty rights of the United States or its citizens in China, including those which relate to the sovereignty, the independence, or the territorial and administrative integrity of the Republic of China, or to the international policy relative to China, commonly known as

SOURCE: Foreign Relations of the United States: Japan, 1931–1941 (2 vols., Washington, D.C., 1943), I, p. 76.

the open door policy; and that it does not intend to recognize any situation, treaty or agreement which may be brought about by means contrary to the covenants and obligations of the Pact of Paris of August 27, 1928, to which Treaty both China and Japan, as well as the United States, are parties. . . .

B. Enforcing the Nine-Power Treaty

THE JAPANESE *navy at the end of January, 1932, launched a large-scale attack upon the Chinese portions of the city of Shanghai. This further instance of aggression, coupled with lack of enthusiasm of the European powers for the Stimson Doctrine, led the Secretary of State into a general statement of American policy toward the Far Eastern crisis. He put it in the form of a public letter dated February 23, 1932, to the chairman of the Foreign Relations Committee, Senator Borah, because that way he would not get any formal replies from Europe, perhaps replies of hostility.*

. . . You have asked my opinion whether, as has been sometimes recently suggested, present conditions in China have in any way indicated that the so-called Nine Power Treaty has become inapplicable or ineffective or rightly in need of modification, and if so, what I considered should be the policy of this Government.

This Treaty, as you of course know, forms the legal basis upon which now rests the "Open Door" policy towards China. That policy, enunciated by John Hay in 1899, brought to an end the struggle among various powers for so-called spheres of interest in China which was threatening the dismemberment of that empire. To accomplish this Mr. Hay invoked two principles (1) equality of commercial opportunity among all nations in dealing with China, and (2) as necessary to that equality the preservation of China's territorial and administrative integrity. These principles were not new in the foreign policy of America. They had been the principles upon which it rested in its dealings with other nations for many years. In the case of China they were invoked to save a situation which not only threatened the future development and sovereignty of that great Asiatic people, but also threatened to create dangerous and constantly increasing rivalries between the other nations of the world. War had already taken place between Japan and China.

SOURCE: *Foreign Relations . . . : 1931–1941, I, pp. 83–87.*

At the close of that war three other nations intervened to prevent Japan from obtaining some of the results of that war claimed by her. Other nations sought and had obtained spheres of interest. Partly as a result of these actions a serious uprising had broken out in China which endangered the legations of all of the powers at Peking. While the attack on those legations was in progress, Mr. Hay made an announcement in respect to this policy as the principle upon which the powers should act in the settlement of the rebellion. . . . He was successful in obtaining the assent of the other powers to the policy thus announced.

In taking these steps Mr. Hay acted with the cordial support of the British Government. In responding to Mr. Hay's announcement . . . Lord Salisbury, the British Prime Minister expressed himself "most emphatically as concurring in the policy of the United States."

For twenty years thereafter the Open Door policy rested upon the informal commitments thus made by the various powers. But in the winter of 1921 to 1922, at a conference participated in by all of the principal powers which had interests in the Pacific, the policy was crystallized into the so-called Nine Power Treaty, which gave definition and precision to the principles upon which the policy rested. . . .

This Treaty thus represents a carefully developed and matured international policy intended, on the one hand, to assure to all of the contracting parties their rights and interests in and with regard to China, and on the other hand, to assure to the people of China the fullest opportunity to develop without molestation their sovereignty and independence according to the modern and enlightened standards believed to maintain among the peoples of this earth. At the time this Treaty was signed, it was known that China was engaged in an attempt to develop the free institutions of a self-governing republic after her recent revolution from an autocratic form of government; that she would require many years of both economic and political effort to that end; and that her progress would necessarily be slow. The Treaty was thus a covenant of self-denial among the signatory powers in deliberate renunciation of any policy of aggression which might tend to interfere with that development. It was believed—and the whole history of the development of the "Open Door" policy reveals that faith—that only by such a process, under the protection of such an agreement, could the fullest interests not only of China but of all nations which have intercourse with her best be served. . . .

It must be remembered also that this Treaty was one of several treaties and agreements entered into at the Washington Conference by the various powers concerned, all of which were interrelated and interdependent. No one of these treaties can be disregarded without disturbing the general understanding and equilibrium which were intended to be accomplished and effected by the group of agreements arrived at in their entirety. The Washington Conference was essentially a disarmament conference, aimed to promote the possibility of peace in the world not only through the cessation of competition in naval armament but also by the solution of various other disturbing problems which threatened the peace of the world, particularly in the Far East. These problems were all interrelated. The willingness of the American government to surrender its then commanding lead in battleship construction and to leave its positions at Guam and in the Philippines without further fortification, was predicated upon, among other things, the self-denying covenants contained in the Nine Power Treaty, which assured the nations of the world not only of equal opportunity for their Eastern trade but also against the military aggrandizement of any other power at the expense of China. One cannot discuss the possibility of modifying or abrogating those provisions of the Nine Power Treaty without considering at the same time the other promises upon which they were really dependent.

Six years later the policy of self-denial against aggression by a stronger against a weaker power, upon which the Nine Power Treaty had been based, received a powerful reinforcement by the execution by substantially all the nations of the world of the Pact of Paris, the so-called Kellogg-Briand Pact. . . .

On January 7th last, upon the instruction of the President, this Government formally notified Japan and China that it would not recognize any situation, treaty or agreement entered into by those governments in violation of the covenants of these treaties, which affected the rights of our Government or its citizens in China. If a similar decision should be reached and a similar position taken by the other governments of the world, a caveat will be placed upon such action which, we believe, will effectively bar the legality hereafter of any title or right sought to be obtained by pressure or treaty violation, and which, as has been shown by history in the past, will eventually lead to the restoration to China of rights and titles of which she may have been deprived.

In the past our Government, as one of the leading powers on the Pacific Ocean, has rested its policy upon an abiding faith in the future of the people of China and upon the ultimate success in dealing with them of the principles of fair play, patience, and mutual goodwill. We appreciate the immensity of the task which lies before her statesmen in the development of her country and its government. The delays in her progress, the instability of her attempts to secure a responsible government, were foreseen by Messrs. Hay and Hughes and their contemporaries and were the very obstacles which the policy of the Open Door was designed to meet. We concur with those statesmen, representing all the nations in the Washington Conference who decided that China was entitled to the time necessary to accomplish her development. We are prepared to make that our policy for the future. . . .

31. Recognition of a Possible Customer and Friend

A. Repaying a Loan

The reasons for recognition of the Soviet Union were at least two-fold —hope of obtaining a new market for American commerce, at a time when business conditions were appalling; and hope also of support for the American position vis-à-vis Japan in Manchuria. Of these two hopes, the first probably was more important. As for any other aspect or aspects of Russian recognition, there was a feeling that the Republican policy of nonrecognition (admittedly begun by President Wilson's last Secretary of State, Bainbridge Colby, in 1920) had lasted too long and that common sense demanded recognition of a government that was in control of its country. There also was a belief among some Americans that the economic system of the Western world, the capitalist system, had failed beginning in 1929 if not before, and that it might be advisable to conclude ties with the regime of a more promising system. The negotiation of recognition was between Foreign Commissar Maxim Litvinov and President Roosevelt, who seems to have enjoyed treating personally with a real, live Communist. Roosevelt's memorandum of November 15, 1933, initialed by both negotiators, set out one of the bases of recognition.

SOURCE: Foreign Relations of the United States: The Soviet Union, 1933–1939 (Washington, D.C., 1952), pp. 26–27.

Mr. Litvinov, at a meeting with the President, the Acting Secretary of the Treasury, and Mr. [William C.] Bullitt, made a "gentleman's agreement" with the President that over and above all claims of the Soviet Government and its nationals against the Government of the United States and its nationals, the Soviet Government will pay to the Government of the United States on account of the Kerensky debt or otherwise a sum to be not less than $75,000,000 in the form of a percentage above the ordinary rate of interest on a loan to be granted to it by the Government of the United States or its nationals, all other claims of the Government of the United States or its nationals and of the Government of the Union of Soviet Socialist Republics or its nationals to be regarded as eliminated.

The President said that he believed confidently that he could persuade Congress to accept a sum of $150,000,000, but that he feared that Congress would not accept any smaller sum. Mr. Litvinov then said he could not on his own authority accept any such minimum, as his Government had already stated that it considered this sum excessive.

Mr. Litvinov said that he had entire confidence in the fair-mindedness of the President and felt sure that when the President had looked into the facts he would not feel that a sum greater than $75,000,000 was justified. So far as he personally was concerned, and without making any commitment, he would be inclined to advise his Government to accept $100,000,000 if the President should still consider such a sum fair.

Mr. Litvinov agreed to remain in Washington after resumption of relations and to discuss with Mr. Morgenthau and Mr. Bullitt the exact sum between the limits of $75,000,000 and $150,000,000 to be paid by the Soviet Government.

B. Establishing Diplomatic Relations

If nothing came of this effort to adjourn the problem of money owed by the Russian government to the government of the United States (the rule being that a change of regime does not invalidate a debt), it was a worthy try by the President. The uncertain nature of the memorandum showed that Roosevelt perhaps never expected to see the money. With

Source: *Foreign Relations . . . : 1933–1939*, pp. 28–29.

this problem out of the way, recognition followed, in an exchange of notes the next day, November 16. After the exchange there was a further exchange in which Litvinov offered and Roosevelt accepted certain specific Russian promises.

. . . I have the honor to inform you that coincident with the establishment of diplomatic relations between our two Governments it will be the fixed policy of the Government of the Union of Soviet Socialist Republics:

1. To respect scrupulously the indisputable right of the United States to order its own life within its own jurisdiction in its own way and to refrain from interfering in any manner in the internal affairs of the United States, its territories or possessions.

2. To refrain, and to restrain all persons in government service and all organizations of the Government or under its direct or indirect control, including the organizations in receipt of any financial assistance from it, from any act overt or covert liable in any way whatsoever to injure the tranquillity, prosperity, order, or security of the whole or any part of the United States, its territories or possessions, and in particular, from any act tending to incite or encourage armed intervention or any agitation or propaganda having as an aim, the violation of the territorial integrity of the United States, its territories or possessions or the bringing about by force of a change in the political or social order of the whole or any part of the United States, its territories or possessions.

3. Not to permit the formation or residence on its territory of any organization or group—and to prevent the activity on its territory or any organization or group, or of representatives or officials of any organization or group—which makes claim to be the Government or makes attempt upon the territorial integrity of, the United States, its territories or possessions; not to form, subsidize, support or permit on its territory military organizations or groups having the aim of armed struggle against the United States, its territories or possessions and to prevent any recruiting on behalf of such organizations and groups.

4. Not to permit the formation or residence on its territory of any organization or group—and to prevent the activity on its territory of any organization or group, or of representatives or officials of any organization or group—which has as an aim the overthrow or the preparation for the overthrow of, or the bringing about by force

of a change in, the political or social order of the whole or any part
of the United States, its territories or possessions.

On November 16, 1933, there were other exchanges between the
President and Foreign Commissar, notably a promise by Litvinov
that the USSR would accord freedom of religion to Americans in
Russia. An exchange provided for drawing of a consular convention. Another specified the right of American nationals in Russia to
obtain information about the Soviet economic system without
making themselves susceptible to prosecution for economic espio-
nage. Another concerned claims arising out of the Russian revolution. Another waived any Russian claims stemming from the
United States army's Siberian expedition at the end of the World
War.

32. Words of Noninvolvement

A. Withholding Arms from Belligerents

A Senate investigation of the munitions industry during the World
War and after, together with other alleged connections between the
government of the United States and the so-called merchants of death,
reinforced the feeling of the nation in the mid-1930s that whatever events
and actions should threaten peace in Europe, they were not the concern
of the United States. The result was a series of neutrality acts defining
American neutral rights and duties that sought to prevent involvement
of the country in a second World War. The first of these pieces of
domestic legislation was an act of Congress dated August 31, 1935.

. . . Resolved by the Senate and House of Representatives of
the United States of America in Congress assembled, That upon
the outbreak or during the progress of war between, or among, two
or more foreign states, the President shall proclaim such fact, and
it shall thereafter be unlawful to export arms, ammunition, or
implements of war from any place in the United States, or possessions of the United States, to any port of such belligerent states, or

Source: Peace and War: United States Foreign Policy, 1931–1941
(Washington, D.C., 1943), pp. 266–67, 271.

to any neutral port for transshipment to, or for the use of, a belligerent country.

The President, by proclamation, shall definitely enumerate the arms, ammunition, or implements of war, the export of which is prohibited by this Act.

The President may, from time to time, by proclamation, extend such embargo upon the export of arms, ammunition, or implements of war to other states as and when they may become involved in such war.

Whoever, in violation of any of the provisions of this section, shall export, or attempt to export, or cause to be exported, arms, ammunition, or implements of war from the United States, or any of its possessions, shall be fined not more than $10,000 or imprisoned not more than five years, or both, and the property, vessel, or vehicle containing the same shall be subject to the provisions of sections 1 to 8, inclusive, title 6, chapter 30, of the Act approved June 15, 1917 . . .

SEC. 6. Whenever, during any war in which the United States is neutral, the President shall find that the maintenance of peace between the United States and foreign nations, or the protection of the lives of citizens of the United States, or the protection of the commercial interests of the United States and its citizens, or the security of the United States requires that the American citizens should refrain from traveling as passengers on the vessels of any belligerent nation, he shall so proclaim, and thereafter no citizen of the United States shall travel on any vessel of any belligerent nation except at his own risk, unless in accordance with such rules and regulations as the President shall prescribe . . .

B. RETAINING FLEXIBILITY

PRESIDENT Roosevelt was not altogether pleased with this act, and issued a statement the same day he approved it, August 31, 1935.

. . . I have approved this joint resolution because it was intended as an expression of the fixed desire of the Government and the people of the United States to avoid any action which might involve us in war. The purpose is wholly excellent, and this joint resolution will to a considerable degree serve that end. . . .

It is the policy of this Government to avoid being drawn into

SOURCE: Peace and War: . . . 1931–1941, p. 272

wars between other nations, but it is a fact that no Congress and no Executive can foresee all possible future situations. History is filled with unforeseeable situations that call for some flexibility of action. It is conceivable that situations may arise in which the wholly inflexible provisions of section I of this act might have exactly the opposite effect from that which was intended. In other words, the inflexible provisions might drag us into war instead of keeping us out. The policy of the Government is definitely committed to the maintenance of peace and the avoidance of any entanglements which would lead us into conflict. At the same time it is the policy of the Government by every peaceful means and without entanglement to cooperate with other similarly minded governments to promote peace. . . .

CONGRESS *in February, 1936, forbade loans to belligerents.*

Resolved by the Senate and House of Representatives of the United States of America in Congress assembled, That section 1 of the joint resolution . . . approved August 31, 1935, be, and the same hereby is, amended by striking out in the first section, on the second line, after the word "assembled" the following words: "That upon the outbreak or during the progress of war between", and inserting therefor the words: "Whenever the President shall find that there exists a state of war between"; and by striking out the word "may" after the word "President" and before the word "from" in the twelfth line, and inserting in lieu thereof the word "shall" . . .

SEC. 2. There are hereby added to said joint resolution two new sections, to be known as sections 1a and 1b, reading as follows:

"SEC. 1a. Whenever the President shall have issued his proclamation as provided for in section 1 of this Act, it shall thereafter during the period of the war be unlawful for any person within the United States to purchase, sell, or exchange bonds, securities, or other obligations of the government of any belligerent country, or of any political subdivision thereof, or of any person acting for or on behalf of such government, issued after the date of such proclamation, or to make any loan or extend any credit to any such government or person . . .

"Whoever shall violate the provisions of this section or of any

SOURCE: *Peace and War: . . . 1931–1941,* pp. 313–14.

regulations issued hereunder shall, upon conviction thereof, be fined not more than $50,000 or imprisoned for not more than five years, or both. Should the violation be by a corporation, organization, or association, each officer or agent thereof participating in the violation may be liable to the penalty herein prescribed. . . ."

C. The Ethics of Neutrality

On the day he signed this second neutrality act, February 29, 1936, Roosevelt took the occasion to restate a "moral embargo" he had instituted the preceding year.

. . . Following the August enactment promptly on October 5, 1935, I issued a proclamation which made effective the embargo with respect to exportations to Italy and Ethiopia, and I have now issued a new proclamation in order to meet the requirements of the new enactment.

The policies announced by the Secretary of State and myself at the time of and subsequent to the issuance of the original proclamation will be maintained in effect. It is true that the high moral duty I have urged on our people of restricting their exports of essential war materials to either belligerent to approximately the normal peacetime basis has not been the subject of legislation. Nevertheless, it is clear to me that greatly to exceed that basis, with the result of earning profits not possible during peace, and especially with the result of giving actual assistance to the carrying on of war, would serve to magnify the very evil of war which we seek to prevent. This being my view, I renew the appeal made last October to the American people that they so conduct their trade with belligerent nations that it cannot be said that they are seizing new opportunities for profit or that by changing their peacetime trade they give aid to the continuation of war.

D. Restricting Trade and Travel

The third neutrality act, January 6, 1937, embargoed shipments to the belligerents in the Spanish Civil War (preceding acts had applied to war between nations). The fourth act, dated May 1, 1937, brought together previous regulations and added two more. One of the additional rules continued to allow, but for a term only of two years (which duly expired May 1, 1939), trade other than munitions so long as it was not carried in American ships and was paid for in advance. The other novel

Source: Peace and War . . . , 1931–1941, p. 315.
Source: Peace and War . . . , 1931–1941, p. 364.

provision of the fourth act concerned Americans traveling aboard belligerent vessels.

SEC. 9. Whenever the President shall have issued a proclamation under the authority of section 1 of this Act it shall thereafter be unlawful for any citizen of the United States to travel on any vessel of the state or states named in such proclamation, except in accordance with such rules and regulations as the President shall prescribe . . .

E. RESTATING AMERICA'S POSITION

AFTER *the Second World War began in September, 1939, another set of rules for American neutrality—the fifth—belatedly became law. The Roosevelt administration had urged passage of an act before outbreak of hostilities, but nothing was done, partly because Senator Borah and other diehards flatly refused to believe that war was coming in Europe. At a White House conference in the summer of 1939, the senator said there would be no war, and cited his own source of information, which turned out to be an article in a left-wing magazine published in London. One has to read between the lines to see the differences of the fifth act from those that preceded.*

Whereas the United States, desiring to preserve its neutrality in wars between foreign states and desiring also to avoid involvement therein, voluntarily imposes upon its nationals by domestic legislation the restrictions set out in this joint resolution; and

Whereas by so doing the United States waives none of its own rights or privileges, or those of any of its nationals, under international law, and expressly reserves all the rights and privileges to which it and its nationals are entitled under the law of nations; and

Whereas the United States hereby expressly reserves the right to repeal, change or modify this joint resolution or any other domestic legislation in the interests of the peace, security or welfare of the United States and its people: Therefore be it

Resolved by the Senate and House of Representatives of the United States of America in Congress assembled,

PROCLAMATION OF A STATE OF WAR BETWEEN FOREIGN STATES

SECTION 1. (a) That whenever the President, or the Congress by concurrent resolution, shall find that there exists a state of war

SOURCE: *Peace and War . . . , 1931–1941,* pp. 494–96, 498–99, 502–03.

between foreign states, and that it is necessary to promote the security or preserve the peace of the United States or to protect the lives of citizens of the United States, the President shall issue a proclamation naming the states involved; and he shall, from time to time, by proclamation, name other states as and when they may become involved in the war. . . .

COMMERCE WITH STATES ENGAGED IN ARMED CONFLICT

Sec. 2. (a) Whenever the President shall have issued a proclamation under the authority of section 1 (a) it shall thereafter be unlawful for any American vessel to carry any passengers or any articles or materials to any state named in such proclamation.

(b) Whoever shall violate any of the provisions of subsection (a) of this section or of any regulations issued thereunder shall, upon conviction thereof, be fined not more than $50,000 or imprisoned for not more than five years, or both. Should the violation be by a corporation, organization, or association, each officer or director thereof participating in the violation shall be liable to the penalty herein prescribed.

(c) Whenever the President shall have issued a proclamation under the authority of section 1 (a) it shall thereafter be unlawful to export or transport, or attempt to export or transport, or cause to be exported or transported, from the United States to any state named in such proclamation, any articles or materials (except copyrighted articles or materials) until all right, title, and interest therein shall have been transferred to some foreign government, agency, institution, association, partnership, corporation, or national. Issuance of a bill of lading under which title to the articles or materials to be exported or transported passes to a foreign purchaser unconditionally upon the delivery of such articles or materials to a carrier, shall constitute a transfer of all right, title, and interest therein within the meaning of this subsection. The shipper of such articles or materials shall be required to file with the collector of the port from or through which they are to be exported a declaration under oath that he has complied with the requirements of this subsection with respect to transfer of right, title, and interest in such articles or materials, and that he will comply with such rules and regulations as shall be promulgated from time to time. Any such declaration so filed shall be a conclusive estoppel against any claim of any citizen of the United States of right, title, or interest in such articles or materials, if such citizen had knowledge of the filing of such declaration; and the exportation or transportation of any articles or materials without filing the declaration required by this subsection shall be a conclusive estoppel against any claim of any citizen of the United States of right, title, or interest in such articles or materials, if such citizen had knowledge of such violation. No loss incurred by any such citizen (1) in connection with the sale or transfer of right, title, and interest in any such articles or materials or (2) in connection with the exportation or transportation of any such copyrighted articles or materials, shall be made the basis of any claim put forward by the Government of the United States.

(d) Insurance written by underwriters on articles or materials included in shipments which are subject to restrictions under the provisions of this joint resolution, and on vessels carrying such shipments shall not be deemed an American interest therein, and no insurance policy issued on such articles or materials, or vessels, and no loss incurred thereunder or by the owners of such vessels, shall be made the basis of any claim put forward by the Government of the United States.

(e) Whenever any proclamation issued under the authority of section 1 (a) shall have been revoked with respect to any state the provisions of this section shall thereupon cease to apply with respect to such state, except as to offenses committed prior to such revocation. . . .

COMBAT AREAS

Sec. 3. (a) Whenever the President shall have issued a proclamation under the authority of section 1 (a), and he shall thereafter find that the protection of citizens of the United States so requires, he shall, by proclamation, define combat areas, and thereafter it shall be unlawful, except under such rules and regulations as may be prescribed, for any citizen of the United States or any American vessel to proceed into or through any such combat area. The combat areas so defined may be made to apply to surface vessels or aircraft, or both. . . .

TRAVEL ON VESSELS OF BELLIGERENT STATES

Sec. 5. (a) Whenever the President shall have issued a proclamation under the authority of section 1 (a) it shall thereafter be unlawful for any citizen of the United States to travel on any vessel of any state named in such proclamation, except in accordance with such rules and regulations as may be prescribed. . . .

SEC. 11. Whenever, during any war in which the United States is neutral, the President shall find that special restrictions placed on the use of the ports and territorial waters of the United States by the submarines or armed merchant vessels of a foreign state will serve to maintain peace between the United States and foreign states, or to protect the commercial interests of the United States and its citizens, or to promote the security of the United States, and shall make proclamation thereof, it shall thereafter be unlawful for any such submarine or armed merchant vessel to enter a port or the territorial waters of the United States or to depart therefrom, except under such conditions and subject to such limitations as the President may prescribe. Whenever, in his judgment, the conditions which have caused him to issue his proclamation have ceased to exist, he shall revoke his proclamation and the provisions of this section shall thereupon cease to apply, except as to offenses committed prior to such revocation. . . .

F. TENTATIVE INVOLVEMENT

THE SIXTH and last act became law on November 17, 1941. Its provisions were pointedly understandable.

Resolved by the Senate and House of Representatives of the United States of America in Congress assembled, That section 2 of the Neutrality Act of 1939 [relating to commerce with States engaged in armed conflict], and section 3 of such Act [relating to combat areas], are hereby repealed.

SEC. 2. Section 6 of the Neutrality Act of 1939 [relating to the arming of American vessels] is hereby repealed; and, during the unlimited national emergency proclaimed by the President on May 27, 1941, the President is authorized, through such agency as he may designate, to arm, or to permit or cause to be armed, any American vessel as defined in such Act. The provisions of section 16 of the Criminal Code [relating to bonds from armed vessels on clearing] shall not apply to any such vessel.

SOURCE: Peace and War . . . , 1931–1941, pp. 787–88.

XI

Good Neighbor in Latin America

After the World War of 1914–18 it became evident that the Panama Canal was secure and that generally the Western Hemisphere was safe from European intervention, and in knowledge of this fact the United States government, after a suitable delay for the sake of appearances, changed its policy toward Latin America from intervention to the friendliness of the good neighbor. In the 1920s trouble still could occur, and an imbroglio in Nicaragua, which in its origins and progress was nothing but a nuisance to the United States, saw an intervention which on the surface looked like the old policy of Theodore Roosevelt. This was the only intervention. In the 1930s the Pan-American movement flourished, and to the delight of the United States it proved possible to obtain the cooperation of the Latin American states when in 1939 and thereafter the Second World War raised the question of the interests of the New World as against those of the Axis powers of the Old.

33. Nicaragua

NICARAGUA as of January 10, 1927, was in the throes of a revolution, and President Calvin Coolidge explained dispassionately to his countrymen why he had intervened.

. . . While conditions in Nicaragua and the action of this Government pertaining thereto have in general been made public, I think the time has arrived for me officially to inform the Congress more in detail of the events leading up to the present disturbances and conditions which seriously threaten American lives and property, endanger the stability of all Central America, and put in jeopardy the rights granted by Nicaragua to the United States for the construction of a canal. It is well known that in 1912 the United States intervened in Nicaragua with a large force and put down a revolution, and that from that time to 1925 a legation guard of American marines was, with the consent of the Nicaraguan Government, kept in Managua to protect American lives and property. In 1923 representatives of the five Central American countries, namely, Costa Rica, Guatemala, Honduras, Nicaragua, and Salvador, at the invitation of the United States, met in Washington and entered into a series of treaties. These treaties dealt with limitation of armament, a Central American tribunal for arbitration, and the general subject of peace and amity. The treaty last referred to specifically provides in Article II that the Governments of the contracting parties will not recognize any other government which may come into power in any of the five Republics through a coup d'état or revolution and disqualifies the leaders of such coup d'état or revolution from assuming the presidency or vice presidency. . . .

The United States was not a party to this treaty, but it was made in Washington under the auspices of the Secretary of State, and this Government has felt a moral obligation to apply its principles in order to encourage the Central American States in their efforts to prevent revolution and disorder. The treaty, it may be noted in passing, was signed on behalf of Nicaragua by Emiliano Chamorro

SOURCE: *Foreign Relations of the United States: 1927* (Washington, D.C., 1942), III, pp. 288–98.

himself, who afterwards assumed the presidency in violation thereof and thereby contributed to the creation of the present difficulty.

In October, 1924, an election was held in Nicaragua for President, Vice President, and members of the Congress. This resulted in the election of a coalition ticket embracing Conservatives and Liberals. Carlos Solorzano, a Conservative Republican, was elected President and Juan B. Sacasa, a Liberal, was elected Vice President. This Government was recognized by the other Central American countries and by the United States. It had been the intention of the United States to withdraw the marines immediately after this election, and notice was given of the intention to withdraw them in January, 1925. At the request of the President of Nicaragua this time was extended to September 1, 1925. Pursuant to this determination and notice, the marines were withdrawn in August, 1925, and it appeared at that time as though tranquility in Nicaragua was assured. Within two months, however, further disturbances broke out between the supporters of General Chamorro and the supporters of the President, culminating in the seizure of the Loma, a fortress dominating the city of Managua. Once in possession of the Loma, General Chamorro dictated an agreement which President Solorzano signed the next day. According to the terms of this agreement the President agreed to substitute supporters of General Chamorro for certain members of his cabinet, to pay General Chamorro $10,000 for the expenses of the uprising, and to grant amnesty to all those who participated in it. Vice President Sacasa thereupon left the country. In the meantime General Chamorro, who, while he had not actually taken over the office of President, was able to dictate his will to the actual Executive, brought about the expulsion from the Congress of 18 members, on the ground that their election had been fraudulent, and caused to be put in their places candidates who had been defeated at the election of 1924. Having thus gained the control of Congress, he caused himself to be appointed by the Congress as designate on January 16, 1926. On January 16, 1926, Solorzano resigned as President and immediately General Chamorro took office. The four Central American countries and the United States refused to recognize him as President. . . .

Notwithstanding the refusal of this Government and of the other Central American Governments to recognize him, General

Chamorro continued to exercise the functions of President until October 30, 1926. In the meantime, a revolution broke out in May on the east coast in the neighborhood of Bluefields and was speedily suppressed by the troops of General Chamorro. However, it again broke out with considerable more violence. The second attempt was attended with some success and practically all of the east coast of Nicaragua fell into the hands of the revolutionists. Throughout these events Sacasa was at no time in the country, having remained in Mexico and Guatemala during this period.

Repeated requests were made of the United States for protection, especially on the east coast, and, on August 24, 1926, the Secretary of State addressed to the Secretary of the Navy the following communication:

> I have the honor to suggest that war vessels of the Special Service Squadron proceed as soon as possible to the Nicaraguan ports of Corinto and Bluefields for the protection of American and foreign lives and property in case that threatened emergencies materialize. The American Chargé d'Affaires at Managua has informed the Department that he considers the presence of war vessels at these ports desirable, and the American Consul at Bluefields has reported that a warship is urgently needed to protect life and property at that port. An attack on The Bluff and Bluefields is expected momentarily.

Accordingly, the Navy Department ordered Admiral Latimer, in command of the special service squadron, to proceed to Bluefields. Upon arriving there he found it necessary for the adequate protection of American lives and property to declare Bluefields a neutral zone. This was done with the consent of both factions, afterwards, on October 26, 1926, reduced to a written agreement, which is still in force. In October [September], 1926, the good offices of the United States were sought by both parties for the purpose of effecting a settlement of the conflict. Admiral Latimer, commanding the special service squadron, brought about an armistice to permit of a conference being held between the delegates of the two factions. The armistice was originally for 15 days and was later extended for 15 days more. At the request of both parties, marines were landed at Corinto to establish a neutral zone in which the conference could be held. Doctor Sacasa was invited to attend this conference but refrained from doing so and remained in Guatemala City. The United States Government did not participate in the conference except to provide a neutral chairman; it simply offered its good offices to make the conference possible and arranged a neutral zone at Corinto at the request of both parties during the time the conference was held. I understand that at this conference General Chamorro offered to resign and permit the Congress to elect a new designate to assume the presidency. The conference led to no result, since just at the time when it seemed as though some compromise agreement would be reached the representatives of Doctor Sacasa suddenly broke off negotiations.

According to our reports, the Sacasa delegates on this occasion stated freely that to accept any government other than one presided over by Doctor Sacasa himself would be a breach of faith with their Mexican allies. Hostilities were resumed on October 30, 1926. On the same date General Chamorro formally turned over the executive power to Sebastian Uriza, who had been appointed designate by the Congress controlled by General Chamorro. The United States Government refused to recognize Señor Uriza, on the ground that his assumption of the Presidency had no constitutional basis. Uriza thereupon convoked Congress in extraordinary session, and the entire 18 members who had been expelled during the Chamorro régime were notified to resume their seats. The Congress which met in extraordinary session on November 10 had, therefore, substantially the same membership as when first convened following the election of 1924. This Congress, whose acts may be considered as constitutional, designated Señor Adolfo Diaz as first designate. At this session of Congress 53 members were present out of a total membership of 67, of whom 44 voted for Diaz and 2 for Solorzano. The balance abstained from voting. On November 11 Señor Uriza turned over the executive power to Diaz, who was inaugurated on the 14th.

The Nicaraguan constitution provides in article 106 that in the absence of the President and Vice President the Congress shall designate one of its members to complete the unexpired term of President. As President Solorzano had resigned and was then residing in California, and as the Vice President, Doctor Sacasa, was in Guatemala, having been out of the country since November, 1925, the action of Congress in designating Señor Diaz was perfectly legal and in accordance with the constitution. Therefore the United States Government on November 17 extended recognition to Señor Diaz. . . .

Immediately following the inauguration of President Diaz and frequently since that date he has appealed to the United States for support, has informed this Government of the aid which Mexico is giving to the revolutionists, and has stated that he is unable solely because of the aid given by Mexico to the revolutionists to protect the lives and property of American citizens and other foreigners. When negotiations leading up to the Corinto conference began, I immediately placed an embargo on the shipment of arms and ammunition to Nicaragua. The Department of State notified the other Central American States, to wit, Costa Rica, Honduras, Salvador, and Guatemala, and they assured the department that they would cooperate in this measure. So far as known, they have done so. The State Department also notified the Mexican Government of this embargo and informally suggested to that Government like action. The Mexican Government did not adopt the suggestion to put on an embargo, but informed the American ambassador at Mexico City that in the absence of manufacturing plants in Mexico for the making of arms and ammunition the matter had little practical importance.

As a matter of fact, I have the most conclusive evidence that arms and munitions in large quantities have been on several occasions since August, 1926, shipped to the revolutionists in Nicaragua. Boats carrying these munitions have been fitted out in Mexican ports, and some of the munitions bear evidence of having belonged to the Mexican Government. It also appears that the ships were fitted out with the full knowledge of and, in some cases, with the encouragement of Mexican officials and were in one instance, at least, commanded by a Mexican naval reserve officer. At the end of November, after spending some time in Mexico City, Doctor Sacasa went back to Nicaragua, landing at Puerto Cabezas, near Bragmans Bluff. He immediately placed himself at the head of the insurrection and declared himself President of Nicaragua. He has never been recognized by any of the Central American Republics nor by any other Government, with the exception of Mexico, which recognized him immediately. As arms and munitions in large quantities were reaching the revolutionists, I deemed it unfair to prevent the recognized Government from purchasing arms abroad, and, accordingly, the Secretary of State has notified the Diaz Government that licenses would be issued for the export of arms and munitions purchased in this country. It would be thoroughly inconsistent for this country not to support the Government recognized by it while the revolutionists were receiving arms and munitions from abroad.

During the last two months the Government of the United States has received repeated requests from various American citizens, both directly and through our consuls and legation, for the protection of their lives and property. The Government of the United States has also received requests from the British Chargé at Managua and from the Italian ambassador at Washington for the protection of their respective nationals. Pursuant to such requests, Admiral Latimer, in charge of the special service squadron, has not only maintained the neutral zone at Bluefields under the agreement of both parties but has landed forces at Puerto Cabezas and Rio Grande, and established neutral zones at these points where considerable numbers of Americans live and are engaged in carrying on various industries. He has also been authorized to establish such other neutral zones as are necessary for the purposes above mentioned.

For many years numerous Americans have been living in Nicaragua developing its industries and carrying on business. At the present time there are large investments in lumbering, mining, coffee growing, banana culture, shipping, and also in general mercantile and other collateral business. All these people and these industries have been encouraged by the Nicaraguan Government. That Government has at all times owed them protection, but the United States has occasionally been obliged to send naval forces for their proper protection. In the present crisis such forces are requested by the Nicaraguan Government, which protests to the United States its inability to protect these interests and states that any measures which the United States deems appropriate for their protection will be satisfactory to the Nicaraguan Government.

In addition to these industries nor in existence, the Government of Nicaragua, by a treaty entered into on the 5th day of August, 1914, granted in perpetuity to the United States the exclusive proprietary rights necessary and convenient for the construction, operation, and maintenance of an oceanic canal. . . .

The consideration paid by the United States to Nicaragua was the sum of $3,000,000. At the time of the payment of this money a financial plan was drawn up between the Nicaraguan Government and its creditors which provided for the consolidation of Nicaragua's obligations. At that time the bondholders holding the Nicaraguan external debt consented to a reduction in interest from 6 to 5 per cent, providing the service of this loan was handled through the American collector of customs, and at the same time a series of internal guaranteed customs bonds amounting to $3,744,-000 was issued by the Nicaraguan Government to pay off the claims which had arisen against it because of revolutionary disturbances from 1909 to 1912. The other outstanding external bonds, amounting on February 1, 1926, to about £772,000, are held in Great Britain. Of the guaranteed customs bonds, $2,867,000 were on February 1, 1926, still in circulation, and of these about $1,000,-000 were held by Nicaraguans, $1,000,000 by American citizens, and the balance by nationals of other countries. The bonds held in the United States are held by the public in general circulation and, so far as the department knows, no American bankers are directly interested in the Nicaraguan indebtedness. This financial plan was adopted by an act of the Congress of Nicaragua on August 31, 1917. The National Bank of Nicaragua was made the depository of all Government revenues. The internal revenues were, as heretofore, to be collected by the Government. Collection of the internal revenue, however, was to be taken over by the collector general of customs, an American citizen appointed by the Nicaraguan Government and approved by the Secretary of State of the United States, if the products should average less than $60,000 a month for three consecutive months. This has never yet been necessary. The proceeds of the customs revenues were to be applied, first, to the payment of such sums as might be agreed upon in the contemplated contracts for the service of the foreign loan, the internal loan, and claims against the Nicaraguan Government. From the balance of the revenue $80,000 a month was to be used for the ordinary budget expenses and an additional $15,000 for extraordinary expenses.

Under this financial plan the finances of Nicaragua have been rehabilitated in a very satisfactory manner. Of the $3,744,000 of internal customs bonds issued in 1917 about $900,000 have been paid. Of the external debt, bonds issued in 1909 amounting to £1,250,000, there now remain only about £770,000. The total public debt of Nicaragua has been reduced from about $22,000,000 in 1917 to $6,625,203 at the beginning of 1926. Furthermore, the country in time of peace has ample revenues for its ordinary budget expenses and a surplus which has been used in extensive public improvements. The Nicaraguan National Bank and the National Railroad, controlling interests in which were formerly owned by American bankers, were repurchased by the Nicaraguan Government in 1920 and 1924, and are now wholly owned by that Government.

There is no question that if the revolution continues American investments and business interests in Nicaragua will be very seriously affected, if not destroyed. The currency, which is now at par, will be inflated. American as well as foreign bondholders will undoubtedly look to the United States for the protection of their interests.

It is true that the United States did not establish the financial plan by any treaty, but it nevertheless did aid through diplomatic channels and advise in the negotiation and establishment of this plan for the financial rehabilitation of Nicaragua.

Manifestly the relation of this Government to the Nicaraguan situation, and its policy in the existing emergency, are determined by the facts which I have described. The proprietary rights of the United States in the Nicaraguan canal route, with the necessary implications growing out of it affecting the Panama Canal, to gether with the obligations flowing from the investments of all classes of our citizens in Nicaragua, place us in a position of peculiar responsibility. I am sure it is not the desire of the United States to intervene in the internal affairs of Nicaragua or of any other Central American Republic. Nevertheless it must be said that we have a very definite and special interest in the maintenance of order and good government in Nicaragua at the present time, and that the stability, prosperity, and independence of all Central American countries can never be a matter of indifference to us. The United States can not, therefore, fail to view with deep concern any serious threat to stability and constitutional government in Nicaragua tending toward anarchy and jeopardizing American interests, especially if such state of affairs is contributed to or brought about by outside influences or by any foreign power. It has always been and remains the policy of the United States in such circumstances to take the steps that may be necessary for the preservation and protection of the lives, the property, and the interests of its citizens and of this Government itself. In this respect I propose to follow the path of my predecessors.

Consequently, I have deemed it my duty to use the powers committed to me to insure the adequate protection of all American interests in Nicaragua, whether they be endangered by internal strife or by outside interference in the affairs of that Republic.

In the spring of 1927, Coolidge sent down Henry L. Stimson who negotiated the Peace of Tipitapa with Sacasa's chief general, José Moncada. Elections followed the next year, supervised by American marines, probably the fairest elections in Nicaraguan history, which elevated Moncada to the presidency. One of Moncada's supporters, Augusto César Sandino, continued in the field as a Nicaraguan Robin Hood, despite the best efforts of a force of 5,480 marines and the marine-trained Guardia Nacional. Sandino's revolt went on for a long time. The Nicaraguan army betrayed him in a truce in 1934, and shot him. Meanwhile the last of the marines had left the country in 1933.

34. A New Policy of Recognition

A. Developing Understanding

PRESIDENT Wilson on March 11, 1913, issued the following statement concerning recognition of revolutionary governments in Latin America, and this policy prevailed until Secretary of State Stimson changed it in 1930.

One of the chief objects of my administration will be to cultivate the friendship and deserve the confidence of our sister republics of Central and South America, and to promote in every proper and honorable way the interests which are common to the peoples of the two continents. I earnestly desire the most cordial understanding and cooperation between the peoples and leaders of America and, therefore, deem it my duty to make this brief statement.

Cooperation is possible only when supported at every turn by the orderly processes of just government based upon law, not upon arbitrary or irregular force. We hold, as I am sure all thoughtful leaders of republican government everywhere hold, that just gov-

SOURCE: *Foreign Relations of the United States: 1913* (Washington, D.C., 1920), p. 7.

ernment rests always upon the consent of the governed, and that there can be no freedom without order based upon law and upon the public conscience and approval. We shall look to make these principles the basis of mutual intercourse, respect, and helpfulness between our sister republics and ourselves. We shall lend our influence of every kind to the realization of these principles in fact and practice, knowing that disorder, personal intrigues, and defiance of constitutional rights weaken and discredit government and injure none so much as the people who are unfortunate enough to have their common life and their common affairs so tainted and disturbed. We can have no sympathy with those who seek to seize the power of government to advance their own personal interests or ambition. We are the friends of peace, but we know that there can be no lasting or stable peace in such circumstances. As friends, therefore, we shall prefer those who act in the interest of peace and honor, who protect private rights, and respect the restraints of constitutional provision. Mutual respect seems to us the indispensable foundation of friendship between states, as between individuals.

The United States has nothing to seek in Central and South America except the lasting interests of the peoples of the two continents, the security of governments intended for the people and for no special group or interest, and the development of personal and trade relationships between the two continents which shall redound to the profit and advantage of both and interfere with the rights and liberties of neither.

From these principles may be read so much of the future policy of this Government as it is necessary now to forecast, and in the spirit of these principles I may, I hope, be permitted with as much confidence as earnestness to extend to the Governments of all the Republics of America the hand of genuine disinterested friendship, and to pledge my own honor and the honor of my colleagues to every enterprise of peace and amity that a fortunate future may disclose.

B. Defining Policy

Perhaps because Stimson had learned at firsthand about Latin American revolutions during the Nicaraguan affair, perhaps because the time simply

Source: *Foreign Relations of the United States: 1930*, I (Washington, D.C., 1945), pp. 387–88.

had come to change the Wilsonian policy, a Department of State press
release of September 17, 1930, set out new rules for recognition.

I have directed Mr. Bliss, our Ambassador to Argentina, to resume normal diplomatic relations with the provisional Argentine Government; and have directed Mr. Dearing, our Ambassador to Peru, to resume normal diplomatic relations with the provisional Peruvian Government; and have directed Mr. Feely, our Minister accredited to Bolivia, to present his letters of credence and resume normal diplomatic relations with the provisional Bolivian Government. This is to be done tomorrow, September eighteenth.

In reaching the conclusion to accord recognition to these three governments, the evidence has satisfied me that these provisional governments are *de facto* in control of their respective countries, and that there is no active resistance to their rule. Each of the present governments has also made it clear that it is its intention to fulfill its respective international obligations and to hold, in due course, elections to regularize its status.

The action of the United States in thus recognizing the present Argentine, Peruvian and Bolivian Governments does not represent any new policy or change of policy by the United States toward the nations of South America or the rest of the world.

I have deemed it wise to act promptly in this matter in order that in the present economic situation our delay may not embarrass the people of these friendly countries in reestablishing their normal intercourse with the rest of the world.

[The Secretary was asked to clarify his statement that this does not represent any change in policy. In reply he stated:]

In acting towards these three Governments, which we are recognizing tomorrow, we are following the regular rules of international law, and the regular policy which has characterized this country ever since the first Secretary of State announced it—Mr. Jefferson in the Administration of President Washington. But with certain countries there are differences made by treaty either with us or between each other. For example, the five Central American countries have entered into a treaty between themselves in which they agreed not to recognize any Government which came into office by virtue of a *coup d'état* or a revolution. That was done in 1923, and although we were not a party to the treaty, we were in hearty accord with it and we agreed on our part that we would follow the same policy with respect to the five Republics who had agreed upon it. . . .

35. Pan-Americanism

A. Cooperation throughout the Americas

WHAT WITH conclusion of the Nicaraguan affair, and announcement of a new policy of recognition, the time had come for the United States to act in cooperation with Latin American states rather than unilaterally. The Roosevelt administration, inaugurated in March, 1933, did just that. At the Seventh International Conference of American States, meeting in Montevideo, delegates on December 26, 1933, signed a Convention on Rights and Duties of States.

ARTICLE 1

The state as a person of international law should possess the following qualifications: a) a permanent population; b) a defined territory; c) government; and d) capacity to enter into relations with the other states.

ARTICLE 2

The federal state shall constitute a sole person in the eyes of international law.

ARTICLE 3

The political existence of the state is independent of recognition by the other states. Even before recognition the state has the right to defend its integrity and independence, to provide for its conservation and prosperity, and consequently to organize itself as it sees fit, to legislate upon its interests, administer its services, and to define the jurisdiction and competence of its courts.

The exercise of these rights has no other limitation than the exercise of the rights of other states according to international law.

ARTICLE 4

States are juridically equal, enjoy the same rights, and have equal capacity in their exercise. The rights of each one do not depend

SOURCE: *Foreign Relations of the United States: 1933* (Washington, D.C., 1950), IV, pp. 214–16.

upon the power which it possesses to assure its exercise, but upon the simple fact of its existence as a person under international law.

ARTICLE 5
The fundamental rights of states are not susceptible of being affected in any manner whatsoever.

ARTICLE 6
The recognition of a state merely signifies that the state which recognizes it accepts the personality of the other with all the rights and duties determined by international law. Recognition is unconditional and irrevocable.

ARTICLE 7
The recognition of a state may be express or tacit. The latter results from any act which implies the intention of recognizing the new state.

ARTICLE 8
No state has the right to intervene in the internal or external affairs of another.

ARTICLE 9
The jurisdiction of states within the limits of national territory applies to all the inhabitants.

Nationals and foreigners are under the same protection of the law and the national authorities and the foreigners may not claim rights other or more extensive than those of the nationals.

ARTICLE 10
The primary interest of states is the conservation of peace. Differences of any nature which arise between them should be settled by recognized pacific methods.

ARTICLE 11
The contracting states definitely establish as the rule of their conduct the precise obligation not to recognize territorial acquisitions or special advantages which have been obtained by force whether this consists in the employment of arms, in threatening diplomatic representations, or in any other effective coercive

measure. The territory of a state is inviolable and may not be the object of military occupation nor of other measures of force imposed by another state directly or indirectly or for any motive whatever even temporarily.

ARTICLE 12
The present Convention shall not affect obligations previously entered into by the High Contracting Parties by virtue of international agreements. . . .

B. SOVEREIGNTY

In a statement to the conferees, the head of the American delegation, Secretary of State Cordell Hull, carefully qualified the American signature to the convention. After making a number of felicitous observations, Hull came to the point in his last few words.

The policy and attitude of the United States Government toward every important phase of international relationships in this hemisphere could scarcely be made more clear and definite than they have been made by both word and action especially since March 4. I have no disposition therefore to indulge in any repetition or rehearsal of these acts and utterances and shall not do so. Every observing person must by this time thoroughly understand that under the Roosevelt Administration the United States Government is as much opposed as any other government to interference with the freedom, the sovereignty, or other internal affairs or processes of the governments of other nations.

In addition to numerous acts and utterances in connection with the carrying out of these doctrines and policies, President Roosevelt, during recent weeks, gave out a public statement expressing his disposition to open negotiations with the Cuban Government for the purpose of dealing with the treaty which has existed since 1903. I feel safe in undertaking to say that under our support of the general principle of non-intervention as has been suggested, no government need fear any intervention on the part of the United States under the Roosevelt Administration. I think it unfortunate that during the brief period of this Conference there is apparently not time within which to prepare interpretations and definitions of

SOURCE: *Foreign Relations . . . : 1933*, IV, pp. 217–18.

these fundamental terms that are embraced in the report. Such definitions and interpretations would enable every government to proceed in a uniform way without any difference of opinion or of interpretations. I hope that at the earliest possible date such very important work will be done. In the meantime in case of differences of interpretations and also until they (the proposed doctrines and principles) can be worked out and codified for the common use of every government, I desire to say that the United States Government in all of its international associations and relationships and conduct will follow scrupulously the doctrines and policies which it has pursued since March 4 which are embodied in the different addresses of President Roosevelt since that time and in the recent peace address of myself on the 15th day of December before this Conference and in the law of nations as generally recognized and accepted. . . .

C. SOLIDARITY

PERHAPS *not satisfied with the results of Montevideo, the Latin American nations at a special conference in Buenos Aires in 1936, which President Roosevelt attended, tried again to pin down the erstwhile Colossus of the North. The conference was rich in resolutions and projects, but two were of special importance. The Declaration of Principles of Inter-American Solidarity and Confederation, signed December 21, made the usual affirmations about sovereignty but stressed the debt problem.*

The Governments of the American Republics, having considered:

That they have a common likeness in their democratic form of government and their common ideals of peace and justice, manifested in the several Treaties and Conventions which they have signed for the purpose of constituting a purely American system tending towards the preservation of peace, the proscription of war, the harmonious development of their commerce and of their cultural aspirations in the various fields of political, economic, social, scientific and artistic activities;

That the existence of continental interests obliges them to maintain solidarity of principles as the basis of the life of the relations of each to every other American nation;

That Pan Americanism, as a principle of American International

SOURCE: *Peace and War* . . . , *1931–1941*, pp. 352–53.

Law, by which is understood a moral union of all of the American Republics in defence of their common interests based upon the most perfect equality and reciprocal respect for their rights of autonomy, independence and free development, requires the proclamation of principles of American International Law; and

That it is necessary to consecrate the principle of American solidarity in all non-continental conflicts, especially since those limited to the American Continent should find a peaceful solution by the means established by the Treaties and Conventions now in force or in the instruments hereafter to be executed,

The Inter-American Conference for the Maintenance of Peace
DECLARES:

1. That the American Nations, true to their republican institutions, proclaim their absolute juridical liberty, their unqualified respect for their respective sovereignties and the existence of a common democracy throughout America;

2. That every act susceptible of disturbing the peace of America affects each and every one of them, and justifies the initiation of the procedure of consultation provided for in the Convention for the Maintenance, Preservation and Reestablishment of Peace, signed at this Conference; and

3. That the following principles are accepted by the American community of Nations:

(a) Proscription of territorial conquest and that, in consequence, no acquisition made through violence shall be recognized;

(b) Intervention by one State in the internal or external affairs of another State is condemned;

(c) Forcible collection of pecuniary debts is illegal; and

(d) Any difference or dispute between the American nations, whatever its nature or origin, shall be settled by the methods of conciliation, or unrestricted arbitration, or through operation of international justice.

D. NONINTERVENTION

An ADDITIONAL *Protocol Relative to Nonintervention, signed December 23rd, made the case against intervention as plainly as words could do. The Senate consented to this protocol without reservation.*

SOURCE: Bevans, comp., Treaties . . . . : 1776–1949, III, p. 345.

Article 1. The High Contracting Parties declare inadmissible the intervention of any of them, directly or indirectly, and for whatever reason, in the internal or external affairs of any other of the Parties.

The violation of the provisions of this Article shall give rise to mutual consultation, with the object of exchanging views and seeking methods of peaceful adjustment.

Article 2. It is agreed that every question concerning the interpretation of the present Additional Protocol, which it has not been possible to settle through diplomatic channels, shall be submitted to the procedure of conciliation provided for in the agreements in force, or to arbitration, or to judicial settlement.

E. Safeguarding Territorial Waters

When war came in Europe in 1939, a meeting of the Pan-American foreign ministers at Panama announced a Declaration of Panama, dated October 3, 1939, establishing a security zone around the Americas south of Canada, which warships of the United States patrolled in vital areas by 1941.

The Governments of the American Republics meeting at Panamá, have solemnly ratified their neutral status in the conflict which is disrupting the peace of Europe, but the present war may lead to unexpected results which may affect the fundamental interests of America and there can be no justification for the interests of the belligerents to prevail over the rights of neutrals causing disturbances and suffering to nations which by their neutrality in the conflict and their distance from the scene of events, should not be burdened with its fatal and painful consequences.

During the World War of 1914–1918 the Governments of Argentina, Brazil, Chile, Colombia, Ecuador and Peru advanced, or supported, individual proposals providing in principle a declaration by the American Republics that the belligerent nations must refrain from committing hostile acts within a reasonable distance from their shores.

The nature of the present conflagration, in spite of its already lamentable proportions, would not justify any obstruction to inter-American communications which, engendered by important

Source: *Foreign Relations of the United States: 1939* (Washington, D.C., 1957), V, pp. 36–37.

interests, call for adequate protection. This fact requires the demarcation of a zone of security including all the normal maritime routes of communication and trade between the countries of America.

To this end it is essential as a measure of necessity to adopt immediately provisions based on the above-mentioned precedents for the safeguarding of such interests, in order to avoid a repetition of the damages and sufferings sustained by the American nations and by their citizens in the war of 1914–1918.

There is no doubt that the Governments of the American Republics must foresee those dangers and as a measure of self-protection insist that the waters to a reasonable distance from their coasts shall remain free from the commission of hostile acts or from the undertaking of belligerent activities by nations engaged in a war in which the said governments are not involved.

For these reasons the Governments of the American Republics Resolve and Hereby Declare:

1. As a measure of continental self-protection, the American Republics, so long as they maintain their neutrality, are as of inherent right entitled to have those waters adjacent to the American continent, which they regard as of primary concern and direct utility in their relations, free from the commission of any hostile act by any non-American belligerent nation, whether such hostile act be attempted or made from land, sea or air.

Such waters shall be defined as follows. All waters comprised within the limits set forth hereafter except the territorial waters of Canada and of the undisputed colonies and possessions of European countries within these limits:

Beginning at the terminus of the United States–Canada boundary in Passamaquoddy Bay, in 44°46′36″ north latitude, and 66°54′11″ west longitude;

Thence due east along the parallel 44°46′36″ to a point 60° west of Greenwich;

Thence due south to a point in 20° north latitude;

Thence by a rhumb line to a point in 5° north latitude, 24° west longitude;

Thence due south to a point in 20° south latitude;

Thence by a rhumb line to a point in 58° south latitude, 57° west longitude;

Thence due west to a point in 80° west longitude;

Thence by a rhumb line to a point on the equator in 97° west longitude;

Thence by a rhumb line to a point in 15° north latitude, 120° west longitude;

Thence by a rhumb line to a point in 48°29′38″ north latitude, 136° west longitude;

Thence due east to the Pacific terminus of the United States–Canada boundary in the Strait of Juan de Fuca.

2. The Governments of the American Republics agree that they will endeavor, through joint representation to such belligerents as may now or in the future be engaged in hostilities, to secure the compliance by them with the provisions of this Declaration, without prejudice to the exercise of the individual rights of each State inherent in their sovereignty.

3. The Governments of the American Republics further declare that whenever they consider it necessary they will consult together to determine upon the measures which they may individually or collectively undertake in order to secure the observance of the provisions of this Declaration.

4. The American Republics, during the existence of a state of war in which they themselves are not involved, may undertake, whenever they may determine that the need therefor exists, to patrol, either individually or collectively, as may be agreed upon by common consent, and in so far as the means and resources of each may permit, the waters adjacent to their coasts within the area above defined.

F. THE DECLARATION OF HAVANA

WITH THE fall of the Low Countries and France in 1940 it seemed advisable to obtain a declaration by the Pan-American foreign ministers of what had long been the policy of the United States, the No-Transfer Principle, that a non-American power holding territory in the Western Hemisphere could not transfer it to another non-American power. The result was the Declaration of Havana of July 30, 1940.

WHEREAS:

1. The status of regions in this Continent belonging to European powers is a subject of deep concern to all of the Governments of the American Republics;

SOURCE: Bevans, comp., *Treaties . . . : 1776–1949*, III, pp. 619–620.

2. As a result of the present European war there may be attempts at conquest, which has been repudiated in the international relations of the American Republics, thus placing in danger the essence and pattern of the institutions of America;

3. The doctrine of inter-American solidarity agreed upon at the meetings at Lima and at Panama requires the adoption of a policy of vigilance and defense so that systems or regimes in conflict with their institutions shall not upset the peaceful life of the American Republics, the normal functioning of their institutions, or the rule of law and order;

4. The course of military events in Europe and the changes resulting from them may create the grave danger that European territorial possessions in America may be converted into strategic centers of aggression against nations of the American Continent;

The Second Meeting of Ministers of Foreign Affairs of the American Republics

Declares:

That when islands or regions in the Americas now under the possession of non-American nations are in danger of becoming the subject of barter of territory or change of sovereignty, the American nations, taking into account the imperative need of continental security and the desires of the inhabitants of the said islands or regions, may set up a regime of provisional administration under the following conditions:

(a) That as soon as the reasons requiring this measure shall cease to exist, and in the event that it would not be prejudicial to the safety of the American Republics, such territories shall, in accordance with the principle reaffirmed by this declaration that peoples of this Continent have the right freely to determine their own destinies, be organized as autonomous states if it shall appear that they are able to constitute and maintain themselves in such condition, or be restored to their previous status, whichever of these alternatives shall appear the more practicable and just;

(b) That the regions to which this declaration refers shall be placed temporarily under the provisional administration of the American Republics and this administration shall be exercised with the two-fold purpose of contributing to the security and defense of the Continent, and to the economic, political and social progress of such regions and,

Resolves:

To create an emergency committee, composed of one representative of each of the American Republics, which committee shall be deemed constituted as soon as two-thirds of its members shall have been appointed. Such appointments shall be made by the American Republics as soon as possible.

The committee shall meet on the request of any signatory of this resolution.

If it becomes necessary as an imperative emergency measure before the coming into effect of the convention approved by this Consultative Meeting, to apply its provisions in order to safeguard the peace of the Continent, taking into account also the desires of the inhabitants of any of the above mentioned regions, the committee shall assume the administration of the region attacked or threatened, acting in accordance with the provisions of the said convention. As soon as the convention comes into effect, the authority and functions exercised by the committee shall be transferred to the Inter-American Commission for Territorial Administration.

Should the need for emergency action be so urgent that action by the committee cannot be awaited, any of the American Republics, individually or jointly with others, shall have the right to act in the manner which its own defense or that of the Continent requires. Should this situation arise, the American Republic or Republics taking action shall place the matter before the committee immediately, in order that it may consider the action taken and adopt appropriate measures.

None of the provisions contained in the present Act refers to territories or possessions which are the subject of dispute or claims between European powers and one or more of the Republics of the Americas.

XII

To Pearl Harbor

Even with a generation and more of retrospect, the events leading to the Japanese attack on the American Pacific fleet at Pearl Harbor seem to have been relentless, inexorable, without much chance of another outcome. Once the Second World War opened in Europe in September, 1939, it was entirely within Japanese tradition to take advantage of Europe's preoccupation. It was also entirely within the American tradition to undertake to protect China against Japanese rapacity. The result was predictable—even if the special circumstance of the beginning of hostilities was shockingly sudden and dire.

36. A Year of Confusion

A. The Influence of Internationalism

As had American Presidents before him, if under differing conditions, President Roosevelt on September 3, 1939, addressed the nation by radio and urged a proper neutrality in the document that follows. Exactly one year later, however, the President sent a message to Congress announcing an executive agreement to trade fifty overage First World War destroyers for bases in British possessions in the New World.

Tonight my single duty is to speak to the whole of America.

Until 4:30 this morning I had hoped against hope that some miracle would prevent a devastating war in Europe and bring to an end the invasion of Poland by Germany.

For 4 long years a succession of actual wars and constant crises have shaken the entire world and have threatened in each case to bring on the gigantic conflict which is today unhappily a fact.

It is right that I should recall to your minds the consistent and at times successful efforts of your Government in these crises to throw the full weight of the United States into the cause of peace. In spite of spreading wars I think that we have every right and every reason to maintain as a national policy the fundamental moralities, the teachings of religion, and the continuation of efforts to restore peace—for some day, though the time may be distant, we can be of even greater help to a crippled humanity.

It is right, too, to point out that the unfortunate events of these recent years have been based on the use of force or the threat of force. And it seems to me clear, even at the outbreak of this great war, that the influence of America should be consistent in seeking for humanity a final peace which will eliminate, as far as it is possible to do so, the continued use of force between nations. . . .

You must master at the outset a simple but unalterable fact in modern foreign relations. When peace has been broken anywhere, peace of all countries everywhere is in danger.

It is easy for you and me to shrug our shoulders and say that conflicts taking place thousands of miles from the continental

United States, and, indeed, the whole American hemisphere, do not seriously affect the Americas—and that all the United States has to do is to ignore them and go about our own business. Passionately though we may desire detachment, we are forced to realize that every word that comes through the air, every ship that sails the sea, every battle that is fought does affect the American future.

Let no man or woman thoughtlessly or falsely talk of America sending its armies to European fields. At this moment there is being prepared a proclamation of American neutrality. This would have been done even if there had been no neutrality statute on the books, for this proclamation is in accordance with international law and with American policy.

This will be followed by a proclamation required by the existing Neutrality Act. I trust that in the days to come our neutrality can be made a true neutrality. . . .

We have certain ideas and ideals of national safety, and we must act to preserve that safety today and to preserve the safety of our children in future years.

That safety is and will be bound up with the safety of the Western Hemisphere and of the seas adjacent thereto. We seek to keep war from our firesides by keeping war from coming to the Americas. For that we have historic precedent that goes back to the days of the administration of President George Washington. It is serious enough and tragic enough to every American family in every State in the Union to live in a world that is torn by wars on other continents. Today they affect every American home. It is our national duty to use every effort to keep them out of the Americas.

And at this time let me make the simple plea that partisanship and selfishness be adjourned, and that national unity be the thought that underlies all others.

This Nation will remain a neutral nation, but I cannot ask that every American remain neutral in thought as well. Even a neutral has a right to take account of facts. Even a neutral cannot be asked to close his mind or his conscience.

I have said not once but many times that I have seen war and that I hate war. I say that again and again.

I hope the United States will keep out of this war. I believe that it will. And I give you assurances that every effort of your Government will be directed toward that end.

As long as it remains within my power to prevent, there will be no blackout of peace in the United States.

B. Exchanging Destroyers for Bases

SHORTLY before the French surrender in June, 1940, Prime Minister Churchill informed President Roosevelt that the British government badly needed destroyers. "We must ask . . . as a matter of life or death," he said, "to be reinforced with these destroyers." This plea placed the President in a quandary, as he would have to prepare Congress for such a request and did not have much time. Moreover, there was considerable danger that Congress would refuse a request. After receiving from Attorney General Robert H. Jackson an opinion that the President had the right to transfer destroyers under an executive agreement, Roosevelt acted. The British ambassador in Washington, Lord Lothian, on September 2, formally offered to the United States the leasing of bases in British territories in the New World.

I have the honour under instructions from His Majesty's Principal Secretary of State for Foreign Affairs to inform you that in view of the friendly and sympathetic interest of His Majesty's Government in the United Kingdom in the national security of the United States and their desire to strengthen the ability of the United States to cooperate effectively with the other nations of the Americas in the defense of the Western Hemisphere, His Majesty's Government will secure the grant to the Government of the United States, freely and without consideration, of the lease for immediate establishment and use of naval and air bases and facilities for entrance thereto and the question and protection thereof, on the Avalon Peninsula and on the southern coast of Newfoundland, and on the east coast and on the Great Bay of Bermuda.

Furthermore, in view of the above and in view of the desire of the United States to acquire additional air and naval bases in the Caribbean and in British Guiana, and without endeavouring to place a monetary or commercial value upon the many tangible and intangible rights and properties involved, His Majesty's Government will make available to the United States for immediate establishment and use naval and air bases and facilities for entrance

SOURCE: Samuel I. Rosenman, ed., *The Public Papers and Addresses of Franklin D. Roosevelt: 1940* (New York, 1941), pp. 392–93.

thereto and the operation and protection thereof, on the eastern side of the Bahamas, the southern coast of Jamaica, the western coast of St. Lucia, the west coast of Trinidad in the Gulf of Paria, in the island of Antigua and in British Guiana within fifty miles of Georgetown, in exchange for naval and military equipment and material which the United States Government will transfer to His Majesty's Government.

All the bases and facilities referred to in the preceding paragraphs will be leased to the United States for a period of ninety-nine years, free from all rent and charges other than such compensation to be mutually agreed on to be paid by the United States in order to compensate the owners of private property for loss by expropriation or damage arising out of the establishment of the bases and facilities in question.

His Majesty's Government, in the leases to be agreed upon, will grant to the United States for the period of the leases all the rights, power, and authority within the bases leased, and within the limits of the territorial waters and air spaces adjacent to or in the vicinity of such bases, necessary to provide access to and defence of such bases, and appropriate provisions for their control.

Without prejudice to the above-mentioned rights of the United States authorities and their jurisdiction within the leased areas, the adjustment and reconciliation between the jurisdiction of the authorities of the United States within these areas and the jurisdiction of the authorities of the territories in which these areas are situated, shall be determined by common agreement.

The exact location and bounds of the aforesaid bases, the necessary seaward, coast and antiaircraft defences, the location of sufficient military garrisons, stores, and other necessary auxiliary facilities shall be determined by common agreement.

His Majesty's Government are prepared to designate immediately experts to meet with experts of the United States for these purposes. Should these experts be unable to agree in any particular situation, except in the case of Newfoundland and Bermuda, the matter shall be settled by the Secretary of State of the United States and His Majesty's Secretary of State for Foreign Affairs. . . .

IN a note of the same day, Secretary Hull accepted the offer.

SOURCE: *Public Papers* . . . , p. 394.

I have received your note of September 2, 1940.

I am directed by the President to reply to your note as follows:

The Government of the United States appreciates the declarations and the generous action of His Majesty's Government as contained in your communication which are destined to enhance the national security of the United States and greatly to strengthen its ability to cooperate effectively with the other nations of the Americas in the defense of the Western Hemisphere. It therefore gladly accepts the proposals.

The Government of the United States will immediately designate experts to meet with experts designated by His Majesty's Government to determine upon the exact location of the naval and air bases mentioned in your communication under acknowledgment.

In consideration of the declarations above quoted, the Government of the United States will immediately transfer to His Majesty's Government fifty United States Navy destroyers generally referred to as the twelve hundred-ton type. . . .

NEXT day, September 3rd, Roosevelt informed Congress.

I transmit herewith for the information of the Congress notes exchanged between the British Ambassador at Washington and the Secretary of State on September 2, 1940, under which this Government has acquired the right to lease naval and air bases in Newfoundland, and in the islands of Bermuda, the Bahamas, Jamaica, St. Lucia, Trinidad, and Antigua, and in British Guiana; also a copy of an opinion of the Attorney General dated August 27, 1940, regarding my authority to consummate this arrangement.

The right to bases in Newfoundland and Bermuda are gifts— generously given and gladly received. The other bases mentioned have been acquired in exchange for 50 of our over-age destroyers.

This is not inconsistent in any sense with our status of peace. Still less is it a threat against any nation. It is an epochal and far-reaching act of preparation for continental defense in the face of grave danger.

Preparation for defense is an inalienable prerogative of a sovereign state. Under present circumstances this exercise of sovereign right is essential to the maintenance of our peace and safety. This

SOURCE: *Public Papers* . . . , pp. 391–92.

is the most important action in the reinforcement of our national defense that has been taken since the Louisiana Purchase. Then as now, considerations of safety from overseas attack were fundamental.

The value to the Western Hemisphere of these outposts of security is beyond calculation. Their need has long been recognized by our country, and especially by those primarily charged with the duty of charting and organizing our own naval and military defense. They are essential to the protection of the Panama Canal, Central America, the northern portion of South America, the Antilles, Canada, Mexico, and our own eastern and Gulf seaboards. Their consequent importance in hemispheric defense is obvious. For these reasons I have taken advantage of the present opportunity to acquire them.

37. Lend-Lease

A. Recognizing Britain's Need

For weeks after the destroyers-bases deal the President wrestled with the problem of covering the British "dollar gap": the British government simply did not have the funds to make necessary purchases of American arms. For a while Roosevelt chose to believe that somehow the British could conduct a sort of sale of their securities, and that anyway the empire was rich and could pay. Gradually these hopes turned to nothing, and in his press conference of December 17, 1940, the President resorted to metaphor.

Now, what I am trying to do is to eliminate the dollar sign. That is something brand new in the thoughts of practically everybody in this room, I think—get rid of the silly, foolish old dollar sign.

Well, let me give you an illustration: Suppose my neighbor's home catches fire, and I have a length of garden hose four or five hundred feet away. If he can take my garden hose and connect it up with his hydrant, I may help him to put out his fire. Now, what do I do? I don't say to him before that operation, "Neighbor, my garden hose cost me $15; you have to pay me $15 for it." What is the transaction that goes on? I don't want $15—I want my garden

Source: *Public Papers* . . . , pp. 607–08.

hose back after the fire is over. All right. If it goes through the fire all right, intact, without any damage to it, he gives it back to me and thanks me very much for the use of it. But suppose it gets smashed up—holes in it—during the fire; we don't have to have too much formality about it, but I say to him, "I was glad to lend you that hose; I see I can't use it any more, it's all smashed up." He says, "How many feet of it were there?" I tell him, "There were 150 feet of it." He says, "All right, I will replace it." Now, if I get a nice garden hose back, I am in pretty good shape.

In other words, if you lend certain munitions and get the munitions back at the end of the war, if they are intact—haven't been hurt—you are all right; if they have been damaged or have deteriorated or have been lost completely, it seems to me you come out pretty well if you have them replaced by the fellow to whom you have lent them.

I can't go into details; and there is no use asking legal questions about how you would do it, because that is the thing that is now under study; but the thought is that we would take over not all, but a very large number of, future British orders; and when they came off the line, whether they were planes or guns or something else, we would enter into some kind of arrangement for their use by the British on the ground that it was the best thing for American defense, with the understanding that when the show was over, we would get repaid sometime in kind, thereby leaving out the dollar mark in the form of a dollar debt and substituting for it a gentleman's obligation to repay in kind. I think you all get it.

B. COMMITMENT: THE LEND-LEASE BILL

THE ADMINISTRATION sponsored a bill that in the House of Representatives received the designation H.R. 1776, more popularly known as the Lend-Lease Bill, which became law on March 11, 1941. In many ways it was the most important single act of the government of the United States between September, 1939, and entrance into war after the attack on Pearl Harbor.

Be it enacted by the Senate and House of Representatives of the United States of America in Congress assembled, That this Act may be cited as "An Act to Promote the Defense of the United States".

SOURCE: Peace and War: . . . 1931–1941, pp. 627–630.

Sec. 2. As used in this Act—

(a) The term "defense article" means—

(1) Any weapon, munition, aircraft, vessel, or boat;

(2) Any machinery, facility, tool, material, or supply necessary for the manufacture, production, processing, repair, servicing, or operation of any article described in this subsection;

(3) Any component material or part of or equipment for any article described in this subsection;

(4) Any agricultural, industrial or other commodity or article for defense.

Such term "defense article" includes any article described in this subsection: Manufactured or procured pursuant to section 3, or to which the United States or any foreign government has or hereafter acquires title, possession, or control.

(b) The term "defense information" means any plan, specification, design, prototype, or information pertaining to any defense article.

Sec. 3. (a) Notwithstanding the provisions of any other law, the President may, from time to time, when he deems it in the interest of national defense, authorize the Secretary of War, the Secretary of the Navy, or the head of any other department or agency of the Government—

(1) To manufacture in arsenals, factories, and shipyards under their jurisdiction, or otherwise procure, to the extent to which funds are made available therefore, or contracts are authorized from time to time by the Congress, or both, any defense article for the government of any country whose defense the President deems vital to the defense of the United States.

(2) To sell, transfer title to, exchange, lease, lend, or otherwise dispose of, to any such government any defense article, but no defense article not manufactured or procured under paragraph (1) shall in any way be disposed of under this paragraph, except after consultation with the Chief of Staff of the Army or the Chief of Naval Operations of the Navy, or both. The value of defense articles disposed of in any way under authority of this paragraph, and procured from funds heretofore appropriated, shall not exceed $1,300,000,000. The value of such defense articles shall be determined by the head of the department or agency concerned or such other depart-

ment, agency or officer as shall be designated in the manner provided in the rules and regulations issued hereunder. Defense articles procured from funds hereafter appropriated to any department or agency of the Government, other than from funds authorized to be appropriated under this Act, shall not be disposed of in any way under authority of this paragraph except to the extent hereafter authorized by the Congress in the Acts appropriating such funds or otherwise.

(3) To test, inspect, prove, repair, outfit, recondition, or otherwise to place in good working order, to the extent to which funds are made available therefor, or contracts are authorized from time to time by the Congress, or both, any defense article for any such government, or to procure any or all such services by private contract.

(4) To communicate to any such government any defense information, pertaining to any defense article furnished to such government under paragraph (2) of this subsection.

(5) To release for export any defense article disposed of in any way under this subsection to any such government.

(b) The terms and conditions upon which any such foreign government receives any aid authorized under subsection (a) shall be those which the President deems satisfactory, and the benefit to the United States may be payment or repayment in kind or property, or any other direct or indirect benefit which the President deems satisfactory.

(c) After June 30, 1943, or after the passage of a concurrent resolution by the two Houses before June 30, 1943, which declares that the powers conferred by or pursuant to subsection (a) are no longer necessary to promote the defense of the United States, neither the President nor the head of any department or agency shall exercise any of the powers conferred by or pursuant to subsection (a); except that until July 1, 1946, any of such powers may be exercised to the extent necessary to carry out a contract or agreement with such a foreign government made before July 1, 1943, or before the passage of such concurrent resolution, whichever is the earlier.

(d) Nothing in this Act shall be construed to authorize or to permit the authorization of convoying vessels by naval vessels of the United States.

(e) Nothing in this Act shall be construed to authorize or to permit the authorization of the entry of any American vessel into a combat area in violation of section 3 of the Neutrality Act of 1939.

SEC. 4. All contracts or agreements made for the disposition of any defense article or defense information pursuant to section 3 shall contain a clause by which the foreign government undertakes that it will not, without the consent of the President, transfer title to or possession of such defense article or defense information by gift, sale, or otherwise, or permit its use by anyone not an officer, employee, or agent of such foreign government.

SEC. 5. (a) The Secretary of War, the Secretary of the Navy, or the head of any other department or agency of the Government involved shall, when any such defense article or defense information is exported, immediately inform the department or agency designated by the President to administer section 6 of the Act of July 2, 1940 (54 Stat. 714), of the quantities, character, value, terms of disposition, and destination of the article and information so exported.

(b) The President from time to time, but not less frequently than once every ninety days, shall transmit to the Congress a report of operations under this Act except such information as he deems incompatible with the public interest to disclose. Reports provided for under this subsection shall be transmitted to the Secretary of the Senate or the Clerk of the House of Representatives, as the case may be, if the Senate or the House of Representatives, as the case may be, is not in session.

SEC. 6. (a) There is hereby authorized to be appropriate from time to time, out of any money in the Treasury not otherwise appropriated, such amounts as may be necessary to carry out the provisions and accomplish the purposes of this Act.

(b) All money and all property which is converted into money received under section 3 from any government shall, with the approval of the Director of the Budget, revert to the respective appropriation or appropriations out of which funds were expended with respect to the defense article or defense information for which such consideration is received, and shall be available for expenditure for the purpose for which such expended funds were appropriated by law, during the fiscal year in which such funds are received and the ensuing fiscal year; but in no event shall any funds so received be available for expenditure after June 30, 1946.

SEC. 7. The Secretary of War, the Secretary of the Navy, and the head of the department or agency shall in all contracts or agreements for the disposition of any defense article or defense information fully protect the rights of all citizens of the United States who have patent rights in and to any such article or information which is hereby authorized to be disposed of and the payments collected for royalties on such patents shall be paid to the owners and holders of such patents.

Sec. 8. The Secretaries of War and of the Navy are hereby authorized to purchase or otherwise acquire arms, ammunition, and implements of war produced within the jurisdiction of any country to which section 3 is applicable, whenever the President deems such purchase or acquisition to be necessary in the interests of the defense of the United States.

Sec. 9. The President may, from time to time, promulgate such rules and regulations as may be necessary and proper to carry out any of the provisions of this Act; and he may exercise any power or authority conferred on him by this Act through such department, agency, or officer as he shall direct.

Sec. 10. Nothing in this Act shall be construed to change existing law relating to the use of the land and naval forces of the United States, except insofar as such use relates to the manufacture, procurement, and repair of defense articles, the communication of information and other noncombatant purposes enumerated in this Act.

Sec. 11. If any provision of this Act or the application of such provision to any circumstance shall be held invalid, the validity of the remainder of the Act and the applicability of such provision to other circumstances shall not be affected thereby.

C. Convoy Difficulties

Once the Lend-Lease Bill had passed Congress, the problem in the spring and summer of 1941 was to ensure that ships with war equipment would get to Great Britain. Almost at once the question of convoying arose: should the United States navy convoy British and American ships at least part of the way to the British Isles? This was a touchy issue, and a section of the act of March 11, 1941, stipulated that nothing in the act should be construed "to authorize or to permit the authorization of convoying vessels by naval vessels of the United States." When a German submarine attacked the United States destroyer Greer, President Roose-

Source: *Peace and War . . . , 1931–1941*, pp. 737–38, 741–43.

velt on September 11, 1941, exactly six months after passage of lend-lease, announced in a radio address that he was authorizing convoying.

The Navy Department of the United States has reported to me that on the morning of September fourth the United States destroyer Greer, proceeding in full daylight towards Iceland, had reached a point southeast of Greenland. She was carrying American mail to Iceland. She was flying the American flag. Her identity as an American ship was unmistakable.

She was then and there attacked by a submarine. Germany admits that it was a German submarine. The submarine deliberately fired a torpedo at the Greer, followed later by another torpedo attack. In spite of what Hitler's propaganda bureau has invented, and in spite of what any American obstructionist organization may prefer to believe, I tell you the blunt fact that the German submarine fired first upon this American destroyer without warning, and with deliberate design to sink her.

Our destroyer, at the time, was in waters which the Government of the United States had declared to be waters of self-defense—surrounding outposts of American protection in the Atlantic.

In the north, outposts have been established by us in Iceland, Greenland, Labrador, and Newfoundland. Through these waters there pass many ships of many flags. They bear food and other supplies to civilians; and they bear matériel of war, for which the people of the United States are spending billions of dollars, and which, by congressional action, they have declared to be essential for the defense of their own land.

The United States destroyer, when attacked, was proceeding on a legitimate mission.

If the destroyer was visible to the submarine when the torpedo was fired, then the attack was a deliberate attempt by the Nazis to sink a clearly identified American warship. On the other hand, if the submarine was beneath the surface and, with the aid of its listening devices, fired in the direction of the sound of the American destroyer without even taking the trouble to learn its identity—as the official German communiqué would indicate—then the attack was even more outrageous. For it indicates a policy of indiscriminate violence against any vessel sailing the seas—belligerent or non-belligerent.

This was piracy—legally and morally. It was not the first nor the last act of piracy which the Nazi Government has committed against the American flag in this war. Attack has followed attack. . . .

This attack on the Greer was no localized military operation in the North Atlantic. This was no mere episode in a struggle between two nations. This was one determined step towards creating a permanent world system based on force, terror, and murder.

And I am sure that even now the Nazis are waiting to see whether the United States will by silence give them the green light to go ahead on this path of destruction.

The Nazi danger to our Western World has long ceased to be a mere possibility. The danger is here now—not only from a military enemy but from an enemy of all law, all liberty, all morality, all religion.

There has now come a time when you and I must see the cold, inexorable necessity of saying to these inhuman, unrestrained seekers of world-conquest and permanent world-domination by the sword—"You seek to throw our children and our children's children into your form of terrorism and slavery. You have now attacked our own safety. You shall go no further."

Normal practices of diplomacy—note-writing—are of no possible use in dealing with international outlaws who sink our ships and kill our citizens.

One peaceful nation after another has met disaster because each refused to look the Nazi danger squarely in the eye until it actually had them by the throat.

The United States will not make that fatal mistake.

No act of violence or intimidation will keep us from maintaining intact two bulwarks of defense: first, our line of supply of matériel to the enemies of Hitler; and second, the freedom of our shipping on the high seas.

No matter what it takes, no matter what it costs, we will keep open the line of legitimate commerce in these defensive waters.

We have sought no shooting war with Hitler. We do not seek it now. But neither do we want peace so much that we are willing to pay for it by permitting him to attack our naval and merchant ships while they are on legitimate business.

I assume that the German leaders are not deeply concerned by what we Americans say or publish about them. We cannot bring about the downfall of Nazism by the use of long-range invective.

But when you see a rattlesnake poised to strike, you do not wait until he has struck before you crush him.

These Nazi submarines and raiders are the rattlesnakes of the Atlantic. They are a menace to the free pathways of the high seas. They are a challenge to our sovereignty. They hammer at our most precious rights when they attack ships of the American flag—symbols of our independence, our freedom, our very life. . . .

Upon our naval and air patrol—now operating in large number over a vast expanse of the Atlantic Ocean—falls the duty of maintaining the American policy of freedom of the seas—now. That means, very simply and clearly, that our patrolling vessels and planes will protect all merchant ships—not only American ships but ships of any flag—engaged in commerce in our defensive waters. They will protect them from submarines; they will protect them from surface raiders.

This situation is not new. The second President of the United States, John Adams, ordered the United States Navy to clean out European privateers and European ships of war which were infesting the Caribbean and South American waters, destroying American commerce.

The third President of the United States, Thomas Jefferson, ordered the United States Navy to end the attacks being made upon American ships by the corsairs of the nations of North Africa.

My obligation as President is historic; it is clear; it is inescapable.

It is no act of war on our part when we decide to protect the seas which are vital to American defense. The aggression is not ours. Ours is solely defense.

But let this warning be clear. From now on, if German or Italian vessels of war enter the waters the protection of which is necessary for American defense they do so at their own peril.

The orders which I have given as Commander-in-Chief to the United States Army and Navy are to carry out that policy—at once.

The sole responsibility rests upon Germany. There will be no shooting unless Germany continues to seek it.

That is my obvious duty in this crisis. That is the clear right of this sovereign nation. That is the only step possible, if we would keep tight the wall of defense which we are pledged to maintain around this Western Hemisphere.

I have no illusions about the gravity of this step. I have not taken it hurriedly or lightly. It is the result of months and months of constant thought and anxiety and prayer. In the protection of your Nation and mine it cannot be avoided.

The American people have faced other grave crises in their history—with American courage and American resolution. They will do no less today.

They know the actualities of the attacks upon us. They know the necessities of a bold defense against these attacks. They know that the times call for clear heads and fearless hearts.

And with that inner strength that comes to a free people conscious of their duty and of the righteousness of what they do, they will—with Divine help and guidance—stand their ground against this latest assault upon their democracy, their sovereignty, and their freedom.

The case of the Greer, which Roosevelt had seized upon to institute convoying, was hardly as the President described it. A British plane had informed the Greer, while en route to Iceland, of the presence of a submarine about ten miles directly ahead. The Greer gave chase, trailing the submarine and broadcasting its position for three hours and twenty-eight minutes, during which the plane dropped four depth charges. The submarine fired a torpedo which crossed the Greer about 100 yards astern. The destroyer answered with a pattern of eight depth charges. The submarine replied with another torpedo that missed the Greer. The chase went on for a while, with more depth charges, and the American ship finally gave up and proceeded to Iceland.

38. Two Statements of Principle

A. THE FOUR FREEDOMS

UNLIKE *President Wilson during the First World War, Roosevelt did not wait until the United States had entered the conflict before setting out American war aims. In an address to Congress on January 6, 1941, he announced what became known as the Four Freedoms.*

. . . In the future days, which we seek to make secure, we look forward to a world founded upon four essential human freedoms.

SOURCE: *Peace and War* . . . , *1931–1941*, p. 611.

The first is freedom of speech and expression—everywhere in the world.

The second is freedom of every person to worship God in his own way—everywhere in the world.

The third is freedom from want—which, translated into world terms, means economic understandings which will secure to every nation a healthy peacetime life for its inhabitants—everywhere in the world.

The fourth is freedom from fear—which, translated into world terms, means a world-wide reduction of armaments to such a point and in such a thorough fashion that no nation will be in a position to commit an act of physical aggression against any neighbor—anywhere in the world.

That is no vision of a distant millennium. It is a definite basis for a kind of world attainable in our own time and generation. That kind of world is the very antithesis of the so-called new order of tyranny which the dictators seek to create with the crash of a bomb.

To that new order we oppose the greater conception—the moral order. A good society is able to face schemes of world domination and foreign revolutions alike without fear.

Since the beginning of our American history we have been engaged in change—in a perpetual peaceful revolution—a revolution which goes on steadily, quietly adjusting itself to changing conditions—without the concentration camp or the quick-lime in the ditch. The world order which we seek is the cooperation of free countries, working together in a friendly, civilized society.

This Nation has placed its destiny in the hands and heads and hearts of its millions of free men and women; and its faith in freedom under the guidance of God. Freedom means the supremacy of human rights everywhere. Our support goes to those who struggle to gain those rights or keep them. Our strength is in our unity of purpose.

To that high concept there can be no end save victory.

B. THE ATLANTIC CHARTER

IN A rendezvous with Prime Minister Churchill at Argentia Bay off Newfoundland, Roosevelt and Churchill on August 14, 1941, announced

SOURCE: *Foreign Relations of the United States: 1941* (Washington, D.C., 1958), I, pp. 368–69.

the Atlantic Charter—the Second World War's equivalent of the Four-
teen Points.

Joint declaration of the President of the United States of
America and the Prime Minister, Mr. Churchill, representing His
Majesty's Government in the United Kingdom, being met together, deem it right to make known certain common principles
in the national policies of their respective countries on which they
base their hopes for a better future for the world.

First, their countries seek no aggrandizement, territorial or other;

Second, they desire to see no territorial changes that do not
accord with the freely expressed wishes of the peoples concerned;

Third, they respect the right of all peoples to choose the form of
government under which they will live; and they wish to see sovereign rights and self government restored to those who have been
forcibly deprived of them;

Fourth, they will endeavor, with due respect for their existing
obligations, to further the enjoyment by all States, great or small,
victor or vanquished, of access, on equal terms, to the trade and to
the raw materials of the world which are needed for their economic
prosperity;

Fifth, they desire to bring about the fullest collaboration between all nations in the economic field with the object of securing,
for all, improved labor standards, economic advancement and
social security;

Sixth, after the final destruction of the Nazi tyranny, they hope
to see established a peace which will afford to all nations the means
of dwelling in safety within their own boundaries, and which will
afford assurance that all the men in all the lands may live out their
lives in freedom from fear and want;

Seventh, such a peace should enable all men to traverse the high
seas and oceans without hindrance;

Eighth, they believe that all of the nations of the world, for
realistic as well as spiritual reasons must come to the abandonment
of the use of force. Since no future peace can be maintained if
land, sea or air armaments continue to be employed by nations
which threaten, or may threaten, aggression outside of their frontiers, they believe, pending the establishment of a wider and
permanent system of general security, that the disarmament of
such nations is essential. They will likewise aid and encourage all

other practicable measures which will lighten for peace-loving peoples the crushing burden of armaments.

39. Pearl Harbor

A. BREAKDOWN OF NEGOTIATIONS

AFTER *toying with the idea of a modus vivendi in regard to Japan, hoping that the Japanese might delay the construction plans for their so-called co-prosperity sphere in Asia, the Roosevelt administration gave up and, in effect, brought to an end the discussions then in progress in Washington by demanding that the Japanese get out of China. The Japanese had been there since 1904. Secretary Hull presented the two Japanese ambassadors in Washington, Kichisaburo Nomura and Saburo Kurusu, with a two-section proposition on November 26, 1941. The first section contained platitudes, but the second got down to business.*

SECTION II

Steps To Be Taken by the Government of the United States and by the Government of Japan

The Government of the United States and the Government of Japan propose to take steps as follows:

1. The Government of the United States and the Government of Japan will endeavor to conclude a multilateral non-aggression pact among the British Empire, China, Japan, the Netherlands, the Soviet Union, Thailand and the United States.

2. Both Governments will endeavor to conclude among the American, British, Chinese, Japanese, the Netherland and Thai Governments an agreement whereunder each of the Governments would pledge itself to respect the territorial integrity of French Indochina and, in the event that there should develop a threat to the territorial integrity of Indochina, to enter into immediate consultation with a view to taking such measures as may be deemed necessary and advisable to meet the threat in question. Such agreement would provide also that each of the Governments party to the agreement would not seek or accept preferential treatment in its trade or economic relations with Indochina and

SOURCE: *Foreign Relations . . . 1931–1941*, II, pp. 769–70.

would use its influence to obtain for each of the signatories equality of treatment in trade and commerce with French Indochina.

3. The Government of Japan will withdraw all military, naval, air and police forces from China and from Indochina.

4. The Government of the United States and the Government of Japan will not support—militarily, politically, economically—any government or regime in China other than the National Government of the Republic of China with capital temporarily at Chungking.

5. Both Governments will give up all extraterritorial rights in China, including rights and interests in and with regard to international settlements and concessions, and rights under the Boxer Protocol of 1901.

Both Governments will endeavor to obtain the agreement of the British and other governments to give up extraterritorial rights in China, including rights in international settlements and in concessions and under the Boxer Protocol of 1901.

6. The Government of the United States and the Government of Japan will enter into negotiations for the conclusion between the United States and Japan of a trade agreement, based upon reciprocal most-favored-nation treatment and reduction of trade barriers by both countries, including an undertaking by the United States to bind raw silk on the free list.

7. The Government of the United States and the Government of Japan will, respectively, remove the freezing restrictions on Japanese funds in the United States and on American funds in Japan.

8. Both Governments will agree upon a plan for the stabilization of the dollar-yen rate, with the allocation of funds adequate for this purpose, half to be supplied by Japan and half by the United States.

9. Both Governments will agree that no agreement which either has concluded with any third power or powers shall be interpreted by it in such a way as to conflict with the fundamental purpose of this agreement, the establishment and preservation of peace throughout the Pacific area.

10. Both Governments will use their influence to cause other governments to adhere to and to give practical application to the basic political and economic principles set forth in this agreement.

B. The Surprise Attack

THE JAPANESE ambassadors presented a memorandum to Secretary Hull on Sunday, December 7, 1941, relating that (according to its last paragraph) "The Japanese Government regrets to have to notify hereby the American Government that in view of the attitude of the American Government it cannot but consider that it is impossible to reach an agreement through further negotiations." The Japanese plan apparently was to present this memorandum almost simultaneously with the attack on Pearl Harbor occurring at 7:50 A.M. Honolulu time—which was 1:20 P.M. Washington time. A regrettable delay put the ambassadors into a very difficult position.

The Japanese Ambassador asked for an appointment to see the Secretary at 1:00 p. m., but later telephoned and asked that the appointment be postponed to 1:45 as the Ambassador was not quite ready. The Ambassador and Mr. Kurusu arrived at the Department at 2:05 p. m. and were received by the Secretary at 2:20.

The Japanese Ambassador stated that he had been instructed to deliver at 1:00 p. m. the document which he handed the Secretary, but that he was sorry that he had been delayed owing to the need of more time to decode the message. The Secretary asked why he had specified one o'clock. The Ambassador replied that he did not know but that that was his instruction.

The Secretary said that anyway he was receiving the message at two o'clock.

After the Secretary had read two or three pages he asked the Ambassador whether this document was presented under instructions of the Japanese Government. The Ambassador replied that it was. The Secretary as soon as he had finished reading the document turned to the Japanese Ambassador and said,

> I must say that in all my conversations with you [the Japanese Ambassador] during the last nine months I have never uttered one word of untruth. This is borne out absolutely by the record. In all my fifty years of public service I have never seen a document that was more crowded with infamous falsehoods and distortions—infamous falsehoods and distortions on a scale so huge that I never

SOURCE: memorandum by Joseph W. Ballantine, Dec. 7, 1941, *Foreign Relations . . . : 1931–1941*, II, pp. 786–87.

imagined until today that any Government on this planet was capable of uttering them.

The Ambassador and Mr. Kurusu then took their leave without making any comment. . . .

C. Declaration of War

PRESIDENT Roosevelt announced the attack to Congress in a short message on Monday, December 8.

Yesterday, December 7, 1941—a date which will live in infamy—the United States of America was suddenly and deliberately attacked by naval and air forces of the Empire of Japan.

The United States was at peace with that Nation and, at the solicitation of Japan, was still in conversation with its Government and its Emperor looking toward the maintenance of peace in the Pacific. Indeed, one hour after Japanese air squadrons had commenced bombing in Oahu, the Japanese Ambassador to the United States and his colleague delivered to the Secretary of State a formal reply to a recent American message. While this reply stated that it seemed useless to continue the existing diplomatic negotiations, it contained no threat or hint of war or armed attack.

It will be recorded that the distance of Hawaii from Japan makes it obvious that the attack was deliberately planned many days or even weeks ago. During the intervening time the Japanese Government has deliberately sought to deceive the United States by false statements and expressions of hope for continued peace.

The attack yesterday on the Hawaiian Islands has caused severe damage to American naval and military forces. Very many American lives have been lost. In addition American ships have been reported torpedoed on the high seas between San Francisco and Honolulu.

Yesterday the Japanese Government also launched an attack against Malaya.

Last night Japanese forces attacked Hong Kong.

Last night Japanese forces attacked Guam.

Last night Japanese forces attacked the Philippine Islands.

Last night the Japanese attacked Wake Island.

SOURCE: *Foreign Relations . . . : 1931–1941*, II, pp. 793–94.

This morning the Japanese attacked Midway Island.

Japan has, therefore, undertaken a surprise offensive extending throughout the Pacific area. The facts of yesterday speak for themselves. The people of the United States have already formed their opinions and well understand the implications to the very life and safety of our Nation.

As Commander-in-Chief of the Army and Navy I have directed that all measures be taken for our defense.

Always will we remember the character of the onslaught against us.

No matter how long it may take us to overcome this premeditated invasion, the American people in their righteous might will win through to absolute victory.

I believe I interpret the will of the Congress and of the people when I assert that we will not only defend ourselves to the uttermost but will make very certain that this form of treachery shall never endanger us again.

Hostilities exist. There is no blinking at the fact that our people, our territory, and our interests are in grave danger.

With confidence in our armed forces—with the unbounded determination of our people—we will gain the inevitable triumph —so help us God.

I ask that the Congress declare that since the unprovoked and dastardly attack by Japan on Sunday, December seventh, a state of war has existed between the United States and the Japanese Empire.

Congress by joint resolution the same day recognized the existence of a state of war between Japan and the United States. Three days later, December 11, Germany and Italy declared war.

XIII

The Second World War

Never in the history of the country had the United States entered a conflict of such proportion as the Second World War, when the nation faced a two-front war and when, clearly, the outcome depended on the success of American arms. It is true that in Europe the Russian armies bore the brunt of the fighting and eventually broke German resistance. That enormous front nonetheless might have stalemated had not the United States entered the war and ensured victory. As for the Pacific war against the Japanese, the war that had brought American entry after the sneak attack at Pearl Harbor, that conflict was almost entirely with American arms and men, the victory on August 14, 1945, an American victory.

40. More Statements of Principles

A. THE UNITED NATIONS DECLARATION

IN BOTH World Wars the government of the United States sought to avoid division of the spoils and generally any specific arrangements for the postwar world until the fighting had finished. This despite the declarations, already mentioned, in 1941. Even so, Americans believed it was necessary to have broad statements of Allied purpose, and within little more than a year after Pearl Harbor there were two of these. Diplomatic representatives of the Allies accredited to the American government signed the first, the United Nations Declaration, at Washington on January 1, 1942.

. . . The Governments signatory hereto,

Having subscribed to a common program of purposes and principles embodied in the Joint Declaration of the President of the United States of America and the Prime Minister of the United Kingdom of Great Britain and Northern Ireland dated August 14, 1941, known as the Atlantic Charter.

Being convinced that complete victory over their enemies is essential to defend life, liberty, independence and religious freedom, and to preserve human rights and justice in their own lands as well as in other lands, and that they are now engaged in a common struggle against savage and brutal forces seeking to subjugate the world, DECLARE:

(1) Each Government pledges itself to employ its full resources, military or economic, against those members of the Tripartite Pact and its adherents with which such government is at war.

(2) Each Government pledges itself to cooperate with the Governments signatory hereto and not to make a separate armistice or peace with the enemies.

The foregoing declaration may be adhered to by other nations which are, or which may be, rendering material assistance and contributions in the struggle for victory over Hitlerism. . . .

SOURCE: *Foreign Relations of the United States: 1942* (Washington, D.C., 1960), I, pp. 25–26.

B. "Unconditional Surrender"

A YEAR later, on January 24, 1943, during the Roosevelt-Churchill conference at Casablanca, the President announced the doctrine of unconditional surrender—that the Allies would accept nothing less than the
unconditional surrender of their foes. The manner in which the President announced this doctrine was later a subject of minor dispute, and
for a short while there was some theorizing that FDR had announced
this important idea without much forethought. The President afterward
said that the notion just "popped into my mind." In fact he had spoken
from notes that afternoon when he and Churchill sat out on chairs on
the grass, with the newspapermen surrounding them.

. . . The President and the Prime Minister, after a complete
survey of the world war situation, are more than ever determined
that peace can come to the world only by a total elimination of
German and Japanese war power. This involves the simple formula
of placing the objective of this war in terms of an unconditional
surrender by Germany, Italy and Japan. Unconditional surrender
by them means a reasonable assurance of world peace, for generations. Unconditional surrender means not the destruction of the
German populace, nor of the Italian or Japanese populace, but
does mean the destruction of a philosophy in Germany, Italy and
Japan which is based on the conquest and subjugation of other
peoples.

The President and the Prime Minister are confident that this is
equally the purpose of Russia, of China, and of all other members
of the United Nations. . . .

THE transcript of the press conference follows.

THE PRESIDENT: This meeting goes back to the successful landing operations last November, which as you all know were initiated
as far back as a year ago, and put into definite shape shortly after
the Prime Minister's visit to Washington in June.

SOURCE: notes by FDR, Jan. 22–23, 1943, *Foreign Relations of the
United States: The Conferences at Washington, 1941–1942, and
Casablanca, 1943* (Washington, D.C., 1968), p. 837.
SOURCE: *Foreign Relations . . . : Washington and Casablanca*,
pp. 726–29.

After the operations of last November, it became perfectly clear, with the successes, that the time had come for another review of the situation, and a planning for the next steps, especially steps to be taken in 1943. That is why we came here, and our respective staffs came with us, to discuss the practical steps to be taken by the United Nations for prosecution of the war. We have been here about a week.

I might add, too, that we began talking about this after the first of December, and at that time we invited Mr. Stalin to join us at a convenient meeting place. Mr. Stalin very greatly desired to come, but he was precluded from leaving Russia because he was conducting the new Russian offensive against the Germans along the whole line. We must remember that he is Commander in Chief, and that he is responsible for the very wonderful detailed plan which has been brought to such a successful conclusion since the beginning of the offensive.

In spite of the fact that Mr. Stalin was unable to come, the results of the staff meeting have been communicated to him, so that we will continue to keep in very close touch with each other.

I think it can be said that the studies during the past week or ten days are unprecedented in history. Both the Prime Minister and I think back to the days of the first World War when conferences between the French and British and ourselves very rarely lasted more than a few hours or a couple of days. The Chiefs of Staffs have been in intimate touch; they have lived in the same hotel. Each man has become a definite personal friend of his opposite number on the other side.

Furthermore, these conferences have discussed, I think for the first time in history, the whole global picture. It isn't just one front, just one ocean, or one continent—it is literally the whole world; and that is why the Prime Minister and I feel that the conference is unique in the fact that it has this global aspect.

The Combined Staffs, in these conferences and studies during the past week or ten days, have proceeded on the principle of pooling all of the resources of the United Nations. And I think the second point is that they have re-affirmed the determination to maintain the initiative against the Axis Powers in every part of the world.

These plans covering the initiative and maintenance of the initiative during 1943 cover certain things, such as united operations conducted in different areas of the world. Secondly, the sending of all possible material aid to the Russian offensive, with the double object of cutting down the manpower of Germany and her satellites, and continuing the very great attrition of German munitions and materials of all kinds which are being destroyed every day in such large quantities by the Russian armies.

And, at the same time, the Staffs have agreed on giving all possible aid to the heroic struggle of China—remembering that China is in her sixth year of the war—with the objective, not only in China but in the whole of the Pacific area, of ending any Japanese attempt in the future to dominate the Far East.

Another point. I think we have all had it in our hearts and heads before, but I don't think that it has ever been put down on paper by the Prime Minister and myself, and that is the determination that peace can come to the world only by the total elimination of German and Japanese war power.

Some of you Britishers know the old story—we had a General called U. S. Grant. His name was Ulysses Simpson Grant, but in my, and the Prime Minister's, early days he was called "Unconditional Surrender" Grant. The elimination of German, Japanese and Italian war power means the unconditional surrender by Germany, Italy, and Japan. That means a reasonable assurance of future world peace. It does not mean the destruction of the population of Germany, Italy, or Japan, but it does mean the destruction of the philosophies in those countries which are based on conquest and the subjugation of other people. . . .

While we have not had a meeting of all of the United Nations, I think that there is no question—in fact we both have great confidence that the same purposes and objectives are in the minds of all of the other United Nations—Russia, China, and all the others.

And so the actual meeting—the main work of the Committee—has been ended, except for a certain amount of resultant paper work—has come to a successful conclusion. I call it a meeting of the minds in regard to all military operations, and, thereafter, that the war is going to proceed against the Axis Powers according to schedule, with every indication that 1943 is going to be an even better year for the United Nations than 1942.

THE PRIME MINISTER: I agree with everything that the President has said. . . .

I hope you gentlemen will find this talk to be of assistance to you in your work, and will be able to build up a good and encouraging story to our people all over the world. Give them the picture of unity, thoroughness, and integrity of the political chiefs. Give them that picture, and make them feel that there is some reason behind all that is being done. Even when there is some delay there is design and purposes, and as the President has said, the unconquerable will to pursue this quality, until we have procured the unconditional surrender of the criminal forces who plunged the world into storm and ruin. . . .

41. The Triumvirs

A. THE BIG THREE CONFERENCES

As DURING the First World War, so in the Second there were the ceremonial—and business—meetings of the leaders of the major Allied powers. But since there was no general peace conference following the Second World War, it was not possible for the Allies to stage a pageant such as occurred at Paris in 1919. Perhaps almost anticipating the lack of a peace conference, the leaders met with considerable ostentation during the course of the war, preserving their unanimity for public view as long as they could. There were three meetings of the Big Three, and at only the first two—Teheran (November 28–December 1, 1943) and Yalta (February 4-11, 1945)—were Roosevelt, Churchill, and Stalin in attendance; by the time of Potsdam (July 17–August 2, 1945), Roosevelt was dead, and in the middle of the meeting the results of the British general election replaced Churchill with Clement Attlee. The first of the Big Three meetings, at Teheran, produced a declaration dated December 1, 1943.

WE—The President of the United States, The Prime Minister of Great Britain, and the Premier of the Soviet Union, have met these four days past in this, the capital of our ally, Iran, and have shaped and confirmed our common policy.

We express our determination that our nations shall work together in war and in the peace that will follow.

As to war—Our military staffs have joined in our round table

SOURCE: Foreign Relations of the United States: 1943, The Conferences at Cairo and Tehran (Washington, 1961), pp. 640-41.

discussions, and we have concerted our plans for the destruction of the German forces. We have reached complete agreement as to the scope and timing of the operations which will be undertaken from the East, West and South.

The common understanding which we have here reached guarantees that victory will be ours.

And as to peace—we are sure that our concord will make it an enduring peace. We recognize fully the supreme responsibility resting upon us and all the United Nations, to make a peace which will command the good will of the overwhelming mass of the peoples of the world, and banish the scourge and terror of war for many generations.

With our diplomatic advisers we have surveyed the problems of the future. We shall seek the cooperation and the active participation of all nations, large and small, whose peoples in heart and mind are dedicated, as are our own peoples, to the elimination of tyranny and slavery, oppression and intolerance. We will welcome them, as they may choose to come, into a world family of democratic nations.

No power on earth can prevent our destroying the German armies by land, their U-boats by sea, and their war plants from the air.

Our attack will be relentless and increasing.

Emerging from these friendly conferences we look with confidence to the day when all peoples of the world may live free lives, untouched by tyranny, and according to their varying desires and their own consciences.

We came here with hope and determination. We leave here, friends in fact, in spirit and in purpose.

B. The Teheran Military Agreement

THE EXISTENCE of a secret military agreement initialed at Teheran on December 1, 1943, was not generally known until after the war, even to the highest officials of the Department of State. The Department was not represented at Teheran, because Roosevelt disliked the prospect of bringing along Secretary Hull. Months after FDR's death a news story from Moscow about special agreements at the wartime conferences caused Secretary of State James F. Byrnes to inquire of President Harry

SOURCE: *Foreign Relations . . . : Cairo and Tehran,* p. 652.

S. Truman—who asked the White House chief of staff, Admiral William D. Leahy (who had served President Roosevelt in the same capacity), to look into the matter. In this way Secretary Byrnes discovered, as he put it in his memoir published in 1947, "how many IOUs were outstanding." It must, of course, have been a great embarrassment to learn of commitments in foreign policy through the newspaper press—no public official should have to undergo such an experience —and Byrnes' memoir shows some of his feeling in this regard. Leahy went to the secret White House operations room, known as the Map Room, and obtained copies of several documents (see also below, pp. 291–299), one of which was the Teheran military agreement. He sent the latter to the Department of State on February 4, 1946, and the Department released it to the press on March 24, 1947.

The Conference:—

(1) Agreed that the Partisans in Yugoslavia should be supported by supplies and equipment to the greatest possible extent, and also by commando operations:

(2) Agreed that, from the military point of view, it was most desirable that Turkey should come into the war on the side of the Allies before the end of the year:

(3) Took note of Marshal Stalin's statement that if Turkey found herself at war with Germany, and as a result Bulgaria declared war on Turkey or attacked her, the Soviet would immediately be at war with Bulgaria. The Conference further took note that this fact could be explicitly stated in the forthcoming negotiations to bring Turkey into the war:

(4) Took note that Operation OVERLORD [the cross-Channel invasion of France] would be launched during May 1944, in conjunction with an operation against Southern France. The latter operation would be undertaken in as great a strength as availability of landing-craft permitted. The Conference further took note of Marshal Stalin's statement that the Soviet forces would launch an offensive at about the same time with the object of preventing the German forces from transferring from the Eastern to the Western Front:

(5) Agreed that the military staffs of the three Powers should henceforward keep in close touch with each other in regard to the impending operations in Europe. In particular it was agreed that a cover plan to mystify and mislead the enemy as regards these operations should be concerted between the staffs concerned.

C. Agreement at Yalta

The Yalta Conference of February 4–11, 1945, was followed by release on February 12th of a communique announcing certain of the conference decisions, including the Yalta Declaration on Liberated Europe —a bill of rights for inhabitants of that area of the Continent. Because the conference occurred before surrender of both Germany (May 8, 1945) and Japan (August 14), the full deliberations became known only after the war. A press leak on March 29, 1945, revealed information about the Yalta decision to accord Russia and the United States three votes in the United Nations Assembly, and eventually the United States government said it would not ask for its own extra Assembly seats. A year later, on February 11, 1946, the Department of State released—after Secretary Byrnes obtained it from Admiral Leahy— the Yalta agreement of exactly one year before, regarding entry of the Soviet Union into the war against Japan.

The leaders of the three Great Powers—the Soviet Union, the United States of America and Great Britain—have agreed that in two or three months after Germany has surrendered and the war in Europe has terminated the Soviet Union shall enter into the war against Japan on the side of the Allies on condition that:

1. The *status quo* in Outer-Mongolia (The Mongolian People's Republic) shall be preserved;

2. The former rights of Russia violated by the treacherous attack of Japan in 1904 shall be restored, viz:

(a) the southern part of Sakhalin as well as all the islands adjacent to it shall be returned to the Soviet Union,

(b) the commercial port of Dairen shall be internationalized, the preeminent interests of the Soviet Union in this port being safeguarded and the lease of Port Arthur as a naval base of the USSR restored,

(c) the Chinese-Eastern Railroad and the South-Manchurian Railroad which provides an outlet to Dairen shall be jointly operated by the establishment of a joint Soviet-Chinese Company it being understood that the preeminent interests of the Soviet Union shall be safeguarded and that China shall retain full sovereignty in Manchuria;

3. The Kuril islands shall be handed over to the Soviet Union.

It is understood, that the agreement concerning Outer-Mongolia

Source: *Foreign Relations of the United States: 1945, The Conferences at Malta and Yalta* (Washington, D.C., 1955), p. 984.

and the ports and railroads referred to above will require concurrence of Generalissimo Chiang Kai-Shek. The President will take measures in order to obtain this concurrence on advice from Marshal Stalin.

The Heads of the three Great Powers have agreed that these claims of the Soviet Union shall be unquestionably fulfilled after Japan has been defeated.

For its part the Soviet Union expresses its readiness to conclude with the National Government of China a pact of friendship and alliance between the USSR and China in order to render assistance to China with its armed forces for the purpose of liberating China from the Japanese yoke.

D. YALTA PROTOCOL

A YEAR later, on March 24, 1947, the Department of State released— together with the secret military agreement at Teheran—the protocol of the proceedings at Yalta, signed by the foreign ministers of Britain, Russia, and the United States on February 11, 1945.

The Crimea Conference of the Heads of the Governments of the United States of America, the United Kingdom, and the Union of Soviet Socialist Republics which took place from February 4th to 11th came to the following conclusions.

1. WORLD ORGANISATION

It was decided:

(1) that a United Nations Conference on the proposed world organisation should be summoned for Wednesday, 25th April, 1945, and should be held in the United States of America.

(2) the Nations to be invited to this Conference should be:

(a) the United Nations as they existed on the 8th February, 1945 and

(b) such of the Associated Nations as have declared war on the common enemy by 1st March, 1945. (For this purpose by the term "Associated Nation" was meant the eight Associated Nations and Turkey). When the Conference on World Organization is held, the delegates of the United Kingdom and United States of America will support a proposal to admit to original membership two Soviet Socalist Republics, i. e. the Ukraine and White Russia.

SOURCE: *Foreign Relations . . . . : Malta and Yalta*, pp. 975–82.

(3) that the United States Government on behalf of the Three Powers should consult the Government of China and the French Provisional Government in regard to the decisions taken at the present Conference concerning the proposed World Organisation.

(4) that the text of the invitation to be issued to all the nations which would take part in the United Nations Conference should be as follows:

INVITATION

"The Government of the United States of America, on behalf of itself and of the Governments of the United Kingdom, the Union of Soviet Socialist Republics, and the Republic of China and of the Provisional Government of the French Republic, invite the Government of _____ to send representatives to a Conference of the United Nations to be held on 25th April, 1945, or soon thereafter, at San Francisco in the United States of America to prepare a Charter for a General International Organisation for the maintenance of international peace and security.

"The above named governments suggest that the Conference consider as affording a basis for such a Charter the Proposals for the Establishment of a General International Organisation, which were made public last October as a result of the Dumbarton Oaks Conference, and which have now been supplemented by the following provisions for Section C of Chapter VI:

C. Voting
1. Each member of the Security Council should have one vote.
2. Decisions of the Security Council on procedural matters should be made by an affirmative vote of seven members.
3. Decisions of the Security Council on all other matters should be made by an affirmative vote of seven members including the concurring votes of the permanent members; provided that, in decisions under Chapter VIII, Section A and under the second sentence of paragraph 1 of Chapter VIII, Section C, a party to a dispute should abstain from voting.

"Further information as to arrangements will be transmitted subsequently.

"In the event that the Government of _____ desires in advance of the Conference to present views or comments concerning the proposals, the Government of the United States of America will be pleased to transmit such views and comments to the other participating Governments."

TERRITORIAL TRUSTEESHIP

It was agreed that the five Nations which will have permanent seats on the Security Council should consult each other prior to the United Nations Conference on the question of territorial trusteeship.

The acceptance of this recommendation is subject to its being made clear that territorial trusteeship will only apply to (a) existing mandates of the League of Nations; (b) territories detached from the enemy as a result of the present war; (c) any other territory which might voluntarily be placed under trusteeship; and (d) no discussion of actual territories is contemplated at the forthcoming United Nations Conference or in the preliminary consultations, and it will be a matter for subsequent agreement which territories within the above categories will be placed under trusteeship.

II. DECLARATION ON LIBERATED EUROPE

The following declaration has been approved:

"The Premier of the Union of Soviet Socialist Republics, the Prime Minister of the United Kingdom and the President of the United States of America have consulted with each other in the common interests of the peoples of their countries and those of liberated Europe. They jointly declare their mutual agreement to concert during the temporary period of instability in liberated Europe the policies of their three governments in assisting the peoples liberated from the domination of Nazi Germany and the peoples of the former Axis satellite states of Europe to solve by democratic means their pressing political and economic problems.

"The establishment of order in Europe and the re-building of national economic life must be achieved by processes which will enable the liberated peoples to destroy the last vestiges of Nazism and Fascism and to create democratic institutions of their own choice. This is a principle of the Atlantic Charter—the right of all peoples to choose the form of government under which they will live—the restoration of sovereign rights and self-government to those peoples who have been forcibly deprived of them by the aggressor nations.

"To foster the conditions in which the liberated peoples may exercise these rights, the three governments will jointly assist the people in any European liberated state or former Axis satellite state in Europe where in their judgment conditions require (a) to establish conditions of internal peace; (b) to carry out emergency measures for the relief of distressed peoples; (c) to form interim governmental authorities broadly representative of all democratic elements in the population and pledged to the earliest possible establishment through free elections of governments responsive to the will of the people; and (d) to facilitate where necessary the holding of such elections.

"The three governments will consult the other United Nations and provisional authorities or other governments in Europe when matters of direct interest to them are under consideration.

"When, in the opinion of the three governments, conditions in any European liberated state or any former Axis satellite state in Europe make such action necessary, they will immediately consult together on the measures necessary to discharge the joint responsibilities set forth in this declaration.

"By this declaration we reaffirm our faith in the principles of the Atlantic Charter, our pledge in the Declaration by the United Nations, and our determination to build in co-operation with other peace-loving nations world order under law, dedicated to peace, security, freedom and general well-being of all mankind.

"In issuing this declaration, the Three Powers express the hope that the Provisional Government of the French Republic may be associated with them in the procedure suggested."

III. DISMEMBERMENT OF GERMANY

It was agreed that Article 12 (a) of the Surrender Terms for Germany should be amended to read as follows:

"The United Kingdom, the United States of America and the Union of Soviet Socialist Republics shall possess supreme authority with respect to Germany. In the exercise of such authority they will take such steps, including the complete disarmament, demilitarisation and the dismemberment of Germany as they deem requisite for future peace and security."

The study of the procedure for the dismemberment of Germany was referred to a Committee, consisting of Mr. Eden (Chairman), Mr. Winant and Mr. Gousev. This body would consider the desirability of associating with it a French representative.

IV. ZONE OF OCCUPATION FOR THE FRENCH AND CONTROL COUNCIL FOR GERMANY.

It was agreed that a zone in Germany, to be occupied by the French Forces, should be allocated to France. This zone would be formed out of the British and American zones and its extent would be settled by the British and Americans in consultation with the French Provisional Government.

It was also agreed that the French Provisional Government should be invited to become a member of the Allied Control Council for Germany.

V. REPARATION

The following protocol has been approved:

1. Germany must pay in kind for the losses caused by her to the Allied nations in the course of the war. Reparations are to be received in the first instance by those countries which have borne the main burden of the war, have suffered the heaviest losses and have organised victory over the enemy.

2. Reparation in kind is to be exacted from Germany in three following forms:

a) Removals within 2 years from the surrender of Germany or the cessation of organised resistance from the national wealth of Germany located on the territory of Germany herself as well as outside her territory (equipment, machine-tools, ships, rolling stock, German investments abroad, shares of industrial, transport and other enterprises in Germany, etc.), these removals to be carried out chiefly for purpose of destroying the war potential of Germany.

b) Annual deliveries of goods from current production for a period to be fixed.

c) Use of German labour.

3. For the working out on the above principles of a detailed plan for exaction of reparation from Germany an Allied Reparation Commission will be set up in Moscow. It will consist of three representatives—one from the Union of Soviet Socialist Republics, one from the United Kingdom and one from the United States of America.

4. With regard to the fixing of the total sum of the reparation as well as the distribution of it among the countries which suffered

from the German aggression the Soviet and American delegations agreed as follows:

"The Moscow Reparation Commission should take in its initial studies as a basis for discussion the suggestion of the Soviet Government that the total sum of the reparation in accordance with the points (a) and (b) of the paragraph 2 should be 20 billion dollars and that 50% of it should go to the Union of Soviet Socialist Republics."

The British delegation was of the opinion that pending consideration of the reparation question by the Moscow Reparation Commission no figures of reparation should be mentioned.

The above Soviet-American proposal has been passed to the Moscow Reparation Commission as one of the proposals to be considered by the Commission.

VI. MAJOR WAR CRIMINALS

The Conference agreed that the question of the major war criminals should be the subject of enquiry by the three Foreign Secretaries for report in due course after the close of the Conference.

VII. POLAND

The following Declaration on Poland was agreed by the Conference:

"A new situation has been created in Poland as a result of her complete liberation by the Red Army. This calls for the establishment of a Polish Provisional Government which can be more broadly based than was possible before the recent liberation of the Western part of Poland. The Provisional Government which is now functioning in Poland should therefore be reorganised on a broader democratic basis with the inclusion of democratic leaders from Poland itself and from Poles abroad. This new Government should then be called the Polish Provisional Government of National Unity.

"M. Molotov, Mr. Harriman and Sir A. Clark Kerr are authorised as a commission to consult in the first instance in Moscow with members of the present Provisional Government and with other Polish democratic leaders from within Poland and from abroad, with a view to the reorganisation of the present Government along the above lines. This Polish Provisional Government of National Unity shall be pledged to the holding of free and unfettered elections as soon as possible on the basis of universal suffrage and secret ballot. In these elections all democratic and anti-Nazi parties shall have the right to take part and to put forward candidates.

"When a Polish Provisional Government of National Unity has been properly formed in conformity with the above, the Government of the U. S. S. R., which now maintains diplomatic relations with the present Provisional Government of Poland, and the Government of the United Kingdom and the Government of the U. S. A. will establish diplomatic relations with the new Polish Provisional Government of National Unity, and will exchange Ambassadors by whose reports the respective Governments will be kept informed about the situation in Poland.

"The three Heads of Government consider that the Eastern frontier of Poland should follow the Curzon Line with digressions from it in some regions of five to eight kilometres in favour of Poland. They recognise that Poland must receive substantial accessions of territory in the North and West. They feel that the opinion of the new Polish Provisional Government of National Unity should be sought in due course on the extent of these accessions and that the final delimitation of the Western frontier of Poland should thereafter await the Peace Conference."

VIII. YUGOSLAVIA

It was agreed to recommend to Marshal Tito and to Dr. Subasic:

(a) that the Tito-Subasic Agreement should immediately be put into effect and a new Government formed on the basis of the Agreement.

(b) that as soon as the new Government has been formed it should declare:

(i) that the Anti-Fascist Assembly of National Liberation (AUNOJ) will be extended to include members of the last Yugoslav Skupstina who have not compromised themselves by collaboration with the enemy, thus forming a body to be known as a temporary Parliament and

(ii) that legislative acts passed by the Anti-Fascist Assemb[l]y of National Liberation (AUNOJ) will be subject to subsequent ratification by a Constituent Assembly;

and that this statement should be published in the communique of the Conference.

IX. ITALO-YUGOSLAV FRONTIER
ITALIO-AUSTRIA FRONTER

Notes on these subjects were put in by the British delegation and the American and Soviet delegations agreed to consider them and give their views later.

X. YUGOSLAV-BULGARIAN RELATIONS

There was an exchange of views between the Foreign Secretaries on the question of the desirability of a Yugoslav-Bulgarian pact of alliance. The question at issue was whether a state still under an armistice regime could be allowed to enter into a treaty with another state. Mr. Eden suggested that the Bulgarian and Yugoslav Governments should be informed that this could not be approved. Mr. Stettinius suggested that the British and American Ambassadors should discuss the matter further with M. Molotov in Moscow. M. Molotov agreed with the proposal of Mr. Stettinius.

XI. SOUTH EASTERN EUROPE

The British Delegation put in notes for the consideration of their colleagues on the following subjects:

(a) the Control Commission in Bulgaria

(b) Greek claims upon Bulgaria, more particularly with reference to reparations.

(c) Oil equipment in Roumania.

XII. IRAN

Mr. Eden, Mr. Stettinius and M. Molotov exchanged views on the situation in Iran. It was agreed that this matter should be pursued through the diplomatic channel.

XIII. MEETINGS OF THE THREE FOREIGN SECRETARIES

The Conference agreed that permanent machinery should be set up for consultation between the three Foreign Secretaries; they should meet as often as necessary, probably about every three or four months.

These meetings will be held in rotation in the three capitals, the first meeting being held in London.

SOURCE: *Foreign Relations of the United States: 1945, The Conference of Berlin* (2 vols., Washington, D.C., 1960), II, pp. 1474–76.

XIV. THE MONTREUX CONVENTION AND THE STRAITS

It was agreed that at the next meeting of the three Foreign Secretaries to be held in London, they should consider proposals which it was understood the Soviet Government would put forward in relation to the Montreux Convention and report to their Governments. The Turkish Government should be informed at the appropriate moment. . . .

E. THE POTSDAM DECLARATION

NOT MUCH came out of the Potsdam Conference (July 17–August 2, 1945) except a pronouncement by the American, British, and Chinese governments—it was impossible for the Russian government to sign, for it did not enter the Far Eastern war until August 8—warning the Japanese to surrender quickly. This Potsdam Declaration did not mention existence of the new atomic weapon, a test device of which had exploded at the proving ground in New Mexico on July 16. In retrospect the Japanese would have done well to have accepted surrender as offered in this declaration of July 26.

(1) We, the President of the United States, the President of the National Government of the Republic of China and the Prime Minister of Great Britain, representing the hundreds of millions of our countrymen, have conferred and agree that Japan shall be given an opportunity to end this war.

(2) The prodigious land, sea and air forces of the United States, the British Empire and of China, many times reinforced by their armies and air fleets from the west are poised to strike the final blows upon Japan. This military power is sustained and inspired by the determination of all the Allied nations to prosecute the war against Japan until she ceases to resist.

(3) The result of the futile and senseless German resistance to the might of the aroused free peoples of the world stands forth in awful clarity as an example to the people of Japan. The might that now converges on Japan is immeasurably greater than that which, when applied to the resisting Nazis, necessarily laid waste to the lands, the industry and the method of life of the whole German people. The full application of our military power, backed by our resolve, *will* mean the inevitable and complete destruction of the Japanese armed forces and just as inevitably the utter devastation of the Japanese homeland.

(4) The time has come for Japan to decide whether she will

continue to be controlled by those self-willed milita[r]istic advisers whose unintelligent calculations have brought the Empire of Japan to the threshold of annihilation, or whether she will follow the path of reason.

(5) Following are our terms. We will not deviate from them. There are no alternatives. We shall brook no delay.

(6) There must be eliminated for all time the authority and influence of those who have deceived and misled the people of Japan into embarking on world conquest, for we insist that a new order of peace, security and justice will be impossible until irresponsible militarism is driven from the world.

(7) Until such a new order is established and until there is convincing proof that Japan's war-making power is destroyed, points in Japanese territory to be designated by the Allies shall be occupied to secure the achievement of the basic objectives we are here setting forth.

(8) The terms of the Cairo Declaration shall be carried out and Japanese sovereignty shall be limited to the islands of Honshu, Hokkaido, Kyushu, Shikoku and such minor islands as we determine.

(9) The Japanese military forces, after being completely disarmed, shall be permitted to return to their homes with the opportunity to lead peaceful and productive lives.

(10) We do not intend that the Japanese shall be enslaved as a race or destroyed as [a] nation, but stern justice shall be meted out to all war criminals, including those who have visited cruelties upon our prisoners. The Japanese government shall remove all obstacles to the revival and strength[en]ing of democratic tendencies among the Japanese people. Freedom of speech, of religion, and of thought, as well as respect for the fundamental human rights shall be established.

(11) Japan shall be permitted to maintain such industries as will sustain her economy and permit the exaction of just reparations in kind, but not those industries which would enable her to rearm for war. To this end, access to, as distinguished from control of raw materials shall be permitted. Eventual Japanese participation in world trade relations shall be permitted.

(12) The occupying forces of the Allies shall be withdrawn from Japan as soon as these objectives have been accomplished and

there has been established in accordance with the freely expressed will of the Japanese people a peacefully inclined and responsible government.

(13) We call upon the Government of Japan to proclaim now the unconditional surrender of all the Japanese armed forces, and to provide proper and adequate assurances of their good faith in such action. The alternative for Japan is prompt and utter destruction.

Shortly after this declaration, which the Japanese government refused to accept, the Second World War in the Far East came to its fiery end. Meanwhile, on August 8, troops of the Soviet Union surged across the Siberian border into Japanese-held Manchuria. The Japanese surrendered on August 14 (the formal surrender was on September 2), after the emperor told a council meeting that his countrymen would have to bear the unbearable. In anguish the war had begun. In the same way it ended.

Note on Sources

For almost a century of American foreign relations, from 1863 to 1950, there is no reliable treaty series to which a student may resort. Hunter Miller ended his magisterial *Treaties and Other International Acts of the United States of America*, 8 vols. (Washington, 1931–48) in July, 1863; and not until after the Second World War did the United States government again begin publishing treaties in an official series with reliable texts. The easiest resource is *Treaties, Conventions, International Acts, Protocols and Agreements between the United States of America and Other Powers: 1776–1937*, 4 vols. (Washington, 1910–38), compiled by William M. Malloy I, II, 1776–1909 (1910), C. F. Redmond, III, 1910–23 (1923), and Edward J. Trenwith, IV, 1923–37 (1938). The Department of State began a *Treaty Series* in pamphlet form in 1908, and an *Executive Agreement Series* in pamphlet form in 1929. A new series has just started: Charles I. Bevans, comp., *Treaties and Other International Agreements of the United States of America: 1776–1949* (Washington, 1968–). Until the latter series fills in the gap left by Hunter Miller the best source for a reliable text is the National Archives.

For the annual summation of the business of the United States including foreign affairs, the President's state of the union message, see James D. Richardson, ed., *Messages and Papers of the Presidents: 1789–1897*, 10 vols. (Washington, 1896–99), or—it is much more easy to use and also comes down to date—Fred L. Israel, ed., *The State of the Union Messages of the Presidents: 1790–1966*, 3 vols. (New York, 1966).

The primary documentary source for American diplomacy in the period covered by the present volume, 1872–1945, is *Foreign Relations of the United States*. This grand compilation began to appear during the Lincoln administration, with documents for 1861 published in 1862. Annual volumes have come out for all the years between then and 1945 with the exception of the year 1869. As the years have passed the number of documents on American foreign relations has increased dramatically, and this increase has become evident in the enlargement of the series. By the early 1920s *Foreign*

Relations was up to two annual volumes, in the latter 1920s up to three, and beginning with 1932 it has needed five or more volumes each year. The year 1945 required twelve. For 1946 there will be eleven volumes, but thereafter the number will be held—by tight compilation—to seven or eight per year.

Foreign Relations, one should add, is not always chronological in its coverage. During the First World War there was such a massive diplomacy that it proved advisable to bring out special volumes and supplements to the annual volumes. The Paris Peace Conference of 1919 produced an enormous record, which appeared in thirteen supplementary volumes. When papers of the late Secretary of State Robert Lansing came back to the Department, it proved necessary to publish the Lansing Papers in two volumes. For diplomacy of a later period there was a special volume on the Soviet Union, 1933–39. A two-volume set came out in 1943 on Japan, 1931–41, ahead of the volumes in the regular annual series. In 1953 certain influential figures on Capitol Hill persuaded Secretary of State John Foster Dulles to have the Department put out special volumes on the top-level wartime conferences and on United States relations with China, 1942–49. In response to this pressure for politically potent material, the conferences of Malta and Yalta came out in 1955, followed by two volumes on Potsdam (1960), a volume on Cairo and Teheran (1961), a volume on the Conferences at Washington in 1941–42 and Casablanca in 1943 (1968), and a volume on the conferences at Washington and Quebec in 1943 (1970). Because the publication of the special volume on China for 1942 proved embarrassing for President Chiang Kai-shek and his American supporters, the special China series was stopped for several years. The Historical Office of the Department of State is now bringing the China volumes out where they belong, that is, along with the regular volumes for each year.

In remarking the progress and problems of *Foreign Relations* it is necessary to point out the gradual increase in time between diplomatic events and publication of documents. In the nineteenth century the annual volumes almost always came out within a year of events, and if some trimming or omissions were necessary this seems to have been managed (the standards of editing *Foreign Relations* were not irreproachable until Tyler Dennett assumed the editorship in the 1920s). As foreign affairs became ever more serious in the twentieth century, the gap of publication widened. By the year 1912 the Department of State was just getting around to publishing *Foreign Relations* for 1908. In 1915 documents appeared for the year 1910. By 1924, admittedly with severe problems in editing for the time of the World War, it was possible to bring out a volume for 1915. The lag of publication worsened until diplomacy for 1927 had documentary publication only in 1942, 1933 in 1950, and 1939 in 1957. The Department was moving toward a "twenty-year rule." With the vast increase in historical interest following the Second World War, there was agitation to bring the time-lag down to perhaps fifteen years, and signs appeared that this might happen. The Historical Office has worked valiantly under the directorship of such distinguished scholars as G. Bernard Noble and (since 1962) William M. Franklin, with its editing in the hands of experts: Richardson Dougall, deputy director, S. Everett Gleason, chief of the *Foreign Relations* division, together with Fredrick Aandahl, Rogers Churchill, and Ralph Goodwin. But at the present writing—1971—the series is running a gap of twenty-five years and each year it is dropping a year behind. Historians are much disturbed not merely to be without the use of *Foreign Relations* for almost all of the postwar period but because access to the archives has been tied to publication of volumes of *Foreign Relations*. The Historical Office is at the bottom of the Department totem pole and the chances for an increase of funds for publication seem almost nonexistent. Indeed the Office is losing "slots" to other offices. This is a pity, for the United States government long has been the world leader in documentary publication and in research access to archives. The American diplomatic record by and large has been a good one, and deserves the support of scholarship.

As for sources of documentation other than *Foreign Relations*, in the mid-1930s the Senate investigation of munitions makers (the merchants of death) inspired the Department of State to produce a two-volume compilation edited by Carlton Savage, *Policy of the United States toward Maritime Commerce in War* (Washington, 1934–36). This work goes back to the Plan of 1776, but is especially strong for the era of the First World War.

A convenient supplement to *Foreign Relations* volumes for the 1930s is the wartime publication *Peace and War: United States Foreign Policy, 1931–1941* (Washington, 1943), which came out at the same time the Department published its two-volume compilation on Japan, 1931–41. Among other things *Peace and War* contains the texts of the neutrality acts. There also is *A Decade of American Foreign Policy: Basic Documents, 1941–1949* (Washington, 1950), which, together with two other volumes, bridges the gap between *Foreign Relations* and a series (which unfortunately has just been discontinued, for lack of personnel in the Historical Office) entitled *American Foreign Policy: Current Documents*.

For light on diplomatic events of the era covered by the present book it sometimes is necessary to go behind or to the side of the documents and employ material from the *Congressional Record* or from special publications by Congress, or resort to material in collections of personal papers such as Elting E. Morison, ed., *Letters of Theodore Roosevelt*, 8 vols. (Cambridge, Mass., 1951–54), Charles Seymour, ed., *The Intimate Papers of Colonel House*, 4 vols. (Boston, 1926–28), and Samuel I. Rosenman, ed., *The Public Papers and Addresses of Franklin D. Roosevelt*, 9 vols. (New York, 1938–50).